W9-BLO-791

Daily Wisdom for Women

Print ISBN 978-1-61626-848-0

eBook Editions:
Adobe Digital Edition (.epub) 978-1-62029-028-6
Kindle and MobiPocket Edition (.prc) 978-1-62029-029-3

Published by Barbour Publishing, Inc., P.O. Box 719, Uhrichsville, Ohio 44683, www.barbourbooks.com

Our mission is to publish and distribute inspirational products offering exceptional value and biblical encouragement to the masses.

Printed in China.

Daily Wisdom for Women

2013 Devotional Collection

Introduction

Experience an intimate connection to your heavenly Father with the *Daily Wisdom for Women* devotional collection. Featuring a powerful devotional reading and prayer for every day of 2013, this beautiful volume provides inspiration and encouragement for your soul. Enhance your spiritual journey with the refreshing readings—and come to know just how deeply and tenderly God loves you.

Created by God

So God created man in his own image, in the image of God he created him; male and female he created them.
Genesis 1:27 NIV

A whole new year stretches out before you, like a crisp carpet of newly fallen snow. What kind of footprints will you leave? Maybe your strides will be gigantic leaps of faith. Or perhaps you will take tiny steps of slow, steady progress. Some imprints might even be creative expressions, woman-sized angels in the snow.

You are a woman; you were created in God's own image. But that isn't the message our world peddles. So what does it mean to be created in God's image? For starters, you have imagination, intellect, and most importantly, a soul. That's the deepest part of your being, where you long to feel whole, loved, cherished, and understood.

But hold the phone: God made you so that He might have an ongoing relationship with you. You need Him and He's promised to always be there for you. Isn't that the kind of life companion you've searched for?

On her fifty-fifth birthday a close friend confided in me that she's never felt really loved by anyone. "That's not true," I told her. "God loves you." Hopefully during this year she'll understand that God has been there all along. She just didn't take time to look in His Word. She didn't take time to feel His love.

Lord, Psalm 139:14 says, "I am fearfully and wonderfully made." Thank You, not only for purposely creating me, but for loving me perfectly.

David's Diary

God, God, save me! I'm in over my head, quicksand under me, swamp water over me; I'm going down for the third time. I'm hoarse from calling for help, bleary-eyed from searching the sky for God.
Psalm 69:1–3 msg

We think of the Book of Psalms as poetry, or even a peek into King David's private diary—over half of the psalms are credited to him. But they were originally verses set to music, compiled as a hymnbook for corporate worship in the temple. Unfortunately, we have no known record of their tunes.

There is a psalm to match every emotion and mood experienced by human beings: joy, anger, frustration, discouragement, loneliness, doubt. Thousands of years after they were written, they still speak to our needs and desires.

But the psalms are much more than beautiful words that parallel our emotions: God is their central focus. Psalms often begin as a heart cry of pain from the psalmist—but they invariably end with a focus on God.

The psalm writers had a very real, genuine relationship with God. They sang praises to God, they got angry with God, they felt abandoned by God, they didn't understand God's slow response. . .and yet they continued to live by faith, deeply convicted that God would overcome.

These ancient prayers remind us that nothing can shock God's ears. We can tell Him anything and everything. He won't forsake us—His love endures forever.

Oh Lord, You know the secrets of my family's hearts. Teach us to talk to You through every emotion and every circumstance. Our focus belongs on You.

Needed: A Strong Spring

My voice shalt thou hear in the morning, O Lord; in the morning will I direct my prayer unto thee, and will look up.
Psalm 5:3 KJV

When Lonnie bought a watch in an army supply in Japan in 1946, he never thought it would still be running today, more than sixty years later. Sometime back, however, he saw that his watch wasn't keeping time as well as it once did. He took it to a watch repairman.

"When do you wind it?" the man asked.

Lonnie told him he winds his watch when he assumes most people wind theirs—if they haven't gone digital.

"Every night before retiring."

"There's your problem," the repairman said. "Your watch gets its hard knocks during the day. That's when it needs to be running on a strong spring. Wind it in the morning and you won't have any problem with it."

And he hasn't.

We need to begin our busy days on a strong spring, too. Not with just a good cup of coffee, but some time spent with our source of strength. Taking five minutes or an hour—or more if we're really disciplined—in prayer and Bible reading can make the difference in our day. No matter if we're facing wresting kids out of bed or fighting traffic all the way to work, that special time can give us a "spring in our step" today.

Thank You, Lord, for another day. Be my source of strength today. In Jesus' blessed name. Amen.

Joy in the Morning

All who seek the Lord will praise him.
Their hearts will rejoice with everlasting joy.
Psalm 22:26 NLT

How grand God is! He knows how dependent we are on Him for the everyday joy we need to carry on. And every day, He provides us with beauty all around to cheer and help us.

It may come through the beauty of flowers or the bright blue sky—or maybe the white snow covering the trees of a glorious winter wonderland. It may be through the smile of a child or the grateful face of the one we care for. Each and every day, the Lord has a special gift to remind us of whose we are and to generate the joy we need to succeed.

In our own pain and frustration, there are times when our eyes don't see the beauty God sends. But if we'll ask, He'll show us. God is faithful to build us up with everything we need to serve Him with joy. What an awesome God we serve!

Lord God, I thank You for Your joy;
I thank You for providing it every day
to sustain me. I will be joyful in You.

Renewal of All Things

Then Peter answered and said to Him, "Behold, we have left everything and followed You; what then will there be for us?" And Jesus said to them, "Truly I say to you, that you who have followed Me, in the regeneration when the Son of Man will sit on His glorious throne, you also shall sit upon twelve thrones, judging the twelve tribes of Israel."
Matthew 19:27–28

Peter, always so practical. Here's what he's really saying: "Lord, when we get to the end, will it have been worth it to follow You?" And Jesus reassures him with a gigantic yes!

How it must have broken Jesus' heart to know His treasured follower would be martyred one day. Perhaps Peter had an inkling about this, too. We see he wanted desperately to know whether life really went on eternally. The Lord went a step further and related that Peter would not only be with Christ, the Son of Man, eternally, but he would have work to do once he arrived in heaven.

None of us will just occupy space in heaven. Our God is always productive. And this job to which Jesus refers, that of judging the twelve tribes of Israel, will be given to the disciples.

Have you ever speculated as to what you might do in heaven? Well, don't worry, it's not going to be anything like what you've done on earth. Your "boss," after all, will be perfect. And the tasks you perform will be custom-tailored to you. "Job satisfaction" will finally fit into our vernacular.

Lord, I can't even imagine what You have in store for me in heaven. Please keep me faithful to complete the duties You've called me to on earth.

He Enjoys You

The Lord your God is in your midst, a mighty one who will save;
he will rejoice over you with gladness; he will quiet you by his love;
he will exult over you with loud singing.
Zephaniah 3:17 ESV

Memory is a powerful part of each one of us. Perhaps you can see your father cheering you on in a sports event or you remember your mother stroking your feverish forehead while you lay sick in bed. With those mental pictures comes a recollection of emotion—how good it felt to be cheered and encouraged—how comforting it was to be loved and attended.

Zephaniah's words remind us that God is our loving parent. Our mighty Savior offers us a personal relationship, loving and rejoicing over us, His children, glad that we live and move in Him. He is the Lord of the universe, and yet He will quiet our restless hearts and minds with His tender love. He delights in our lives and celebrates our union with Him. We can rest in His affirmation and love, no matter what circumstances surround us.

Lord, help me remember that You are always with me and that You delight in me. Remind me that I am Your child and that You enjoy our relationship.

"Perfect Peace and Rest"

For thus said the Lord GOD, the Holy One of Israel,
"In returning and rest you shall be saved; in quietness and in trust shall be your strength." But you were unwilling.
ISAIAH 30:15 ESV

Some of the saddest words in the Bible are found at the end of Isaiah 30:15: "But you were unwilling." Here the Lord sets before His people a simple formula to the extreme difficulties of life they were experiencing. By returning to God's ways and resting in Him, they could be safe from the enemies who sought to destroy them. In quieting their spirits and trusting in God, they could be strengthened for the battles ahead. But they were unwilling. Instead they wanted to flee God's presence.

Frances Ridley Havergal's devotion to God throughout her short life is seen in her many hymns. The nineteenth-century English woman's life was riddled with pain and sickness, yet she sought the Lord through it all. In her hymn "Like a River Glorious," she depicts the peace and rest God offers as a mighty river, growing fuller and deeper each day. The refrain summarizes God's promise to each of us: "Stayed upon Jehovah, hearts are fully blest; finding, as He promised, perfect peace and rest."

Father, I'm tired of trying to outrun my problems.
May Your peace flow through me like a mighty river,
bringing rest to my soul.

Seeking Wisdom

To receive instruction in wise behavior, righteousness, justice and equity; to give prudence to the naive, to the youth knowledge and discretion, a wise man will hear and increase in learning, and a man of understanding will acquire wise counsel, to understand a proverb and a figure, the words of the wise and their riddles.

Proverbs 1:3–6

When asked by God what he wished for, Solomon answered, "Wisdom." Looking back over your life, if you'd been afforded this same opportunity in your early twenties, what would your response have been?

Like most of us, at that age wisdom probably wasn't high on your priority list. Instead of asking God or your parents for direction, you more likely turned to your peers.

Natalie, a strikingly beautiful girl who'd just turned seventeen, found the advances of an older man extremely difficult to resist. Disregarding all the precepts she'd learned from years of Sunday school, Natalie turned instead to a non-Christian girlfriend for advice. "Go for it!" the friend encouraged with gusto.

A decade later that friend has been married and divorced. Natalie herself found out too late that her "boyfriend" already had a wife and baby.

Satan may be out of the garden but he still finds his way into vulnerable areas of our lives. But God is with you, even in times of sinful temptation. He's promised to give you the power to withstand such moral crises.

Lord, surround me with friends who know You and Your Word. Surround me in a crisis so I can still hear Your voice of wisdom and reason.

Sweet Aroma

The heartfelt counsel of a friend is as sweet as perfume and incense.
PROVERBS 27:9 NLT

When you think of the word *comfort*, what comes to mind? Maybe it's a favorite pair of jeans or a well-worn sweatshirt. It might be chocolate or homemade mac and cheese—foods that soothe in a difficult time. Or perhaps it's a luxurious bubble bath, complete with candles and relaxing music.

While all these things can bring temporary relief, God's Word tells us that finding true comfort is as simple as sharing heart-to-heart with a friend. Whether it's over coffee, dessert, or even on the phone, a cherished friend can offer the encouragement and God-directed counsel we all need from time to time.

Friendships that have Christ as their center are wonderful relationships blessed by the Father. Through the timely, godly advice these friends offer, God speaks to us, showering us with comfort that is as sweet as perfume and incense. So what are you waiting for? Make a date with a friend and share the sweet aroma of Jesus!

Jesus, Your friendship means the world to me.
I value the close friendships You've blessed me with, too!
Thank You for the special women in my life.
Show me every day how to be a blessing to them,
just as they are to me.

Full of Grace

Let your conversation be always full of grace, seasoned with salt, so that you may know how to answer everyone.
COLOSSIANS 4:6 NIV

Inflection. Tone of voice. Attitude. Maybe you remember your mom saying, "It's not what you say, but how you say it." Words not only convey a message, they also reveal the attitude of our hearts. When our conversation is full of grace, even difficult truths can be communicated effectively. But how do we season our words with grace?

Grace is undeserved favor that extends unconditional love to another. Whether you're communicating with friends, family, or coworkers, it's important to show that you value them. Put their needs above your own. Communicate truth within the context of love. Show compassion and forgiveness. Demonstrate understanding and an openness to receive their input. Respect their opinion. Rather than striving to drive home your point, try to understand theirs. Seek to build them up. Convey encouragement and hope. Be positive.

When our conversations are full of grace, people will enjoy communicating with us. They will walk away blessed by the love we have shown. Today, in your conversations, extend God's grace to those hungry to experience His love.

Dear Lord, may I view each conversation as an opportunity to extend Your grace to others. May my words be a blessing. Amen.

Keeping a Clean Heart

Therefore, having these promises, beloved, let us cleanse ourselves from all filthiness of the flesh and spirit, perfecting holiness in the fear of God.
2 CORINTHIANS 7:1 NKJV

Her new home had white ceramic tile floors throughout. Upon seeing them, visiting friends and family often asked, "Won't they show every speck of dirt?"

"Yes, but at least I can tell if I need to clean them," replied the new home owner, explaining her thinking that the better she could see the dirt the better chance she had of keeping them sparkling clean.

"So how often do you have to clean them—once a week?" her friends asked.

"More like every day," she replied, laughing at their horrified faces.

Keeping a clean heart requires similar diligence and regular upkeep. While Jesus Himself cleanses us from all unrighteousness, as believers we need to be on the lookout for temptations and situations that might cause us to fall into sin in the first place. Reading the Bible reminds us that God is holy and that He expects us to strive for holiness in our thoughts and actions. As we pray daily, God shows us areas in our character or behaviors that are displeasing to Him and that need a thorough cleaning.

Like the home owner who enjoyed knowing her floors were clean, there is joy and peace knowing our hearts can be clean, too.

"Create in me a clean heart, O God, and renew a steadfast spirit within me" [Psalm 51:10 NKJV]. Amen.

He Keeps His Promises

"For I know the plans I have for you," declares the Lord, "plans to prosper you and not to harm you, plans to give you hope and a future."
Jeremiah 29:11 niv

Unimaginable. That must describe the hopelessness the disciples felt as they saw their Master die on the cross. All the promises they held dear—all their feelings of hopeful expectation—were shot down with those final words: "It is finished."

Some of Jesus' followers may have remembered His earlier words assuring them of His return. But in the face of certain death, those words of victorious life must have been hard to accept.

We all experience moments of hopelessness in our earthly journeys. The death of our dreams, the crashing down of our hopes, the promises of God seemingly unfulfilled. . .we are no more immune to disappointment than Jesus' disciples were.

In the end, though, Jesus' promises held true—He did prevail no matter how dark that first Good Friday looked. We can always trust the words of our Lord. He knows the plans He has for us, and He has the power to see them through.

Hope and a future, prosperity and peace—we can trust that, even when things seem hopeless, God is still at work, carrying out His promises.

*Thank You, Jesus, for being at work in my life.
Thank You for having a perfect plan and for keeping
Your promises. Give me faith to believe in You even
when it seems like everything is going wrong.*

Trials Have a Purpose

Then Joseph said to his brothers, "Please come closer to me." And they came closer. And he said, "I am your brother Joseph, whom you sold into Egypt. And now do not be grieved or angry with yourselves, because you sold me here; for God sent me before you to preserve life."
GENESIS 45:4–5

How many of us could forgive as Joseph did? His jealous siblings had kidnapped him, thrown him into a pit, and then allowed him to be sold into slavery. Yet Joseph trusted that from God's perspective, not his own, his trials had a purpose.

Joseph walked through his humiliating ordeal with his eyes focused on the Lord. He continued not only to love his brothers but to find forgiveness in his heart for them. Studying his life has enabled me to look at my own situation differently: God can accomplish miracles in the midst of trials.

Is there a hurt so deep inside that you have never shared it with another human being? Perhaps someone in your own family has rejected or betrayed you. Remember the pain suffered by Joseph; remember the anguish of Jesus Christ, who was betrayed by one as close as a brother, Judas Iscariot. God knows your pain and He is strong enough to remove any burden.

Lord, sometimes I want to enjoy my agony a while longer. Show me the brilliance of Your forgiveness that I might trust You in the trial and not miss the outcome You've planned.

A Prosperous Soul

Beloved, I wish above all things that thou mayest prosper and be in health, even as thy soul prospereth.
3 JOHN 1:2 KJV

Twenty-first-century women do everything conceivable to keep their bodies and their minds in good shape. They work out, watch their calories and carbs, and take excellent care of their skin and teeth. On the outside, many women appear to be in excellent health. But what about their souls? What would it profit a woman to be completely fit on the outside and have a sin-sick soul?

Maybe you're one of those women who thrive on staying in shape. Perhaps you even put your external body on the front burner of your life, paying particular attention to diet, exercise, and appearance. As you think about your overall health, consider your soul. Have you given your heart and life to the Lord Jesus Christ? If so, are you spending time with Him? Praying? Reading His Word? These things are necessary for a healthy soul.

Today's scripture is so encouraging. God wants us to prosper and He loves for us to be in good health, even as our souls prosper. If we really think about that, we have to conclude that the health of our soul is even more important than our physical health. Spend some time today giving your soul a workout.

Lord, sometimes I pay more attention to the outside than the inside. I care more about what people can see than what they can't. Today I draw near to You. Make me healthy. . .from the inside out.

Self-Examination

Let us test and examine our ways, and return to the LORD!
LAMENTATIONS 3:40 ESV

What if you could follow yourself around for the day, carefully examining all that you do? Look at your schedule—your choice of activities, the people you talk to, the things you listen to and watch, the habits being formed, the thoughts you think. Maybe your heart desires intimacy with God, but a real day in your life leaves no time for solitude. God often speaks to us in the stillness and silent spaces. How will we hear Him if we're never still?

Taking time to reflect, to think, and to examine oneself is a necessary step in moving toward intimacy with God. Before we can turn back to Him, we must repent of the things that moved us away from Him in the first place. As we set aside time for solitude and reflection, the Holy Spirit will gently show us these things if we ask. He will show us the sins we need to confess and give us the grace of repentance. Experiencing forgiveness, our fellowship with our heavenly Father is restored.

Lord, help me to still myself before You and be willing to examine my ways. Speak to me through Your Holy Spirit of what is wrong in my life. Give me the gift of repentance and allow me to enjoy the sweetness of Your forgiveness.

The New Me

*Therefore, if anyone is in Christ, he is a new creation;
the old has gone, the new has come!*
2 Corinthians 5:17 niv

Are you in Christ? Is He consistently Lord of your life? Then you are a new creation.

Regardless of your past, regardless of the circumstances you may have faced, you're a new creation. All the past guilt is gone—vanished, obliterated—and everything is new.

It's true that some of us live with the consequences of past choices. Maybe our children are the result of premarital sex—but they are nonetheless marvelous miracles of God. Maybe today's health problems result from years of unwise and harmful choices—but God says the guilt is all in the past, gone. Everything is new. What's history is done and over—and Jesus has replaced your old with His new: new peace, new joy, new love, new strength.

Since God Himself sees us as a new creation, how can we do any less? We need to choose to see ourselves as a new creation, too. And we can, through God's grace.

If you are "in Christ," you are a new creation. Be glad. Give thanks. Live each day as the new creation you have become through Jesus.

Father, I'm so thankful that You are a God of grace—and I thank You that I am a new creation. Please give me the spiritual eyes to see myself as a new creation, looking past the guilt of yesterday's choices.

A Refuge from Our Despair

Hear my cry, O God; give heed to my prayer. from the end of the earth I call to Thee, when my heart is faint; lead me to the rock that is higher than I. For Thou hast been a refuge for me, a tower of strength against the enemy. Let me dwell in Thy tent forever; let me take refuge in the shelter of Thy wings.

Psalm 61:1–4

King David, writer of this psalm, composed it as a song, acknowledging God as his rock. He clung with tenacity to the fact that no matter how desperate his situation appeared, God was as immovable as a huge rock or boulder. Although David's trials may differ from yours, you, too, can use strong coping mechanisms.

First, David acknowledged God remained all powerful, despite life circumstances. And second, David looked back at God's past rescues. "O my God, my soul is in despair within me; therefore I remember Thee from the land of the Jordan, and the peaks of Hermon, from Mount Mizar. Deep calls to deep at the sound of Thy waterfalls; all Thy breakers and Thy waves have rolled over me. The Lord will command His lovingkindness in the daytime; and His song will be with me in the night, a prayer to the God of my life" (Psalm 42:6–8).

Lord, I search for a way through the torrents of despair. How precious is the knowledge that You hear and care.

Make a Choice

Do not let your hearts be troubled (distressed, agitated). You believe in and adhere to and trust in and rely on God; believe in and adhere to and trust in and rely also on Me.
John 14:1 amp

Some days are full of joy and peace; others are not. When we face the inevitable dark days in life, we must choose how we respond. We bring light to the darkest of days when we turn our face to God. Sometimes we must let in trusted friends and family members to help on our journey toward solving our problems.

David knew much distress and discomfort when he cried out, "God is our Refuge and Strength" (Psalm 46:1 amp). Matthew Henry's commentary says of Psalm 46, "Through Christ, we shall be conquerors. . . . He is a Help, a present Help, a Help found, one whom we have found to be so; a Help at hand, one that is always near; we cannot desire a better, nor shall we ever find the like in any creature."

Knowing that Christ is at the center of our battles—and that we can trust Him—lends peace and stills the weakest of hearts. Rely on Him to lead you through the darkest days.

Oh Lord, still my troubled heart. Let me learn to rely on You in all circumstances. Thank You, Father, for Your everlasting love.

His Perfect Strength

"My grace is sufficient for you, for my power is made perfect in weakness." Therefore I will boast all the more gladly about my weaknesses, so that Christ's power may rest on me.
2 CORINTHIANS 12:9 NIV

How do you define stress? Perhaps you feel it when the car doesn't start or the toilet backs up or the line is too long at the grocery store. Or maybe your source of stress is a terrible diagnosis, a late-night phone call, a demanding boss, or a broken relationship. It's probably a combination of all of these things. You might be able to cope with one of them, but when several are bearing down at once, stress is the inevitable result.

It has been said that stress results when our perceived demands exceed our perceived resources. When the hours required to meet a deadline at work (demand) exceed the number of hours we have available (resources), we get stressed. The most important word in this definition is *perceived*. When it comes to stress, people have a tendency to do two things. One, they magnify the demand ("I will *never* be able to get this done") and two, they fail to consider all of their resources. For the child of God, this includes His mighty strength, which remains long after ours is gone.

In an uncertain world, it is difficult to say few things for sure. But no matter what life throws our way, we can be confident of this: Our demands will *never* exceed God's vast resources.

Strong and mighty heavenly Father,
thank You that in my weakness I can always
rely on Your perfect strength. Amen.

Wisdom Calls Out

Does not wisdom call, and understanding lift up her voice? On top of the heights beside the way, where the paths meet, she takes her stand; beside the gates, at the opening to the city, at the entrance of the doors, she cries out: "To you, O men, I call. . . . For wisdom is better than jewels; and all desirable things can not compare with her."
PROVERBS 8:1–4, 11

Dream books, that's what my grandmother called catalogues. When I was young we'd view them together, imagining that we'd buy all sorts of jewels and trinkets. As I grew older I realized that none of those things we had circled really meant anything to Granny. This wise woman valued people, giving generously of her time to anyone in need.

Although she never went to college, Granny had a natural wisdom about people, an understanding of their hearts, that doesn't come from most books. Her wisdom came from knowing and living out the precepts in one book, the Bible, God's Word.

Wisdom calls to all of us, but some of us are just better listeners. Notice in this passage that wisdom is found "on top of the heights beside the way, where the paths meet . . ." Wisdom is a choice. We can walk right past it.

Wisdom is also "beside the gates, at the opening to the city, at the entrance of the doors. . . ." Wisdom is at the very precipice of every decision.

Lord, You lay before me a path of righteousness. Please help me desire to walk with You!

Unchained!

For you did not receive a spirit that makes you a slave again to fear, but you received the Spirit of sonship. And by him we cry, "Abba, Father."
ROMANS 8:15 NIV

Imagine how difficult life would be inside prison walls. No sunlight. No freedom to go where you wanted when you wanted. Just a dreary, dark existence, locked away in a place you did not choose, with no way of escape.

Most of us can't even imagine such restrictions. As Christians we have complete freedom through Jesus Christ, our Lord and Savior. No limitations. No chains.

Ironically, many of us build our own walls and choose our own chains. When we give ourselves over to fear, we're deliberately entering a prison the Lord never intended for us. We don't always do it willfully. In fact, we often find ourselves behind bars after the fact, then wonder how we got there.

Do you struggle with fear? Do you feel it binding you with its invisible chains? If so, then there's good news. Through Jesus, you have received the Spirit of sonship. A son (or daughter) of the most-high God has nothing to fear. Knowing you've been set free is enough to make you cry, "Abba, Father!" in praise. Today, acknowledge your fears to the Lord. He will loose your chains and set you free.

Lord, thank You that You are the great chain-breaker! I don't have to live in fear. I am Your child, Your daughter, and You are my Daddy-God!

Don't Give In

But you'll welcome us with open arms when we run for cover to you. Let the party last all night! Stand guard over our celebration. You are famous, God, for welcoming God-seekers, for decking us out in delight.
PSALM 5:11–12 MSG

From time to time, we can lose hope and become discouraged despite all the blessings surrounding us. When this happens, we need to remember Paul's words about the certainty of God's promises and realize that our God will never forsake us.

When we have those down-in-the-dumps days, we should encircle ourselves with encouragers, Christian friends who can hold up our arms, like Moses, when we're unable to continue the journey. We can reach for God's Word, which breathes life into our spirits. Moments of prayer will connect us to the Life-Giver and refresh us.

Worry and discouragement are spiritual traps that sap our energy and cover us with a cloud of gloom. These evil twins can be dispelled by praise. Turn on the radio, hum an old hymn, read a psalm aloud. We can choose to praise and look for joy in spite of our circumstances. David did. Paul and Silas did. We can, too.

God has promised to give us peace and joy in spite of our trials and struggles. Let's reach out to Him and shed our veil of darkness for a mantle of praise.

Heavenly Father, I lift my eyes to the heavens and ask for Your peace. Thank You for Your love and care. Thank You for standing by my side. I praise Your name.

Lay It at the Cross

"Come to me, all you who are weary and burdened, and I will give you rest. Take my yoke upon you and learn from me. . .you will find rest for your souls. For my yoke is easy and my burden is light."
Matthew 11:28–30 niv

Does life sometimes get you down? Often when we experience difficulties that weigh us down, we hear the old adage "Lay it at the cross." But how do we lay our difficulties at the cross?

Jesus gives us step-by-step guidance in how to place our difficulties and burdens at the foot of the cross. First, He invites us to come to Him; those of us who are weary and burdened just need to approach Jesus in prayer. Second, He exchanges our heavy and burdensome load with His easy and light load. Jesus gives us His yoke and encourages us to learn from Him. The word *yoke* refers to Christ's teachings, Jesus' *way* of living life. As we follow His teachings, we take His yoke in humility and gentleness, surrendering and submitting ourselves to His will and ways for our lives. Finally, we praise God for the rest He promises to provide us.

Do you have any difficulties in life, any burdens, worries, fears, relationship issues, finance troubles, or work problems that you need to "lay at the cross"? Jesus says, "Come."

Lord, thank You for inviting me to come and exchange my heavy burden for Your light burden. I praise You for the rest You promise me. Amen.

I Am a Friend of God

When Jesus saw their faith, he said, "Friend, your sins are forgiven."
Luke 5:20 NIV

Friendships are critical to women, and godly friendships are the best. Can you even imagine a world without your girlfriends in it? Impossible! Who would you share your hopes and dreams with? Your goals and aspirations? Oh, what a blessing women of God are! They breathe hope and life into us when we need it most. They laugh along with us at chick flicks. They cry with us when our hearts are broken.

Isn't it amazing to realize God calls us His friend? He reaches out to us with a friendship that goes above and beyond the very best the world has to offer. Best of all, He's not the sort of friend who loses touch or forgets to call. He's always there. And while your earthly friends might do a good job of comforting you when you're down, their brand of comfort doesn't even begin to compare with the Lord's. He knows just what to say when things go wrong, and knows how to throw an amazing celebration when things go well for you.

Today, thank the Lord—not just for salvation, not just for the work He's done in your heart, not just for the people and things He's placed in your life—but for calling you His friend.

Oh Lord, I'm so blessed to be called Your friend! You're the best one I'll ever have. Thank You for the kind of friendship that supersedes all boundaries.

A Woman of Folly

The woman of folly is boisterous, she is naive, and knows nothing. And she sits at the doorway of her house, on a seat by the high places of the city, calling to those who pass by, who are making their paths straight: "Whoever is naive, let him turn in here," and to him who lacks understanding she says, "Stolen water is sweet; and bread eaten in secret is pleasant." But he does not know. . .the depths of Sheol.

Proverbs 9:13–18

This woman is beyond sanguine. She *is* the party, not just the life of it! But how did she end up this way, sitting at the doorway of her house and calling out to those who pass by?

Perhaps life has just sort of happened to her, and she lost the battle before she even knew what the war was about. When she was young, all the road signs appeared to be filled with possibilities. But now that she's getting older the options are fewer. She's sitting on a suitcase in an abandoned train station, waiting for the whistle to blow again.

This woman is not only content to wreak havoc on her own life, but she entices those who wanted to go the right way to join her on this road to nowhere. The passage describes her as "naive," because surely if she'd known better she'd have chosen more wisely.

Have you ever felt like this woman? Did you start out with endless options and then begin purchasing tickets to oblivion? With Christ it's not too late to cash in that pass to nowhere. With Christ your life will have direction.

Lord, please provide me with a true picture of myself. Guide me to the place You envision for me.

Shining Light

"You are the light of the world. A city on a hill cannot be hidden."
Matthew 5:14 NIV

Jesus' disciples knew all about darkness. Centuries before electricity had been harnessed to provide light, individuals made do with fires and oil lamps. When the sun went down, darkness ruled.

So when Jesus told His followers that they are the light of the world, the image meant a great deal to them. Light that overtakes the darkness—light to illuminate the way to the Savior. What an amazing concept!

Jesus tells us twenty-first-century followers to be light, too, boldly and unashamedly flooding the darkness that surrounds us. How do we do it? First, by living the life God calls us to—not sinless, but forgiven. Second, by sprinkling our conversations with evidence of our faith. Did something good happen? Share that blessing with others and give God the credit for it. When someone asks about the peace they see in you, share the joy of Jesus.

Being a light of the world is not about being a Bible thumper or bashing others over the head with religion. It's about living out genuine faith that allows Christ's light to break through our everyday lives. With that goal in mind, shine!

Jesus, You are my true light. Even though I alone can't shine as brightly as You, I ask that You shine through me as I seek to follow after You. I know I won't be perfect, but I also know that Your grace has me covered. Amen.

Lead Goose

Jethro replied: That isn't the best way to do it.
You and the people who come to you will soon be worn out.
The job is too much for one person; you can't do it alone.
EXODUS 18:17–18 CEV

The V formation of flying geese is a fascinating example of aerodynamics. Each bird flies slightly above the bird in front of it, resulting in a reduction of wind resistance. It also helps to conserve the geese's energy. The farther back a goose is in formation, the less energy it needs in the flight. The birds rotate the lead goose position, falling back when tired. With this instinctive system, geese can fly for a long time before they must stop for rest. This is an example of God's wisdom displayed in the natural world.

We often find ourselves as a lead goose. We have a hard time recognizing signs of exhaustion in ourselves. Even harder is falling back and letting someone else have a chance to develop leadership skills. Deep down we think that no other goose could get the gaggle where it needs to go without getting lost or bashing into treetops.

Jethro, Moses' father-in-law, came for a visit as the Israelites camped near the mountain of God. Jethro found Moses to be on the brink of exhaustion. "You will wear yourself out and these people as well," he told Moses. Jethro recommended that Moses delegate responsibilities. Moses listened and implemented everything Jethro suggested, advice that benefited the entire nation of Israel.

Dear Lord, help me to know when to fall back and rest,
letting someone else take the lead. Teach me
to serve You in any position. Amen.

Voice of the Shepherd

"My sheep listen to my voice; I know them, and they follow me."
John 10:27 niv

Next time you're around a group of children, watch for this fascinating phenomenon: At Sunday school or the day-care center, even with upwards of thirty kids playing, crying, or quietly looking at books, a child will hear her own mother's voice as soon as she enters the room. As soon as Mom acknowledges the teacher or helper, her child, instantly honing in on her voice, will look up to see her face. None of the other kids stop playing because she's not their mom—her voice doesn't catch their attention. Only a mother's child hears that one special voice above the ruckus.

It should be the same way for us as God's children. We may be engrossed in our day, running after children, throwing supper together, nursing a cold—but when our Lord speaks, we should hear Him because we as His children know His voice.

God's voice is distinct—and when we become part of His family, we learn to recognize it. The more we tune in to that distinct voice, the more we'll hear it.

Let's be like the child, eager to hear a parent's loving voice.

Lord, I know I am Your child—yet often I find it difficult to hear Your voice over the noise of my life. Please give me ears to hear Your still, small voice, and the strength and faith to obey what You say to me.

Forsaken by God?

My God, my God, why hast Thou forsaken me?
Far from my deliverance are the words of my groaning.
Psalm 22:1

Have you ever cried out to God with such despairing utterances as these? I have. Amid the deep black void of a moonless night, my loneliness threatened to pull me into a swirling, spiraling eddy of emptiness. The sound of my own raspy voice screamed out from my inmost being: "God, if You really exist, show me how to find You! I don't know where You are!" Church hadn't met my needs. People who promised love only provided pain. While my clenched fists beat against my bedroom wall, twelve years' worth of tears, a maelstrom of anger, hurt, and frustration, flowed freely.

He showed me the cross. The year was 1973. I left my knapsack of grief on the bloodstained ground beneath His wooden cross. And I never looked back. He has met my every need in surprising, miraculous, and incredible ways.

Jesus, separated from the Father because of our sin, reached the ear of God with His own desperation. He experienced for us this ultimate terror. . .that we would never be forsaken or walk alone the road that leads to Calvary.

Where are you today? On the road, walking toward Him? Sitting down, too bewildered to even formulate questions? Or are you kneeling, as I did, right at His bleeding feet?

Lord, no matter what hazards are down the road,
You've got a signpost ready to hang on whatever
misleading marker is already in the ground.
And the Son is shining ahead!

Holy Spirit Prayers

We do not know how to pray as we should, but the Spirit Himself intercedes for us with groanings too deep for words; and He who searches the hearts knows what the mind of the Spirit is, because He intercedes for the saints according to the will of God.
ROMANS 8:26–27

Many times the burdens and troubles of our lives are too complicated to understand. It's difficult for us to put them into words, let alone know how to pray for what we need. And unless we know someone who has been through similar circumstances, we can feel isolated and alone.

But we can always take comfort in knowing that the Holy Spirit knows, understands, and pleads our case before the throne of God the Father. Our groans become words in the Holy Spirit's mouth, turning our mute prayers into praise and intercession "according to the will of God."

We can be encouraged, knowing that our deepest longings and desires, maybe unknown even to us, are presented before the God who knows us and loves us completely. Our names are engraved on His heart and hands. He never forgets us; He intervenes in all things for our good and His glory.

Father, I thank You for the encouragement these verses bring. May I always be aware of the Holy Spirit's interceding on my behalf.

Giver of Good Things

For the LORD God is a sun and shield; the LORD will give grace and glory; no good thing will He withhold from those who walk uprightly.
PSALM 84:11 NKJV

Worry is such a useless practice, like spinning wheels on a vehicle that takes you nowhere. And yet we women are notorious for it. The Bible advises us to let each day take care of itself. We are promised that God will provide for us.

Psalm 84:11 says that God is not a withholder of good things from His children. He knows us. He created us and put in us our own unique dreams, preferences, and hopes. When you begin to worry, read this verse. Put it on your bulletin board at work and your bathroom mirror at home. Read it aloud each time that worry begins to creep in.

Your heavenly Father is not "the big man upstairs" looking down upon you and laughing at the unfulfilled desires in your life. He wants to give you good things. Often His timing is different from ours, but His plan is always to bless and never to harm us. Look for the blessings in each day, and keep bringing your desires before the Lord in expectation.

Father, sometimes I wonder why You don't just pour down from heaven the blessing that I cry out for. Give me patience, and help me to see the good gifts from You in each day—even the small ones. Amen.

People Pleaser vs. God Pleaser

We are not trying to please men but God, who tests our hearts.
1 THESSALONIANS 2:4 NIV

Much of what we say and do stems from our desire to be accepted by others. We strive to make a certain impression, to shed the best light possible on ourselves. Wanting to be viewed as successful, we may decide to exaggerate, embellish, or even lie. It's difficult to be true to ourselves when we care so much about the acceptance and opinions of others. Impression management is hard work, so it's good to know God has a better plan!

Rather than being driven by the opinions of others, strive to live your life for God alone and to please Him above all else. God knows our hearts. He perceives things as they truly are. We cannot fool Him. When we allow ourselves to be real before Him, it doesn't matter what others think. If the God of the universe has accepted us, then who cares about someone else's opinion?

It is impossible to please both God and man. We must make a choice. Man looks at the outward appearance, but God looks at the heart. Align your heart with His. Let go of impression management that focuses on outward appearance. Receive God's unconditional love and enjoy the freedom to be yourself before Him!

Dear Lord, may I live for You alone.
Help me transition from a people pleaser
to a God pleaser. Amen.

To Touch Jesus' Cloak

*And a woman who had a hemorrhage for twelve years,
and had endured much at the hands of many physicians,
and had spent all that she had and was not helped at all,
but rather had grown worse, after hearing about Jesus,
came up in the crowd behind Him, and touched His cloak.
For she thought, "If I just touch His garments, I shall get well."*
Mark 5:25–28

This woman is frantic. Each time she's received the report of a gifted healer, she's traversed far and wide to find a cure. The wonder is that this dear woman could survive for twelve long years. For that phrase, "endured much," means she "suffered something or experienced evil." She'd become a challenge to physicians of that day.

In one last-ditch effort she reaches out to touch the garment of Jesus as He passes by. She doesn't bother to call out to Him or even ask for help. Somehow she knows that His very holiness can heal her physically.

"And immediately Jesus, perceiving in Himself that the power proceeding from Him had gone forth, turned around in the crowd and said, 'Who touched My garments?' " (Mark 25:30). The disciples think He's "losing it" for sure.

"But the woman fearing and trembling, aware of what had happened to her, came and fell down before Him, and told Him the whole truth" (Mark 25:33). She's been miraculously healed and now she demonstrates her faith by worshiping at Jesus' feet. Does your faith shine through even in small gestures?

*Lord, You heal me when I come to You,
by renewing my spirit and deepening my faith.
I worship Your majesty and power.*

A New Name

"To everyone who is victorious I will give some of the manna that has been hidden away in heaven. And I will give to each one a white stone, and on the stone will be engraved a new name that no one understands except the one who receives it."
Revelation 2:17 NLT

As a teenager, Darlene didn't like her name. It reminded her of the teenagers portrayed on *The Mickey Mouse Club*. That wasn't her! So she experimented with other names. Around other Darlenes, she used her middle name. She wrote stories under the pen name Heather.

Later, Darlene learned that the sound of her name reflected its meaning: darling or beloved. Not only that, she discovered that her parents had chosen her middle name, Hope, from 1 Corinthians 13:13. Every time they spoke her name, they were saying, "We love you. We have hope for your future." Darlene felt like she had received a brand-new name.

God will give each of His children a new name, reflecting something unique and special in our lives. When Abram, which means "exalted father," was ninety-nine, God changed his name to *Abraham*, meaning "father of many." When Jacob, which means "deceiver," wrestled with God, the Lord changed his name to *Israel*, "he struggles with God." God looks into our inmost being and gives us a name that carries the essence of our new creation in Christ.

What might your new name be?

Dear Lord, I look forward to the day when I will receive my new name, one that reflects the very essence of who I am in You.

The Great Gift Giver

Every good and perfect gift is from above,
coming down from the Father of the heavenly lights,
who does not change like shifting shadows.
JAMES 1:17 NIV

Do you know a true gift giver? We all give gifts on birthdays and at Christmas, when we receive wedding invitations, and when a baby is born. But do you know someone with a real knack for gift giving? She finds all sorts of excuses for giving gifts. She delights in it. A true gift giver has an ability to locate that "something special." When shopping for a gift, she examines many items before making her selection. She knows the interests and preferences, the tastes and favorites of her friends and family members. She chooses gifts they will like—gifts that suit them well.

God is a gift giver. He is, in fact, the Creator of all good gifts. He finds great joy in blessing you. The God who made you certainly knows you by name. He knows your tastes and preferences. He even knows your favorites and your dreams. Most important, God knows your needs.

So in seasons of waiting in your life, rest assured that gifts chosen and presented to you by the hand of God will be worth the wait.

God, sometimes I am anxious. I want what I want,
and I want it now. Calm my spirit and give me the
patience to wait for Your perfect gifts. Amen.

Tuesday
February 5

An Extravagant God

Change your life, not just your clothes. Come back to God, your God. And here's why: God is kind and merciful. He takes a deep breath, puts up with a lot, this most patient God, extravagant in love.
Joel 2:13 msg

There are times when we are exhausted and discouraged and we allow our minds to roam to dark places. Despair and disappointment set in. A woe-is-me attitude prevails. How do we rise from the doldrums? How do we continue? We turn our faces toward the Lord God and know that He is in control.

Scripture tells of God's mercy and loving-kindness. It speaks to us to come back to God. This doesn't necessarily mean a change of circumstances, but a change of heart. And this change is a choice we intentionally make. It's not necessary to be in a church building or revival tent. While many changes happen there, ours can be in our closet, our car, our office. We reach inwardly to the Highest and ask for His mercy. And scripture says He is merciful.

Focusing on the negative—choosing despair—doesn't bring life. Voluntarily focusing on Jesus will. Praise Him for all your blessings: They are there, look for them! Some might be tiny, others magnificent. But they're all because of our Lord Jesus Christ. He is a most patient God and extravagant in His love.

Heavenly Father, I praise Your name. You are extravagant in Your love, filling me to overflowing! I am grateful for all You've done.

Jesus Is Tempted by Satan

And the devil said to Him, "If You are the Son of God, tell this stone to become bread." And Jesus answered him, "It is written 'Man shall not live on bread alone.' "
LUKE 4:3–4

Have you ever found yourself so tempted to sin that you ached all the way to your soul? Christ understands that pull toward evil.

Satan wasn't just present in the wilderness to "bug" the Lord Jesus Christ. This was a full-on, frontal attack. And the stakes were high. For if Christ succumbed to Satan's snare, He would be ineligible to make that perfect sacrifice on the cross as the Lamb of God without blemish.

In this first temptation, Satan intimated that there must be something wrong with the Father's love for the Son since He allowed Him to go hungry. Satan's fiery darts of doubt were aimed directly at the Triune God.

With the second temptation, Satan led Christ upward for a better view of "all the kingdoms of the world." Satan attempted to get Christ to bypass the cross and seize the power.

The third temptation involved a literal leap of faith. For Satan declared that Jesus prove Himself as the Son of God and stand on the pinnacle of the temple and throw Himself down. This time the evil one meant to question the Father's faithfulness toward the Son. After all, the Scriptures did say that God would give His angels charge concerning Him.

Lord, I thank You for Your Son's perfect victory over Satan.

Hurt by Others' Choices

God heard the boy crying. The angel of God called from Heaven to Hagar, "What's wrong, Hagar? Don't be afraid. God has heard the boy and knows the fix he's in."
GENESIS 21:17 MSG

A slave during early biblical times, Hagar had little say in her life decisions—others made them for her. Because of the infertility of her mistress, Sarah, Hagar became the concubine of Sarah's husband, Abraham, and gave birth to Ishmael.

At first, Hagar's hopes soared. Her son would become Abraham's heir, rich and powerful beyond her wildest dreams! However, the surprise appearance of Isaac, the late-life son of Sarah and Abraham, destroyed Hagar's fantasies of a wonderful future. Sarah wanted Hagar and Ishmael out of their lives. Abraham, though upset, loaded Hagar with water and food and told her to take Ishmael into the unforgiving desert.

When their water supply failed, Hagar laid her dehydrated son under a bush and walked away crying because she could not bear to watch Ishmael die. But God showed Hagar a well of water. Quickly she gave her child a drink. Both survived, and "God was on the boy's side as he grew up" (Genesis 21:20 MSG).

God is also on our side when we suffer because of others' choices. Even when we have lost hope, God's plan provides a way for us and those we love.

Heavenly Father, when my world seems out of control, please help me love and trust You—even in the deserts of life.

Overwhelmed by Life

"The waves of death swirled about me; the torrents of destruction overwhelmed me. . . . In my distress I called to the LORD. . . . From his temple he heard my voice; my cry came to his ears."
2 SAMUEL 22:5, 7 NIV

Some days the "dailyness" of life seems like a never-ending grind. We get up, eat, work, rest—and do it again the next day. Then when tragedy strikes, we're swept up in grief. What once seemed doable now seems a huge challenge. Depression sinks its claws deep into our spirit. Fatigue sets in, and we are overwhelmed: Life is hard. We may be tempted to question, "Is this all there is?"

Here's the good news: There's more. God never meant for us to simply exist. He created us for a specific purpose. He longs for us to make a difference and show others His love and grace. What's more, He never asked us to do life alone. When the waves of death swirl around us, and the pounding rain of destruction threatens to overwhelm us, we can cry out to our heavenly Father, knowing that He will not let us drown. He will hear our voice, and He will send help.

So, next time you feel that you can't put one foot in front of the other, ask God to send you His strength and energy. He will help you to live out your purpose in this chaotic world.

Lord, thank You for strengthening me when the "dailyness" of life, and its various trials, threatens to overwhelm me.

Ask for Directions

The wicked in his proud countenance does not seek God;
God is in none of his thoughts.
Psalm 10:4 nkjv

Do the laundry, wash the dishes, shop for groceries, cook dinner, work a full day, drive the kids to soccer practice, the list of a busy woman's duties goes on and on. Entwined within those chores are the mental challenges of making wise decisions, dealing with relationships, raising the kids well—again, the list goes on.

Somewhere along the way we got the idea that it is wrong to ask for help. But you can't live the Christian life like that. It's impossible. You can't possibly forge through life alone, managing to make wise decisions while you resist temptations and recover from failures. If you don't ask for help, you won't stand a chance.

Women often tease that men would rather drive around lost for hours instead of stopping to ask for directions. But how often, in your own day, do you stop for a moment and ask the Father for directions? Jesus, knowing that He needed guidance from His Father, constantly sought His will by praying and asking for it. Instead of trying to find His own way through the day, Jesus fully depended on directions from above and actively pursued them.

Jesus, forgive me for my pride and for not asking
You for directions. Please show me the way to go
and lead me in it. Help me to hear Your leading
and then to follow it. Amen.

Fishers of Men

"Come, follow me," Jesus said,
"and I will make you fishers of men."
MATTHEW 4:19 NIV

Walking beside the glistening blue waters of the Sea of Galilee, Jesus saw two brothers casting their fishing nets. When He spoke the words recorded above, Peter and Andrew must have been intrigued. But Jesus didn't invent the phrase "fishers of men." Philosophers and teachers of that day used this term to describe those who captured men's minds.

The passage goes on to say that Peter and Andrew immediately left their nets and followed Jesus. But this wasn't their first invitation to follow Him. They had gone with Jesus to Capernaum and Galilee and later returned to their trade of fishing. However, this particular invitation was to full-time ministry and they responded wholeheartedly.

But why did Christ want these fishermen? Peter and Andrew were men of action who knew how to get a job done without quitting or complaining. Their tenacity would be an asset to Christ's ministry of soul winning.

Jesus came not only to save but to teach men and women how to have true servants' heart. The substance of ministry is service. When the apostles agreed to follow Christ, they accepted the call on His terms, not theirs.

Lord, show me clearly where I can be of
service within my local body of believers.
Perhaps there's a small hand in the Sunday
school just waiting to be held.

Melting Point

If anyone builds on the foundation with gold, silver, costly stones, wood, hay, or straw, each one's work will become obvious. . . because it will be revealed by fire.
1 Corinthians 3:12–13 hcsb

Wood, hay, and straw—they all burn. We use them as kindling and fuel. Apply a flame to each and they leap to life—providing light and heat until they're totally consumed.

Gold and silver, though, are different. They don't burn; they *melt*. As they turn from solid to liquid, the impurities of their natural state burn away.

In a similar way, tribulation reveals the quality of our inner lives. Trials consume the worthless parts of our character, activities, and spending habits. What isn't consumed melts, turning our stability on its head. Then we're prepared for a reformation of what remains.

When we consider what we say, do, purchase, or pursue, we can use today's verse as our standard. Is our pursuit *ignitable*—temporary and unimportant—or is it *malleable*—something that can be reshaped and used as God directs?

What happens when the fires of tribulation blow through our lives? Do we reach an ignition point or a melting point?

O Lord God, You test me to transform me into the image of Your Son. Teach me to invest in what will last and not that which passes away.

David Called Him Lord

And Jesus answering began to say, as He taught in the temple, "How is it that the scribes say that the Christ is the son of David? David himself said in the Holy Spirit, 'The Lord said to my Lord, "Sit at My right hand, until I put thine enemies beneath Thy feet."' David himself calls Him 'Lord'; and so in what sense is He his son?" And the great crowd enjoyed listening to Him. And in His teaching He was saying: "Beware of the scribes. . .who devour widows' houses, and for appearance's sake offer long prayers; these will receive greater condemnation."

Mark 12:35–38, 40

In this age where all of us are overly conscious of being politically correct, it's difficult to understand how extremely direct Christ was being here. The Pharisees, after all, enjoyed a position in which their motives and actions were seldom questioned.

Christ had just explained to the Pharisees that the reason they couldn't comprehend what would take place in the Resurrection was because they understood neither the Scriptures nor the power of God (Mark 12:24).

All of us are responsible not only to read the Word of God with understanding but also to have discernment concerning the clergy who minister to us. Is their primary goal to make sure their flock is ultimately led to God's glory?

Am I like those in the crowd who simply "enjoyed listening" to Christ? Help me take time to know You, Lord.

Take My Hand

*I have no regrets. I couldn't be more sure of my ground—
the One I've trusted in can take care of what he's trusted me to do.*
2 Timothy 1:11–12 msg

Ever feel like giving up? Throwing in the towel? Some days it's hard to find the resolve to persevere. Despite our human frailties, our heavenly Father is there to grab our hands and pull us to our feet. He isn't impressed with what we do in life, but how we tackle each day. He wants us to gaze at Him and know He's there to take care of us despite the overwhelming odds life brings.

Paul could have given in. The man was shipwrecked, beaten, imprisoned, and persecuted, and yet he kept on giving the Lord praise. He preached the good news of Jesus and faced the consequences of his actions. Few of us will face the same persecution, but we have the same Spirit within us that Paul did. He told Timothy he had no regrets because he was sure of the One he served.

Are you sure today of the One you serve? When coming to grips with difficulties, do you turn to the Creator of the universe and ask for help? You should. He's available. Just reach out and take His hand. He'll be there.

*Lord, teach me Your love. Let me feel Your embrace.
I choose to trust in You. Amen.*

How Do I Love Thee?

This is what real love is: It is not our love for God; it is God's love for us. He sent his Son to die in our place to take away our sins.
1 JOHN 4:10 NCV

If the word *love* were banned from popular music, radio stations and songwriters would go out of business. Even the Internet would shrink without this word, so key to human existence. All around the world, people search for someone to care. They chat with strangers, post videos, pay for profiles—anything to find the real love they crave.

Few prove successful—because we human beings are hard to love! Even our charity often wears a disguise. We give so we will receive attention, prestige, or assurance that other people will respect us. Some of us even think our little five-and-dime "love" will obtain a place for us in heaven, as if God were a headwaiter to be bribed.

The Bible tells us He does not *need* our love. He *is* love. God the Father, God the Son, and God the Spirit love each other in perfect eternal unity and joy. If God had done the logical thing, He would have wiped out us troublesome humans and created a new race, one that would worship Him without question.

But He would rather die than do that.

Oh Lord, when I presume on Your love, please forgive me. Open my eyes to Your magnificent generosity so I can worship with my whole heart, in a way that pleases You.

Light in the Darkness

I will lead blind Israel down a new path, guiding them along an unfamiliar way. I will brighten the darkness before them and smooth out the road ahead of them.

Isaiah 42:16 NLT

In the dim moonlight, we can sometimes find our way in the darkness of our homes. In familiar places we know the lay of the land. At best we will make our way around the obstacles through memory and shadowy outline. At worst, we will lightly stumble into an armchair or a piano bench. When all else fails, we know where the light switch is and, blindly groping in the darkness, we can turn on the light to help us find our way.

But when we walk in the darkness of unfamiliar places, we may feel unsettled. Not sure of our bearings, not knowing where the light switch is, we become overwhelmed, afraid to step forward, afraid even to move. At those times, we need to remember that our God of light is always with us. Although we may not see Him, we can rest easy, knowing He is ever-present in the darkness of unknown places, opportunities, and challenges.

God will never leave us to find our way alone. Realize this truth and arm yourself with the knowledge that no matter what the situation, no matter what the trial, no matter how black the darkness, He is ever there, reaching out for us, helping us find our way. Switch on the truth of His light in your mind, and walk forward, knowing He is always within reach.

Lord, be my Light. Guard me in the darkness of these days. Make my way straight and the ground I trod smooth. And if I do stumble, catch me! In Jesus' name, I pray. Amen.

Hope

Why are you downcast, O my soul?
Why so disturbed within me? Put your hope in God,
for I will yet praise him, my Savior and my God.
PSALM 42:5–6 NIV

If you've ever been depressed, you're not alone. Depression can be caused by circumstances, biology, environment, or a combination of all of those things. Research indicates that as many as 25 percent of Americans suffer from depression at some point in their lives.

We are blessed with scriptural accounts of godly people like David and Jeremiah who struggled with depression. These stories let us know that it's a normal human reaction to feel overcome by the difficulties of life.

While feeling this way is normal, it doesn't have to be the norm. As Christians, we have hope. Hope that our circumstances will not always be the way they are right now. Hope that no matter how dismal the world situation seems to be, God wins in the end. Hope that eternity is just on the other side.

Hope is like a little green shoot poking up through hard, cracked ground. When you're depressed, do what David and Jeremiah did—pour out your heart to God. Seek help from a trusted friend or godly counselor.

Look for hope. It's all around you, and it's yours for the taking.

Father, even when I am depressed, You are still God.
Help me to find a ray of hope in the midst
of dark circumstances. Amen.

The Original "Me Generation"

And He called the twelve together, and gave them power and authority over all the demons, and to heal diseases. And He sent them out to proclaim the kingdom of God, and to perform healing. And He said to them, "Take nothing for your journey, neither a staff, nor a bag, nor bread, nor money; and do not even have two tunics apiece. And whatever house you enter, stay there, and take your leave from there."
LUKE 9:1–3

Remember what it was like as a kid to dream about having unlimited powers? Such fantasies have inspired cartoonists to create a variety of superheroes. In our hearts we know that these superheroes aren't real men and women. Human beings, if nothing else, are full of flaws, phobias, and fears.

He instructed His apostles not to take any possessions or provisions with them. Jesus wanted them to learn to rely fully on Him. But their lack of faith rendered them too weak to exercise this authority.

These were the men Christ had trained, empowered, and prepared to bring the Gospel message first to the Jews and then the Gentiles. They had been with Christ on a daily basis, learning from His example how to reach out with compassion to those in need. But instead they displayed both selfishness and a lack of love. How could they be left in charge of disseminating the Gospel? And yet they were God's Plan A.

Lord, how grateful I am that Your Holy Spirit worked in the lives of these apostles, molding them into strong men of faith. Help me to become unselfish with my time that many more will hear the Gospel.

Fear-Free

You will not fear the terror of night, nor the arrow that flies by day.
Psalm 91:5 niv

Were you afraid of the dark when you were a little girl? It's hard to be comfortable when you can't see what's out there, right? Even as a big girl, the nighttime hours can still be a little scary. Seems like we're most vulnerable to fears and failures in the wee hours, when the darkness closes in around us.

So, how do you face the "terror of night" without fear? You have to grasp the reality that God is bigger and greater than anything that might evoke fear. He's bigger than financial struggles. He's bigger than job stress. He's even bigger than relational problems. Best of all, He can see in the dark. He knows what's out there and can deal with it. All it takes is one sentence from Him: *"Let there be light!"* and darkness dispels.

We serve an awesome and mighty God, One who longs to convince us He's mighty enough to save us, even when the darkness seeps in around us. So don't fear what you can't see. Or what you *can* see. Hand over that fear and watch God-ordained faith rise up in its place.

Father, I'm glad You can see in the dark. Sometimes I face the unseen things of my life with fear gripping my heart. I release that fear to You today. Thank You for replacing it with godly courage.

Be a God-Pleaser

*Am I now trying to win the approval of men, or of God?
Or am I trying to please men? If I were still trying to please men,
I would not be a servant of Christ.*
GALATIANS 1:10 NIV

Sometimes we work ourselves to the bone because we have no choice. Other times, we do it to win the approval of others.

Today, let's be honest with ourselves. Are we run-down? Worn out? If that's the result of situations we can't control, let's ask the Lord to give us the strength we need to keep going. But if we're exhausted because we're afraid of letting someone down or hurting his or her feelings, it might be time to reassess. If we're up to our eyebrows in work, overlooking other options for the people under our care, then we might be caught up in the "man-pleaser" game.

Here's how the game works: We do our best to make others happy—at any expense. Our health, our finances, our time. We sacrifice in unbalanced ways because we're concerned about what people will think of us.

Today, let's aim to be God-pleasers. Let's do the things *He* calls us to—nothing more and nothing less.

*Lord, You see my heart. You know what struggles
I have in accomplishing these tasks. Redirect my
thoughts, Father, to pleasing You rather than men.*

Pack Up!

The LORD had said to Abram, "Leave your native country, your relatives, and your father's family, and go to the land that I will show you. . . . I will bless you. . . and you will be a blessing to others."
GENESIS 12:1–2 NLT

"Honey, we're moving!" Kayla's husband called to tell her. His company had offered him a big promotion—in another state. Her response? Fat, sloppy tears. She hoped her weeping would change his mind.

Kayla ended up loving her new home.

In God's wisdom, He likes to shake us up a little, stretch us out of our comfort zone, push us out on a limb. Yet we resist the change, cling to what's known, and try to change His mind with fat, sloppy tears.

God seems to have a fondness for change. His first words to Abram were, "Get packing. Say good-bye to your pals in glitzy Ur. I have something better in mind for you" (author's paraphrase).

Are you facing a big change? It might not be a change of address. It could be running for a seat on the school board or going on a short-term mission trip. God wants us to be willing to embrace change that He brings into our lives. Even unbidden change. You may feel as if you're out on a limb, but don't forget that God is the tree trunk. He's not going to let you fall.

Holy, loving Father, in every area of my life, teach me to trust You more deeply. Amen.

When Fear Paralyzes

And a certain young man was following Him, wearing nothing but a linen sheet over his naked body; and they seized him. But he left the linen sheet behind, and escaped naked. And they led Jesus away to the high priest; and all the chief priests and the elders and the scribes gathered together. And Peter had followed Him at a distance, right into the courtyard of the high priest; and he was sitting with the officers, and warming himself at the fire. Now the chief priests and the whole Council kept trying to obtain testimony against Jesus to put Him to death; and they were finding none.
Mark 14:51–55

Suddenly you awake at one in the morning to the sound of the doorknob being turned, followed by the sound of creaking boards. Your heart leaps into your throat. What do you do?

When John Mark, the writer of this Gospel, learned that Jesus had been captured by the Roman guards and a trial was pending, he grabbed the sheet off his bed and ran to observe the events himself.

We know John Mark escaped the threatening situation. Yet Jesus Christ remained in the eye of the storm, well aware of the situation yet in perfect sync with the Father. When fear paralyzes, help is only a prayer away.

*Lord, I believe in all that You are,
both God and Man.*

Talking to God

One of his disciples said to him, "Lord, teach us to pray, just as John taught his disciples." He said to them, "When you pray, say: 'Father, hallowed be your name, your kingdom come. Give us each day our daily bread.' "
LUKE 11:1–3 NIV

Ruth was a Christian, but she struggled in her prayer life. How could she be worthy of speaking to the supreme Creator of the universe? He already knew everything in her mind.

Lord, she thought, *I don't know what to say. How can I possibly pray to You? Do You even hear my insignificant requests?*

Yes, God hears—and, although He knows what we need before we even ask Him, He *wants* us to pray. He even gave us instruction on how to pray. Our prayers don't have to be long or eloquent or even particularly organized. When Jesus taught His disciples to pray, the sample wasn't wordy. He simply taught the disciples to give God glory and to come to Him and ask for their daily needs.

But Luke 11 teaches us something beyond just an outline for prayer. The story shows clearly that if we ask God to teach us how to pray, He will. It's all part of the prayer—ask God to lead you, then speak to Him from the heart.

Let's make it a habit to pray every day. Like the saying goes, practice makes perfect.

Dear God, teach me how to pray. Remind me that my words don't have to be profound. You're just looking for earnest thoughts from the heart.

Fix Your Eyes

So we fix our eyes not on what is seen, but on what is unseen. For what is seen is temporary, but what is unseen is eternal.
2 Corinthians 4:18 niv

The majestic oak's enormous trunk was three feet in diameter. For more than one hundred years, buds had formed each spring and leaves had dropped each fall. But one spring, the leaves were not as plentiful as in previous years. That summer the leaves suddenly turned brown. Soon it was painfully obvious that the great white oak had died.

What a visual reminder that the things of this world will someday pass away. Although the oak had lived many years, it no longer produced oxygen—no longer shaded the backyard. Even trees have life spans.

There are very few things that can be counted on to last forever. Souls are eternal; they remain even when our earthly bodies decay. We need to see beyond the physical by focusing on the spiritual. There is life beyond what we are experiencing in this moment.

Spend your energy and resources on those things that will last: your relationships with your heavenly Father and with others. Love God. Love people. Then you won't fear being cut down like the majestic oak. You will live into eternity in the Lord's presence.

Dear Lord, help me keep an eternal focus and perspective in this life. Allow me to "see" what is unseen. Amen.

Say What?

Don't fool yourself into thinking that you are a listener when you are anything but, letting the Word go in one ear and out the other. Act on what you hear!
JAMES 1:22 MSG

Have you ever been introduced to someone and immediately forgotten the person's name? Similarly, have you ever tried to talk to someone who is engrossed in a television show? "Yeah, I'm listening," the person replies in a less-than-attentive voice.

James seems to be in a similar situation. He is frustrated by those who pretend to listen and yet do not apply what they have heard. Like a person who sits through a speech and afterward cannot list the main points, so the people to whom James writes have heard the Word of God and cannot—or will not—apply it.

So often we find ourselves tuning out the minister on Sunday morning or thinking about other things as we read our Bibles or sing hymns of praise. We look up at the end of a sermon, a stanza, a chapter, and we don't know what we've heard, sung, or read. We pretend to hear, but we are really letting the Word of God go in one ear and out the other. Our minds must be disciplined to really listen to God's Word. Then we must do the more difficult thing—*act* on what we've finally heard.

Dear Lord, please teach me to be attentive to Your Word. Help me to act on the things You teach me so that mine becomes a practical faith. Amen.

Martha and Mary

A woman named Martha welcomed Him into her home. And she had a sister called Mary, who moreover was listening to the Lord's word, seated at His feet. But Martha was distracted with all her preparations; and she came up to Him, and said, "Lord, do You not care that my sister has left me to do all the serving alone? Then tell her to help me."
Luke 10:38–40

Isn't this just how we feel when the men in our household excuse themselves from the table as soon as the first dirty dish appears? Martha, ever the perfect hostess, was left to do all the work. It didn't seem fair.

However, what Martha really desired was a release from her compulsive neatness. And that's when the Lord presented her with a process for "chilling out."

" 'Martha, Martha, you are worried and bothered about so many things; but only a few things are necessary, really only one, for Mary has chosen the good part, which shall not be taken away from her' " (Luke 10:41–42). In other words, all the busyness that now preoccupied Martha didn't really matter. Jesus was here and she was passing up a tremendous opportunity to learn from Him.

After all, who knew better than Christ how to put the pressures of life into perspective? He had only three years in which to establish His ministry, train up His disciples, and present the Gospel. Yet we see no record of Him hurrying others or running at a frantic pace.

Have you taken time to get to know your Lord? Perhaps your life, like Martha's, is missing the best part.

Lord, I pray for peace today from my busy schedule so I may learn at Your knee.

Humble Service Is Pure Religion

Pure religion and undefiled before God and the Father is this, to visit the fatherless and widows in their affliction, and to keep himself unspotted from the world.
James 1:27 KJV

She was not a "great" Christian. She didn't do "marvelous things for God." She was no missionary like Amy Carmichael or Gladys Aylward. Books and movies won't be written about her.

Her short life was spent in a rural area of Pennsylvania. But decades after her death, she is still remembered for her many acts of kindness.

Her children remember, too. Often they sat in the car alone, waiting as she visited the sick in the hospital or the bereaved at the funeral home. Often they sat politely on dusty chairs as she visited shut-ins, and sat quietly in the backseat as she talked to the widows she drove around in her car.

Those kids helped her sort clothes for the poor and for children on mission fields. And they watched in amazement on her last Christmas, when she was in the final stages of cancer, as she left her home to visit her elderly friends at a nursing home.

Although the world did not recognize her good works, God did.

Her religion was pure and undefiled before Him.

Dear Father, I want so much to do great things for You—but there's never time because I'm so busy caring for the needy around me. Please remind me that greatness in Your eyes comes in humility and lowliness, in caring for those who have afflictions. Thank You for the many opportunities You give me to serve.

Red High Heels

Don't be concerned about the outward beauty of fancy hairstyles, expensive jewelry, or beautiful clothes. You should clothe yourselves instead with the beauty that comes from within, the unfading beauty of a gentle and quiet spirit, which is so precious to God.
1 Peter 3:3–4 NLT

Fashion gurus love to tell women what to wear. Many like to recommend one pair of red shoes—preferably sassy high heels—to spice up a lady's wardrobe. Proponents of the advice say having one special pair of shoes to wear when feeling down or depressed can turn a woman's whole day around, making her feel beautiful and powerful.

While fashion trends are fun and we all want to look well-groomed, we can't forget where true beauty and power come from. Wasn't it Jesus who taught us not to place our treasure in physical things like our bodies or worry about where our clothes will come from? He promises to provide for us.

Shoes scuff, necklaces break, and fabric fades, but true beauty starts from within. When we allow God to dress our spirits in robes of love, joy, peace, patience, kindness, goodness, faithfulness, gentleness, and self-control, our inner beauty will far outshine anything we put on our physical bodies.

Dear Father, I want to be a woman whose inner beauty far surpasses my outer beauty, so that when people see me they are pointed to You and rejoice in Your creation.

Where Do You Take Refuge?

Be gracious, O God, for man has trampled upon me; fighting all day long he oppresses me. My foes have trampled upon me all day long, for they are many who fight proudly against me. When I am afraid, I will put my trust in Thee. In God, whose word I praise, in God I have put my trust; I shall not be afraid. What can mere man do to me?
PSALM 56:1–4

When my father was away during World War II, my mom, sister, and I lived with my grandparents. At the time I was only three years old or so. Frequently, I'd hide under their long, wooden porch, making my world a little smaller, I suppose. Looking out through the latticed covering, somehow I felt safe.

David wrote this psalm when the Philistines had seized him in Gath. These Philistines had been enemies of the Israelites for a long time. At one point they'd even stolen the ark of the covenant. They'd probably never forgiven David for killing their giant, Goliath. I wonder if David reflected during his present predicament, remembering the time in his youth when he'd faced that giant with only five smooth stones and a sling. He had called upon his God to deliver him, and the Lord had prevailed (1 Samuel 17:37–50).

Where do you go for refuge? I run to the arms of my loving Father, just as David did in his own crisis. And He always comes through.

O Lord, You alone are my refuge and strength.
Help me to come to You first in a crisis.

Microwave Faith?

And so after waiting patiently,
Abraham received what was promised.
Hebrews 6:15 niv

Pop a little bag into the microwave, and in two minutes you have hot, delicious popcorn. Unfortunately, faith doesn't always work the same way.

Imagine what Abraham wondered nine months after his conversation with God. He had been promised a son. Abraham believed God. His faith was credited to him as righteousness (Genesis 15:6). Nine months later, he was still waiting. Even nine years later, there was no sign of the promised child. Each passing day brought an opportunity for doubt. But Abraham "considered him faithful who had made the promise" (Hebrews 11:11 niv). Abraham looked past the facts. He was not swayed by the circumstances. He simply believed God and many years later, received his son.

How many times have you given up on the promises of God because circumstances told you something different? It's not too late. Pick up your faith. Determine to see those promises come to pass.

Heavenly Father, I thank You that You are faithful.
Your Word does not return void. I ask You to
forgive me for doubting You. I believe Your Word.
I praise You and glorify You in advance for the
promises You are bringing into my life.

It's All Good

And we know that all things work together for good to them that love God, to them who are the called according to his purpose.
ROMANS 8:28 KJV

Barren for life. A seventeen-year-old girl received news from her doctor that she would never conceive children. Questions flooded her mind: *What guy would want to marry me? What about my love of children?* Yet amid the questions came a gentle whisper: *"We know that* all things *work together for good to them that love God"* (emphasis added). She didn't understand how, but she trusted the Lord to fulfill His promise. He did. Over the next thirty years, she became a wife, a mother, and a grandmother.

God can and does use all things in our lives for His good purpose. Remember Joseph in the cistern, Daniel in the lions' den, and Jesus on the cross? The Lord demonstrated His resurrection power in each of those cases. He does so in our lives as well. He brings forth beauty from ashes.

What are you facing that seems impossible? What situation appears hopeless? What circumstance is overwhelming you? Believe God's promise. It is easy to trust God when things are going well. And when we choose to trust Him in uncertain times, we receive a peace that gives us hope that sustains us. We are not disappointed, because God always keeps His promises. Our response is to trust Him.

Dear Lord, thank You that You work all things together for Your good purpose. May I trust You to fulfill Your purpose in my life. Amen.

Calmed by His Love

"The LORD your God is in your midst, a mighty one who will save; he will rejoice over you with gladness; he will quiet you by his love; he will exult over you with loud singing."
ZEPHANIAH 3:17 ESV

What is causing you unrest today? Inadequacy? Lack of strength? Poor finances?

God wants you to know that He is with you. He sees your circumstances, your concerns, your worries. And He wants you to know that He's the mighty One who will save you. He is rejoicing over you with gladness, exulting over you with loud singing. Why?

Because He loves you. And He wants to wrap you in His love that's like a thick comforter on a cold winter evening. He wants us to rest in His love. For only His love can calm the fear that hinders you from doing what He's tasked you to do.

God's love sent His Son to die for you, that you might receive everything you need pertaining to life and godliness. His love enables you to keep on going even when you're ready to give up. His love allows you to rest, to gain strength, to be still in the midst of the storm that is raging all around you. The waters will not rise enough to drown you, nor will the raging fire consume you.

Father, I thank You for the gift of Your love. It calms me, it soothes me, it gives me peace in the middle of the storm. Please fill me with Your love and peace today.

When Everyone in Heaven Rejoices

"Or what woman, if she has ten silver coins and loses one coin, does not light a lamp and sweep the house and search carefully until she finds it? And when she has found it, she calls together her friends and neighbors, saying, 'Rejoice with me, for I have found the coin which I had lost!' In the same way, I tell you, there is joy in the presence of the angels of God over one sinner who repents."
LUKE 15:8–10

This Scripture brings back a certain trip to the beach. As my husband and I were about to relax in our travel trailer at a California beach, I realized I had misplaced my expensive sunglasses. Frantically retracing my steps, I hunted through both the trailer and the car. We even called the AAA office where we had made a quick stop to secure a few maps. However, the sunglasses never materialized.

How ecstatic this woman was to find this missing coin she'd considered lost forever. When a young girl in Israel married she began wearing a headband containing ten silver coins. This band carried the same significance as our modern wedding rings. To lose one would have been nothing short of a catastrophe.

Jesus compared the woman's deep joy to the celebration that goes on in heaven when a sinner repents and "Son-beams" of peace finally flood into the soul. It's the feeling of "wholeness" a person hungers for all her life.

Lord, I am grateful that Your Word has penetrated the core of my own heart. Hallelujah!

Commitment Challenges

Remember me for this, my God, and do not blot out what I have so faithfully done for the house of my God and its services.
NEHEMIAH 13:14 TNIV

Have you ever sacrificed precious "leisure" hours to serve on a church committee, count offerings, or weed church flower beds? Despite your work and home schedule, you agree to co-teach Bible school—only to receive a phone call the night before from your partner. She has decided to go on vacation instead! Now, surrounded by hyper kindergarteners, you wonder what you did to deserve this.

Nehemiah felt the same way. A governor during Old Testament times, he spearheaded the rebuilding of Jerusalem's broken walls, then spent years encouraging his countrymen to worship Yahweh. He organized priests and Levites and served as a spiritual lay leader. He managed the practical affairs of the temple, including schedules, payments, and distributions. Nehemiah fought enemies, settled internal squabbles and—and—*and!* His days never seemed long enough. He grew discouraged when trusted fellow workers in God's house placed their priorities elsewhere. Between crises, Nehemiah took a deep breath and prayed the above prayer.

More than twenty-five hundred years later, God tells the story of Nehemiah's perseverance in the Bible. Like you, Nehemiah may not have seen his reward as soon as he wanted. But now he is enjoying it forever.

So will you.

Lord Jesus, when I feel tired and unappreciated as I serve others, let Your applause be enough for me.

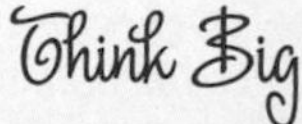

Think Big

"For as the sky soars high above earth, so the way I work surpasses the way you work, and the way I think is beyond the way you think."

ISAIAH 55:9 MSG

Anne heard a missionary speak at church, and a dream to serve in China was born in her heart. After graduation from high school, she would go.

But World War I began and kept her dream on hold. She began a teaching career that spanned the years until she retired at sixty-five. On the day of her retirement, she filled out an application to serve as a missionary, but was rejected because of her age. Undecided about her future, she packed her car and drove north to a small town in need of a teacher.

Anne continued to pray about her heart's desire. In the late '60s, an age discrimination bill was passed. Anne filled out the form to become a missionary and went to China. She had a big dream—one large enough for God to fill.

We should dream big and ask God for direction in life. We humans are impatient and want what we want right now. But our Father in heaven knows better. He has created a world that unfolds according to His timetable.

We must dream, think big, and wait for God to reveal the plan. He's in control.

Dear Lord, You know my heart's desire. Help me to wait upon Your answer for my life. Amen.

Our Prayer Requests

In the morning, O Lord, you hear my voice; in the morning I lay my requests before you and wait in expectation.
Psalm 5:3 niv

When my children were young the only way I could ensure having a special quiet time of prayer was to get up earlier than anyone else in the house. On weekdays this translated to 5:30 a.m. Settled into one particular chair, I read my Bible and then prayed for each member of our family. Although I never made a big deal about this habit, occasionally the kids would catch a glimpse of me there as they began their own busy days.

On Sunday evenings I would ask my husband and children for any particular things they'd like me to pray about that week. Such concerns as tests, projects, or schoolwork that were due, and once in a while class bullies or teachers were voiced. (Whenever "teachers" came up, I figured my child had been given a great deal of homework and resented it.)

Often in the morning I'd find little folded notes on my prayer chair. Now that our children are raised, I wish I'd saved some of those crumpled "last-minute additions" always written on notebook paper. But I do have memories of the celebrating we did when one of those prayers was answered.

Are you laying your own requests before the Lord?

Lord, I wander around like those who have no hope, forgetting to ask You for wise solutions to my dilemmas. Help me remember to come to You before I start my day.

Financial Strain

"No one can serve two masters. Either he will hate the one and love the other, or he will be devoted to the one and despise the other. You cannot serve both God and Money."
Matthew 6:24 niv

Do you ever get nervous when you watch the news and see reports about the stock market? Does your head spin when you see the prices rise at the gas pump? Can you feel your heart race when you look at your bills in comparison to your bank statement? Even though many of our day-to-day activities depend on money, it's important to remember that money is not a provider or sustainer. Only God can provide for you and sustain you. When we begin to focus on and worry about money, then we are telling God that we don't trust Him.

As you feel yourself start to worry about money, stop and change your focus from wealth to God. Thank Him for what He has provided for you and then humbly ask Him to give you wisdom about your financial situation. Be at peace as you remember that you can absolutely trust God to provide for you and to sustain you.

Dear God, help me not to worry but to trust that You will provide for me. Help me to be devoted to You only. Amen.

A Discerning Woman

*Wisdom reposes in the heart of the discerning
and even among fools she lets herself be known.*
Proverbs 14:33 niv

Dorothy, a precious older woman, faithfully attended my Bible study group each week despite the fact that she suffered from congestive heart failure. She was the kind of person one treasured as a gift, knowing the time with her would be all too brief. She shared the contents of her heart freely, no longer restricted behind the confining walls of decorum. From her perspective, the word *cherish* didn't exist in her husband's vocabulary.

We would pray and cry together over the grief her marriage had caused her soul. And then she'd sit and play a beautiful hymn on the piano. This is the way the Lord ministered to her pain. Confident of her eternal destination, she exuded serenity, wisdom, peace, and love. And the Lord called her home that year because He valued her tremendously. She's buried in a cemetery near my house and I smile when I pass by, knowing she's found a refuge where the music never stops and people never cry.

Today's proverb says that "wisdom reposes in the heart of the discerning." How well Dorothy understood this. And although she couldn't change her husband's heart, her own was filled with wisdom. She'd learned the art of holding life like a kite, giving it enough room to float freely and then watching as it returned to her.

*Lord, everyone has a cross to bear.
But because You bore Calvary's cross for me,
I have the hope of eternal life.*

Release the Music Within

Those who are wise will find a time and a way to do what is right.
ECCLESIASTES 8:5 NLT

Miss Lilly is a talented woman. Without the luxury of taking one lesson, she plays the violin with grace and ease. Her oil paintings exude warmth, character, and charm. And her ability to retain information would challenge a twenty-year-old college student. But in her eighty years, Lilly has merely dabbled in the gifts God has entrusted to her.

"Never had the time, and too late to start!" she insists, as she discusses her unfulfilled dreams and what she would do differently if she could "do it all over again." So her talents are undeveloped, unused, and unappreciated by a world waiting for Lilly's God-given abilities to touch, bless, and stir them.

It has been said that many people go to their graves with their music still in them. Do you carry a song within your heart, waiting to be heard?

Whether we are eight or eighty, it is never too late to surrender our hopes and dreams to God. A wise woman trusts that God will help her find the time and manner in which to use her talents for His glory as she seeks His direction.

Let the music begin.

Dear Lord, my music is fading against the constant beat of a busy pace. I surrender my gifts to You and pray for the time and manner in which I can use those gifts to touch my world. Amen.

God's Foolishness Is Man's Wisdom

*For the foolishness of God is wiser than man's wisdom,
and the weakness of God is stronger than man's strength.*
1 Corinthians 1:25 niv

Cindy reached a fork in the road, facing a troubling decision about a choice she needed to make. Which was the right path? She felt a vagueness and an uncertainty about what to do.

Finally, after time in prayer, she felt the Holy Spirit's prompting to move forward. The choice she felt led to make didn't entirely make sense—but she decided to follow the prompting anyway. Only afterward, as she looked back, did she realize God had mysteriously guided her to the right decision.

This is faith in God. Sometimes, He'll lead us to act contrary to common sense. Did it "make sense" to have Jesus Christ die for our sins? How could a man, hanging on a cross outside Jerusalem, take away our sins? It's foolishness. Impossible!

But with God, all things are possible. He asks us to simply take Him at His Word—and we have plenty of evidence, both biblical and in our own lives, that shows us we can believe Him.

Believing God can seem like foolishness—at least in the world's eyes—but we know the deep peace that comes with that decision.

*Lord, teach me to pray and to listen for
Your guidance. I thank You that You go before
me in every choice, even the confusing ones!
I can move forward with confidence,
knowing You are with me.*

Reach Out

But people who aren't spiritual can't receive these truths from God's Spirit. It all sounds foolish to them and they can't understand it, for only those who are spiritual can understand what the Spirit means.
1 CORINTHIANS 2:14 NLT

Imagine yourself visiting France but unable to speak the language. Everywhere you go, people are conversing in a tongue that you cannot decipher. Although you're lost, asking for directions seems useless. You drive around aimlessly, confused by street signs that don't make sense. People honk as you enter the exits and yell as you navigate the roundabouts. Even though you're trying your hardest, the French judge you as an idiot.

In the same way, unbelievers may feel confused trying to navigate the unfamiliar territory of spiritual truth. They don't have the ability to understand it because they don't have the Holy Spirit as a teacher to guide them. The Bible may not make sense to them, but don't be quick to judge. Hope isn't lost!

God likely has placed unbelievers in your life that He wants you to reach out to. Share your faith with them in words and actions they can understand. Pray the Lord opens their hearts to receive Jesus as Lord and Savior. Then the Holy Spirit will dwell with them, giving them the ability to comprehend spiritual truth. Pray that these lost "tourists" will find Jesus soon!

Dear Lord, help me not judge those that don't know You. Instead, may I pray that You intercede to show them the way. Amen.

Weary Days

Why art thou cast down, O my soul? and why art thou disquieted in me? hope thou in God: for I shall yet praise him for the help of his countenance. O my God, my soul is cast down within me: therefore will I remember thee from the land of Jordan, and of the Hermonites, from the hill Mizar.
Psalm 42:5–6 kjv

It's easy for life's responsibilities and commitments to drag us down. Each day seems like a repeat of the day before. The morning alarm becomes our enemy, and the snooze button becomes our considerate companion. Our hard work often goes unappreciated. Nothing feels accomplished. Our soul yearns for something more.

If we accept it, God's constant goodness can be our delight. In the mornings, instead of our groaning and hiding beneath the pillows, God desires for us to communicate with Him. His voice could be the first one that we hear each day. As we roll over and stretch, we can then say, "I love You, God. Thank You for another day of life."

Our willingness to speak with God at the day's beginning shows our dependence on Him. We can't make it alone. It is a comforting truth that God never intended for us to trek through the hours unaccompanied. He promises to be with us. He also promises His guidance and direction as we meet people and receive opportunities to serve Him.

Getting started is as simple as removing our head from beneath the pillows and telling God good morning.

Lord, refresh my spirit and give me joy for today's activities. Amen.

The Gift of Manna

*They asked, and He brought quail,
and satisfied them with the bread of heaven.*
PSALM 105:40

Who wouldn't welcome the delivery of frec bread on their doorstep each morning? Well, the Israelites had it made and they still complained. "Same old, same old," they'd have cried out in today's vernacular. A one-day supply of this sticky, white, honey-flavored nourishment, called manna, covered the ground each morning. After gathering it, the Israelites ground it between two millstones or beat it with a mortar, boiled it in the pot, and made cakes with it. The taste was similar to cakes baked with oil (Numbers 11:8).

However, after forty years, the thought of waking up to this substance didn't exactly entice one to crawl out of their tent in anticipation.

After repeated complaints, God gave the Israelites some quail to eat (Numbers 11:31). No matter how God cared for them, the Israelites found something to criticize.

Another life-giving bread is symbolically offered to us under the new covenant. Jesus said, " 'I am the living bread that came down out of heaven; if anyone eats of this bread, he shall live forever; and the bread also which I shall give for the life of the world is My flesh' " (John 6:51). Christ Himself compared the two breads: " 'This is the bread which came down out of heaven; not as the fathers ate, and died, he who eats this bread shall live forever' " (John 6:58).

*Lord, I long to live forever
in Your glorious presence.*

Restoration

He maketh me to lie down in green pastures: he leadeth me beside the still waters. He restoreth my soul.
Psalm 23:2–3 KJV

Dumb, helpless, straying sheep. The fluffy creatures don't know any better than to wander away from the herd and get tangled in underbrush. The animals need a shepherd who acts in their best interest and protects them from harm.

That's us—sheep. We wander away from the fold and get caught in the underbrush of the world. We leave the flock and become tired, hungry, and thirsty. Our wandering ways leave us sick in mind, spirit, and body.

We need the Good Shepherd—Jesus. He searches for us when we go astray. He pulls us out of the pits we've fallen into. He removes the thorns from our hides. During the heat of tribulation, He places us in His shadow where we can rest. He slakes our thirst with His living water, the Holy Spirit. He restores our souls. We know His voice and follow Him.

God watches over us day and night, no matter where we are. He tends our wounds, guards us, and builds us back up for the challenges of life. When we are lost, we need only listen for the voice of our Shepherd.

Lord, my Shepherd, I shall not want. Teach me to lie still in Your green pastures and drink of Your quiet waters. Please restore my soul.

Mutual Delight Society

He brought me forth also into a large place:
he delivered me, because he delighted in me.
2 SAMUEL 22:20 KJV

Did you know you are part of a mutual delight society? If you're a Christian, God delights in you, and you delight in Him, too (Psalm 37:4). Over and over, scripture refers to this two-sided enjoyment. How could anyone, believer or not, have missed it?

Sadly, non-Christians don't understand this mutual-delight organization. They think Christians spend their time moping and complaining or sitting in church. All they can see are the things Christians don't do and no longer enjoy or the things they, as unbelievers, wouldn't like doing. The faithless miss out on the larger picture: Sin is no longer fun for those who delight in God. It's more wonderful to live for Him than engage in the sin.

If a sliver of the light of Christian joy pierces the unbelievers' lives, Satan blocks it so they can't see what they might be missing. He can't let them know that loving God can be fun!

The woman who delights in God has God delighting in her, too. His plans for her future are beautiful because she has experienced His salvation. No good thing will He deny her (though her definition of a good thing and His may differ at times).

Do you delight in God? Then share the news. Help others join this mutual delight society today.

Thank You, Lord, for inviting me
to share Your delights. Amen.

SUNDAY
MARCH 17
ST. PATRICK'S DAY

Vocalizing a Prayer

"And when you are praying, do not use meaningless repetition, as the Gentiles do, for they suppose that they will be heard for their many words."
MATTHEW 6:7

Remember kneeling beside your bed and praying when you were a kid? Why did it all seem so simple then? We just talked to God like He was really there and kept our requests short and simple.

Then, as you got older, the lengthy and spiritual prayers of the "older saints" became intimidating. So, where's the balance? Reading a little further in this passage from Matthew, at verse 9, Jesus gives us His own example for prayer. If you can remember the acrostic ACTS, you'll have an excellent formula for prayer: Adoration, Confession, Thanksgiving, and Supplication.

As we come before the Lord we first need to honor Him as Creator, Master, Savior, and Lord. Reflect on who He is and praise Him. And because we're human we need to confess and repent of our daily sins. Following this we should be in a mode of thanksgiving. Finally, our prayer requests should be upheld. My usual order for requests is self, family members, and life's pressing issues. Keeping a prayer journal allows for a written record of God's answers.

Your prayers certainly don't have to be elaborate or polished. God does not judge your way with words. He knows your heart. He wants to hear from You.

Lord, Your Word says that my prayers rise up to heaven like incense from the earth. Remind me daily to send a sweet savor Your way!

Answered Prayer

Delight yourself in the LORD;
and He will give you the desires of your heart.
PSALM 37:4

Sometimes our heartfelt prayers receive a "yes" from God. Sometimes, it's a "no." At other times, we get back only a "not yet."

Have you heard anyone quote today's scripture, saying that God will give us the desires of our hearts? Some believe the verse means that a Christian can ask for anything—health, money, possessions, you name it—and get exactly what she wants. But this passage actually teaches something much deeper.

Note the first part of Psalm 37:4: "Delight yourself in the LORD." A woman who truly delights herself in the Lord will naturally have the desires of her heart—because her heart desires only God and His will.

Our Father takes no pleasure in the things of this world—things that will all wither and die. Neither should we.

So what pleases God? He loves it when we witness for Him, live right, and instruct others in His Word. If those are things that we also truly desire, won't He grant us the "desires of our heart" and let us see people brought into the kingdom? Won't we have a life rich in spiritual growth?

Lord, please help me see where my desires
are not in line with Your will—so that the
things that I pursue are only and always
according to Your own desires.

Protecting Angels

For he will command his angels concerning you to guard you in all your ways.
Psalm 91:11 niv

The SUV was completely totaled after being rear-ended by a semitruck. After flipping end over end, the SUV landed upright. Mangled pieces from the vehicle were scattered along the highway.

It was hard to imagine anyone surviving in such an accident, but the five occupants—a husband and wife and their three granddaughters—walked away from the scene with minor injuries.

Have you ever experienced a miraculous accident like this? It wasn't luck that kept you safe; it was the protecting hands of God's angels watching over and keeping you safe, just as the angels did for the family in the SUV.

Take great comfort in knowing that God loves you so much that you are being guarded and protected by an elite group of heavenly host.

Dear Lord, no matter where I go, in my heart I always know that Your angels are with me night and day, keeping me safe in every way. Amen.

Music in the Morning

It is good to give thanks to the LORD, and to sing praises to Thy name, O Most High; to declare Thy lovingkindness in the morning, and Thy faithfulness by night, with the ten-stringed lute, and with the harp; with resounding music upon the lyre. For Thou, O LORD, hast made me glad by what Thou hast done, I will sing for joy at the works of Thy hands.

PSALM 92:1–4

It's spring! Pollen is in the air and, thanks to the regeneration of life, multiplying rapidly! When I'm stuck working inside, glued to my computer chair, I hunger for some melodious tunes to bolster my sagging spirit.

This particular psalm was actually written for a Sabbath celebration. If you ever attend a Messianic service, you'll discover that believers in Yeshua (Jesus' Hebrew name) definitely have the market cornered on celebrating. They sing, dance, and rejoice in finding their Savior. It's the kind of merriment God designed for us to enjoy with Him. And it's probably the closest reenactment of heavenly worship you'll find on this earth.

Interspersed among all those "begats" that bog us down in the book of Genesis there's a "who's who of professions." "Adah gave birth to Jabal; he was the father of those who dwell in tents and have livestock. And his brother's name was Jubal; he was the father of those who play the lyre and pipe" (Genesis 4:20–21). It seems the human family has found joy in music since almost the beginning of time.

Lord, thank You for music and the way it uplifts my spirits. No matter what time of day or season, I rejoice in worshiping You.

Powerful One

He who forms the mountains, creates the wind, and reveals his thoughts to man, he who turns dawn to darkness, and treads the high places of the earth—the Lord God Almighty is his name.
Amos 4:13 niv

Ever pondered the power of our Lord God Almighty? Meditating on God's power can soothe our biggest worries and calm our deepest fears.

The Word of God speaks often of His power—we know He created our universe in less than a week. But if that's too much to comprehend, consider the enormity of a single mountain or ocean. Those vast, mighty things came into being simply by God's voice—and they're only a tiny fraction of everything He made. What power!

The Lord opens the morning curtains to reveal the dawn and pulls the sky shades back at night to bring darkness. He plots the course of the wind, arranges for rainfall, and causes grass, crops, and trees to grow. He feeds the gigantic whales of the ocean, and every tiny little bird. If our Lord has enough knowledge and power to handle these jobs, surely He can (and will!) look after us.

Problems that seem insurmountable to us are simply a breath to Him. Let's not be anxious today—God holds each one of us in the palm of His hand.

Lord God, You are my provider. Thank You for holding such power—and for choosing me to be Your child. Please give me a greater understanding of who You are, helping me to remember that You, the Lord God Almighty, love me.

Simply Silly

A cheerful disposition is good for your health.
PROVERBS 17:22 MSG

Jeanne Calmont died at the age of 122, after outliving twenty-seven French presidents, and entered the *Guinness Book of World Records* as the world's oldest woman. When asked the secret of her longevity, she replied, "Laughter!"

It's a scientifically proven fact that laughter lowers blood pressure and strengthens the immune system. It helps overcome depression. In short, laughter is good medicine. A "spoonful" each day will add much to our lives.

Paul had so much joy that he sang and won his jailers to Christ. Imagine the effect we could have on our world today if our countenance reflected the joy of the Lord all of the time: at work, at home, at play. Jesus said, "I have told you this so that my joy may be in you and that your joy may be complete" (John 15:11 NIV).

Is your cup of joy full? Have you laughed today? Not a small smile, but laughter. Maybe it's time we looked for something to laugh about and tasted joy. Jesus suggested it.

Lord, help me find joy this day. Let me laugh and give praises to the King. Amen.

Finding the Messiah

He found first his own brother, Simon, and said to him, "We have found the Messiah" (which translated means Christ).
John 1:41

I'll never forget the day that I accepted Jesus Christ as my Savior. I'd been drawn to church twice that day, aware that my soul ached for peace. So many Christians had told me that all I needed to do was "pray and ask Christ into my life." But that seemed overly simplistic. How could this action change my life?

A short time before, while recovering from a compression fracture in my back, I began attending a Bible study. Now those Scriptures I'd heard there began to come back to me. It wasn't a matter of reciting words. Instead, asking Christ into my life meant being willing to trade all the emptiness and estrangement within my soul for the completeness that He alone could provide.

At the age of twenty-nine, on Father's Day, I prayed to receive Christ, relinquishing control of my life to the Lord.

Andrew, speaking in today's Scripture, also found the Messiah and couldn't wait to tell his brother, Peter. That's how we all feel when God's light is at last turned on inside the dungeon of our souls.

How blessed for Andrew that his brother responded and they shared the love of the Lord together. In many families this never happens. Perhaps in reading this you understand what it means to be ridiculed because of your faith in Christ.

Lord, I pray for strength to share Your love with unbelieving family members.

Action–Figure Easter

We will not hide these truths from our children; we will tell the next generation about the glorious deeds of the LORD.
PSALM 78:4 NLT

Michelle opened the big picture Bible to Jesus' donkey-riding entry into Jerusalem and smiled down at her children busy assembling their props. Seven-year-old Michael spread palmetto fronds across the toothpick road he'd carefully laid across the living room carpet. Five-year-old Kyla mounted the Jesus doll on My Little Pony and began the trek down the winding path amid cries of "Hosanna!" from her dad, who had lined a battalion of green army men along the roadside. Toddler Josh clutched the round pillow that was to become the stone rolled in front of the shoe-box tomb after Jesus' crucifixion on a cross formed from pencils rubber-banded together.

The Good Friday tradition of acting out the Easter week story had begun when Michael was in diapers and had evolved into a much-anticipated family production. A real Jesus doll had been purchased, but the rest of the cast was assembled—with much imagination—from the toy box. As Michelle read the Easter story aloud, beginning with Palm Sunday and ending with Jesus' glorious resurrection, the children acted out each scene.

Michelle treasured her children's delight each Easter morning when they sprang from their beds to find the grave handkerchief discarded and Jesus miraculously sitting atop the shoe-box tomb, His little plastic arms raised triumphantly in the air.

Risen Savior, help us use every opportunity to instill in our children the marvelous truths of our faith, so that Your love may be as a precious heirloom to future generations. Amen.

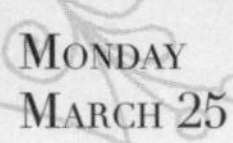

Anxious Anticipations

I am not saying this because I am in need, for I have learned to be content whatever the circumstances.
PHILIPPIANS 4:11 NIV

Have you ever been so eager for the future that you forgot to be thankful for the present day?

We anxiously await the weekend, our next vacation, retirement, or some other future event. Maybe we're eager to start a new chapter in our life because we've been frustrated with our current responsibilities.

Those of us who have raised children have felt a similar pull. We looked ahead to their first steps, their school days, their weddings. In all the daily responsibilities, we sometimes wished the kids would "just grow up." Then they did—and we missed those little ones and their mischievous antics, wishing we could turn back the clock.

Humans have a tendency to complain about the problems and irritations of life. It's much less natural to appreciate the good things we have—until they're gone. While it's fine to look forward to the future, let's remember to reflect on all of *today's* blessings—the large and the small—and appreciate all that we do have.

Thank You, Lord, for the beauty of today. Please remind me when I become preoccupied with the future and forget to enjoy the present.

The Passover Lamb

"Slay the Passover lamb. And take a bunch of hyssop and dip it in the blood which is in the basin, and apply some of the blood that is in the basin to the lintel and the two doorposts; and none of you shall go outside of his house until morning. For the LORD will pass through to smite the Egyptians; and when He sees the blood on the lintel and on the two doorposts, the LORD will pass over the door and will not allow the destroyer to come to your houses to smite you."
EXODUS 12:21–23

This Scripture passage paints a comprehensive picture of the Passover.

Each year this symbolic Passover meal is re-created. The man of the house reads Exodus 12:14. Then his wife puts on her head covering and lights two candles. Using circular motions with her hands above the candles, she then closes her eyes and says a specific prayer.

Four cups of wine or grape juice represent sanctification, the cup of plagues (visited on Egypt), the cup of redemption by Messiah, and the cup of praise to God as the King of the Universe.

Other symbols include parsley, which represents produce, likened to Israel as a seed and growing to maturity; a hidden matzoh bread, denoting Christ in the tomb; the shank bone of the Passover lamb; bitter herbs, commemorating their slavery; and karoset, an apple mixture akin to the mortar of the bricks they made in Egypt as slaves.

We can celebrate the Passover with joy and thanksgiving, knowing for certain that the long-awaited Messiah has come, and will come again!

Lord Jesus Christ, I thank You for being my promised Messiah and Passover Lamb. I thank You for Your sacrifice so that my sins could be forgiven.

Refreshing Gift

For we have great joy and consolation in your love, because the hearts of the saints have been refreshed by you, brother.
PHILEMON 1:7 NKJV

Unsure whether she could continue in the race, the woman looked ahead. A small stand wasn't far down the road. She could see the line of cups at the edge of the table—drinks set out to refresh the runners. The sight encouraged her enough to give her the needed confidence to finish the race.

Encouragement is a wonderful gift. Simple gestures mean so much to those around us. We don't have to make big, splashy scenes to give someone a boost. Our smile can lift someone who is discouraged. A sincere thank-you or a quick hug conveys a wealth of love, gratitude, and appreciation. We all have the opportunity to make small overtures to those around us.

Jesus always took the time for those who reached out to Him. In a crowd of people, He stopped to help a woman who touched Him. His quiet love extended to everyone who asked, whether verbally or with unspoken need.

God brings people into our path who need our encouragement. We must consider those around us. Smile and thank the waitress, the cashier, the people who help in small ways. Cheering others can have the effect of an energizing drink of water so that they will be able to finish the race with a smile.

Jesus, thank You for being an example of how to encourage and refresh others. Help me to see their need and to be willing to reach out. Amen.

Give It All

Jesus looked him hard in the eye—and loved him! He said, "There's one thing left: Go sell whatever you own and give it to the poor. All your wealth will then be heavenly wealth. And come follow me." The man's face clouded over. This was the last thing he expected to hear, and he walked off with a heavy heart. He was holding on tight to a lot of things, and not about to let go.
Mark 10:21–22 msg

It wasn't the response the rich young ruler wanted to hear. Things usually went his way. His position and prestige afforded him that.

But these straightforward, piercing words, blended with the love in Jesus' eyes, troubled the man's soul. It just was too much. He understood just what was being asked of him—everything! The pain in his heart was reflected on his face and in his posture as he slumped away. The truth was, this ruler was not ready to relinquish his all for Jesus.

What has Christ asked *you* to let go of? What are you holding tightly to? Most of us don't have great wealth (we might wish for that kind of "problem"), but are we willing to give up what we *do* have to serve Him?

Outwardly, we may look fine. But inwardly? Are our motives pure? Do we have an "underground" thought life? Is there anger bubbling beneath our calm surface?

The stresses of caregiving can bring such trouble spots to light in our lives. Today let's face the truth of exactly who we are and give up those things that prevent us from wholeheartedly serving Jesus.

Lord, show me what I need to relinquish to You. Help me to abandon everything to freely and joyfully serve You.

What Is Written on Your Heart?

These commandments that I give you today are to be upon your hearts. . . . Write them on the doorframes of your houses and on your gates.
DEUTERONOMY 6:6, 9 NIV

In many Jewish homes today, there is a small container attached to the doorway. Inside the box is a tiny scroll containing the words of Deuteronomy 6:9. This is known as a mezuzah and serves as a tangible reminder of God's ancient covenant with the Israelites and His desire to have first place in their lives.

In the Old Testament, God's law was written on scrolls and passed down from generation to generation. In the New Testament, we learn that Jesus both fulfilled the old covenant and introduced a new covenant. This new covenant is written on our hearts (see Hebrews 10:16). God's Word is our scroll and it confirms the truths that He has already written on our hearts through the Holy Spirit. In spite of this, we sometimes forget.

What are some practical ways you can remind yourself, each day, of the truth of God's Word? Copy verses on index cards to carry with you, or better yet, commit them to memory. Listen to the Bible on tape or to songs composed from scripture. Whatever you do, always be looking for fresh ways to remember the truth that God has written on your heart.

Father, thank You for writing Your truth upon my heart. Help me to look for tangible reminders of Your truth. Amen.

Look Around

Come and see the works of God;
He is awesome in His doing toward the sons of men.
Psalm 66:5 nkjv

We tend to think of encouragement as coming in the way of cards, phone calls, gifts, or efforts performed on our behalf. Isn't it wonderful how God uses people to encourage us? But when the cards or calls don't come, we're wise to look at the other ways God can send us encouragement.

First, He uplifts us through His Word. Just by reading the Bible, we're reminded of the grace and love God has for us. Then there's His creation. Watching a bird fly, seeing a squirrel scramble up a tree, and observing a beautiful flower or a wonderful sunrise are just a few ways God reminds us of His power. Encouragement can also be found by remembering what God has done for us.

If it's been a while since you received a phone call, visit, or card, don't grow discouraged, thinking that God isn't aware of your needs. He's creative in His encouragement—just take the time to look for it.

Dear God, I thank You for all the ways You encourage me. May I not overlook Your blessings because they didn't come in the form I expected.

SUNDAY
MARCH 31
EASTER SUNDAY

Jesus Prepares His Disciples

And He took the twelve aside and said to them, "Behold we are going up to Jerusalem, and all things which are written through the prophets about the Son of Man will be accomplished. For He will be delivered up to the Gentiles, and will be mocked and mistreated and spit upon, and after they have scourged Him, they will kill Him; and the third day He will rise again."

LUKE 18:31–33

As you read today's Scripture you've probably either just celebrated Easter or are anticipating this solemn season of remembrance of Christ's sacrifice on Calvary's cross.

Jesus had traveled with the Twelve, eaten meals with them, spoken of what it meant to truly abide in God, and lived out a sinless life before them. Now His time on earth drew to its inevitable close. Jesus began preparing His disciples for the time He'd be gone from them. He needed to help them accept His death, understand the reason for it, and strengthen them for all this would mean once they could no longer be with Him face-to-face.

In these last days, did they ponder the precious words He spoke at their last supper together? " 'I glorified Thee on earth, having accomplished the work which Thou hast given Me to do. I manifested Thy name to the men whom Thou gavest Me out of the world; Thine they were, and thou gavest them to Me, and they have kept Thy word' " (John 17:4, 6). What is Jesus saying to you?

Lord, I know the days ahead may be difficult. Help me realize, like the disciples, that You are always with me, to the end.

Thinking of Others

Do nothing out of selfish ambition or vain conceit, but in humility consider others better than yourselves. Each of you should look not only to your own interests, but also to the interests of others.
Philippians 2:3–4 niv

The apostle Paul, along with Timothy, founded the church at Philippi. Paul's relationship with this church was always close. The book of Philippians is a letter he wrote to this church while he was imprisoned for preaching the gospel.

Paul knew the Philippians had been struggling with jealousy and rivalry. He encouraged them in his letter to think of others. He reminded them that this was the attitude of Jesus, who took on the role of a servant and humbled Himself for us, even to His death on the cross.

In the final chapter of Philippians, we read the well-known verse that says, "I can do everything through him who gives me strength" (Philippians 4:13 niv). We can do everything through Christ Jesus who gives us strength. That includes putting others before ourselves. That includes replacing "I deserve. . ." with "How can I serve?"

When you start to look out for "number one," remember that your God is looking out for you. You are His precious daughter. As you allow Him to take care of you, it will free up space in your heart and allow you to look to the needs of others.

Father, You have made me to be a part of something much larger than myself. Focus my attention on those around me and not only on my own needs. Amen.

Wimps for Jesus?

Wherefore lift up the hands which hang down, and the feeble knees; and make straight paths for your feet, lest that which is lame be turned out of the way; but let it rather be healed.
Hebrews 12:12–13 KJV

God's discipline sometimes leaves us feeling limp—and not too bright.

"How could I do such a thing? Why didn't I stop to think, read the Bible, and pray about the situation?"

All Christians live through these humbling experiences, because we all make mistakes—sometimes big ones. Washed up and wiped out, we wonder why Jesus bothers with us. We want to give up. Satan would like nothing better. "What's the use?" he whispers. "You've embarrassed yourself and God, and there's no way you will ever hold up your head again." We let our Bibles gather dust and stop going to church. When we see other Christians around town, we hide! We also find ourselves spending time and energy in paths that aggravate our pain rather than heal it.

As always, God presents better solutions for our problems. He disciplines us for the same reason a mother corrects her children: out of love. Ultimately, parents want their kids to lead healthy, productive lives. How can we think God wants any less for us?

Lord Jesus, You gave Your life that I might be healed of my sin and weakness. Please help me to obey You, trusting that You know what You're doing in my life.

Knowing God's Precepts

Teach me Thy statutes. Make me understand the way of Thy precepts, so I will meditate on Thy wonders. My soul weeps because of grief; strengthen me according to Thy word. Remove the false way from me, and graciously grant me Thy law.
PSALM 119:26–29

Have you ever felt as if you've reached the end of the road and the only choice ahead of you is a brick wall? When you reach that point the only remedy is to look up! God is waiting for you to come to your senses.

In these verses we learn the principles that can set things right. The first, revival, occurs when we truly "seek the Lord with all our hearts." Martin Luther, an Augustinian monk, recognized that the precepts he learned from studying the Scriptures didn't mesh with the teachings of the Roman Catholic Church. Therefore, in 1517, he openly stated his objections to the Catholic Church by nailing his Ninety-five "Theses" to the door of the church at Wittenberg. This began the revival that led to the formation of the Protestant church.

Confession of sin is the beginning of true hope. For when we acknowledge that we've failed, God can use our broken and contrite heart, through the Holy Spirit, to mold us anew.

Understand and walk in the way of the precepts by meditating on God's Word. If you're not participating in an in-depth Bible study, consider finding or starting one.

Lord, teach me Your ways, that I might live out Your precepts before my family and loved ones.

Wish List

But they cried the more, saying, Have mercy on us, O Lord, thou Son of David. And Jesus stood still, and called them, and said, What will ye that I shall do unto you?
MATTHEW 20:31–32 KJV

The two blind men heard that Jesus was passing by. They called out a generic plea. "Have mercy on us!"

The man they addressed as Lord and Son of David stopped in His tracks. He responded with a simple question: "What do you want?"

Wasn't it obvious? Jesus knew their thoughts and what their hearts desired. But that wasn't enough. They had to verbalize their request: "We want our *sight*"—the one thing they could not receive without divine intervention. Jesus answered their prayer by opening their eyes—and they responded by following Him.

God wants us to bring specific needs to Him. Do you need a job? Tell Him how much salary you need, what kind of work you like to do, and where you want to commute. Do you need a new home? Tell Him exactly what you'd like.

God doesn't *need* us to tell Him our desires. He already knows them. But He delights in going above and beyond what we can ask for. He loves to demonstrate His lavish love. Even if He doesn't give us what we want, it's because He has something better in store.

God wants us to bring the wishes of our hearts to Him in prayer.

Heavenly Father, I thank You that You care about the smallest details of my life. Teach me the joy of specific prayer.

Running on Empty

I have observed something else under the sun.
The fastest runner doesn't always win the race,
and the strongest warrior doesn't always win the battle.
ECCLESIASTES 9:11 NLT

Jan struggled to be the best at everything she tried. She worked harder than anyone in her office, joined nearly every ministry at her church, taught wonderful Bible studies, and gave the best parties of anyone in her women's group. She cooked better, dressed better, kept a better home, and was never seen in public without her game face on.

There was only one problem. Before long, Jan was running on empty. She had little left to give. Her quest to appear perfect before a watching world crumbled around her. Not only was she not perfect, she couldn't keep up with the crazy schedule anymore.

Can you relate to this woman? Are you trying too hard? Always rushing here and there, involving yourself in a dozen things? Has keeping up appearances become an issue? Watch out. Before long, you might be running on empty, too.

Lord, I'm so tired! I've taken on too much.
My heart was in the right place, but somewhere along
the way I got off-track. Redirect me, Father. Show me
what to give up and what to stick with. Amen.

The Rainbow

I have set my rainbow in the clouds, and it will be the sign of the covenant between me and the earth. . . Whenever the rainbow appears in the clouds, I will see it and remember the everlasting covenant between God and all living creatures of every kind on the earth.
Genesis 9:13, 16 niv

Before sunrise the rain beat furiously against our trailer, rous-ing me from a deep sleep. Once it subsided the birds chirped sweetly and I raised the window shade to peek outside. Stretching boldly across the gray clouds lay a vibrant semicircle of color. And slightly above it arched another, more muted bow. "God, You really outdid Yourself this time!" I shouted, waking my husband who reluctantly nodded and then threw the covers over his head. A minute later I flew out the door for a better vantage point.

Every day God freely displays His blessings. Are we too busy or disinterested to appreciate their wonder? Even if we've forgotten He's there, reminders are all around for He is the God of covenants. In a world where promises (or covenants) are disregarded routinely, I need God's kind of stability.

Have you ever made a covenant or a vow to God only to find that life's circumstances prevented you from keeping it? Perhaps it was a marriage vow. In my own marriage there have been times when just honoring that vow has taken every bit of courage and strength I have. Without God's intervention my stubborn flesh would never stay one more day and watch for His miracles of change and hope.

Lord, only You can renew my weary spirit
and fill me with fresh expectation.
Keep my eyes on Your rainbows!

A Hospitable Heart

After [Lydia] was baptized, along with everyone in her household, she said in a surge of hospitality, "If you're confident that I'm in this with you and believe in the Master truly, come home with me and be my guests." We hesitated, but she wouldn't take no for an answer.
ACTS 16:15 MSG

Lydia, a dealer in purple cloth, worked hard at her trade. The Bible does not tell us much else about her except that she was a worshipper of God.

One day during their travels, Paul and his companions stopped to pray by the river outside the city gate of Philippi. They met a group of women there that included Lydia. She listened to Paul's message and accepted Jesus. After Lydia was baptized, she insisted the men come home with her and be her guests. As was customary for a hostess, she likely prepared and served them food and gave them a place to rest and pray. She showed hospitality in the name of the Lord.

You can follow Lydia's lead. Whether your home is small or large, you can choose to be hospitable. Invite a friend who needs a pick-me-up to join you for a meal during the week. Ask a single mom and her children to come over for a pizza and movie night. If elderly neighbors are unable to get out, take your hospitality to them! Bake them some cookies or take them flowers from your garden.

Father, give me a heart for hospitality. May I always serve others in Your name. Amen.

Fearfully and Wonderfully Made

For Thou didst form my inward parts; Thou didst weave me in my mother's womb. I will give thanks to Thee, for I am fearfully and wonderfully made; wonderful are Thy works, and my soul knows it very well. My frame was not hidden from Thee, when I was made in secret, and skillfully wrought in the depths of the earth. Thine eyes have seen my unformed substance; and in Thy book they were all written, the days that were ordained for me, when as yet there was not one of them.
PSALM 139:13–16

Are you one of those people who picks up a new book and reads the last page first? Well, if your life could be compared to a book, only God knows the "ending" as well as the beginning. Despite the "pages" in the middle that might prove disappointing at times, God has a definite purpose for your life. And if you are in His will, the last page will have a very happy ending!

As we survey this "sea of humanity," we can feel as insignificant as a grain of sand. And yet one granule piled on top of another makes for a gorgeous beach.

Each of us has not only an inborn sense that there is a God, but also an understanding that we possess a designed intent. Your parents aren't responsible for your creation, God is. Had He not willed your very existence, you would not have happened. God wants to use your life to further His kingdom.

Lord, please renew my understanding that You created me in Your own image and likeness with a body, mind, and spirit.

Guilt-Free

So now there is no condemnation
for those who belong to Christ Jesus.
Romans 8:1 NLT

Every one of us has messed up—some of us big-time. Fortunately, we serve the God of second chances.

He tells us in 1 John 1:9, "If we confess our sins, he is faithful and just and will forgive us our sins and purify us from all unrighteousness" (NIV).

When we confess our failures, repent, and move on, God wipes those mistakes away—He sees the child He created, who is washed in the blood of Jesus.

"Therefore," Romans 8:1 says, "[there is] now no condemnation (no adjudging guilty of wrong) for those who are in Christ Jesus, who live [and] walk not after the dictates of the flesh, but after the dictates of the Spirit" (AMP).

Whatever we've done wrong, let's stop condemning ourselves. If we've confessed those sins, there is no need for our feelings of guilt.

Guilt has held back the blessings of God long enough! Let it go! Have faith in the blood that cleanses *all* sins—past, present, and future.

"Even if we feel guilty, God is greater than our feelings, and he knows everything" (1 John 3:20 NLT).

Father God, I thank You that You have forgiven me.
Help me to forgive myself—and to let go of the guilt
that keeps me from becoming the person You say that I
am. Your Word is true, and I choose to believe
what You say over what I feel.

Tough Faith

These people of faith died not yet having in hand what was promised, but still believing. How did they do it? They saw it way off in the distance, waved their greeting, and accepted the fact that they were transients in this world.
Hebrews 11:13 msg

Sometimes Renee felt that she could not stand one more day of her complicated life. Her husband, Tony, spent Sundays racing stock cars instead of going to church. Their daughter struggled at school. Renee had run out of ideas to help her. Although Renee's siblings lived nearby, too, her elderly parents always seemed to call Renee for a ride to the doctor's office. Even the dog dragged his dish to her! Renee tried hard to balance her days in a godly way. Whatever happened to the abundant life that was supposed to be hers as a Christian?

Renee—and most of us—want to identify with the triumphant heroes listed in Hebrews 11, the "Faith Chapter." God protected them as they succeeded in doing great things for Him. We would rather forget others mentioned who did not achieve their goals during their lifetimes, suffering injustice and hardship. But God has not forgotten them—or Renee and other heroines who faithfully follow Him. They may see few results from their obedience, but their great reward will last an eternity.

Father, when I am sick and tired of doing good, help me to say good-bye to earthly expectations and wave hello to Your forever love. Amen.

Praise and Dance

Praise the LORD! Praise God in His sanctuary; praise Him in His mighty expanse. Praise Him for His mighty deeds; praise Him according to His excellent greatness. Praise Him with timbrel and dancing. . . Let everything that has breath praise the LORD. Praise the LORD!

PSALM 150:1–2, 6

In other words, "Praise Him with all you've got to make noise with!" Isn't that what true worship is, using our entire beings to give Him the glory He deserves?

I know people who believe that dancing is a sin. But God said He wanted His people dancing and praising Him. This worshipful motion accompanied the psalms as they were sung.

In just this one psalm we are given a formula for worship.

Whom are we to praise? The Lord! Where are we to praise? Wherever His congregation gathers. For what are we praising? For who He is, what He's done, and the way He's done it. How are we to praise? With our voices, our instruments, and our bodies as we dance in worship.

You've heard people say, "I don't need church, I can worship God anywhere." They usually mean that formal church service usurps precious moments spent in personal pursuits. They are denying any accountability to God.

The church is God's provision for all the spiritual and physical needs of His people. In a society that has become so mobile as to practically abandon the idea of closeness with extended family, the church picks up the slack.

*Lord, help me to yield my spirit
up to You in true worship.*

She Gave, and He Gave Back

Then Peter arose and went with them. When he was come, they brought him into the upper chamber: and all the widows stood by him weeping, and shewing the coats and garments which Dorcas made, while she was with them.
Acts 9:39 KJV

Dorcas had spent her life as a servant. She was a follower of Christ who was "full of good works and almsdeeds" (Acts 9:36 KJV) that she did continually. Scripture does not itemize her works, but we do know that she sewed coats and garments and took care of many widows.

She was the type of woman who could have "worked herself to death." People like Dorcas are often so busy caring for others that they fail to care about themselves. Of course, we can't say that for sure about Dorcas.

But we definitely know that when she died, many people grieved. And when they heard that the apostle Peter was nearby, they asked him to come—apparently believing he could raise the dead.

That's exactly what Peter did. Through his prayer, he raised Dorcas and returned her to service.

Dorcas had given her life to serve God, and God had given it back.

"For whosoever will save his life shall lose it: and whosoever will lose his life for my sake shall find it" (Matthew 16:25 KJV).

When you give your life to serve others, you are honoring God—and finding life.

Lord Jesus, I don't understand why You would give Your life for me. There is nothing greater that I can do on earth than to give my life for You in service to others. Please strengthen me for this joyful task.

Infinite and Personal

*Am I a God at hand, saith the LORD, and not a God afar off? . . .
Do not I fill heaven and earth?*
JEREMIAH 23:23–24 KJV

Back in the 1950s, the Union of Soviet Socialist Republics sent up its first satellite, *Sputnik*. At that time, communism held Russia in its tightfisted grip. Everyone who was anyone in the USSR was a communist and an atheist. Not long after *Sputnik*, the Russian cosmonauts circled Planet Earth. After their return to earth, one cosmonaut made this announcement to the world: "I saw no God anywhere."

When U.S. astronauts finally made it into space some months later, one remarked, "I saw God everywhere!"

Our worldview determines the way we see reality. The cosmonaut didn't expect to see God, and he didn't. The astronaut didn't see anything more or less than his Russian counterpart, but he came away with an entirely different response. God says that He is both close at hand and over all there is. The late theologian and philosopher Francis Schaeffer called Him the infinite-personal God.

Whether your day is crumbling around you or is the best day you have ever had, do you see God in it? If the "sky is falling" or the sun is shining, do you still recognize the One who orders all the planets and all your days? Whether we see Him or not, God tells us He is there. And He's here, too—in the good times and bad.

Lord, empower me to trust You when it's hard to remember that You are near. And help me to live thankfully when times are good. Amen.

Known by God

But if anyone loves God, he is known by God.
1 Corinthians 8:3 esv

How do we show that we love God? Is it by church attendance? Giving? Doing good deeds? Prayer? These may be manifestations of our love for God, or they may be things we do out of a sense of duty; but loving God is first and foremost a response to being known and loved by God. We can't muster emotion or feeling toward God nor do we love Him simply by willing ourselves to acts of obedience. We begin to love God when we grasp what it means to be known by God.

He knit us together in our mothers' wombs.

He knows the number of hairs on our heads.

He knows every quirk of our personality and gave us every talent that we have.

He accepts us as we are because of Christ's sacrifice for us.

He has compassion for our weakness.

He forgives our sins.

He longs to commune with us.

He delights to hear our prayers.

He desires to help us, strengthen us, and bless us.

He has given us the Holy Spirit as our comforter, our helper, and our teacher.

He wills all this for us before we ever turn to Him in repentance. We need to reacquaint ourselves with the gospel often, to meditate on what Christ has done for us, and to remember that He first loved us.

Lord, renew my love for You.
Help me to remember that You knew me
and loved me before I ever knew You.

Taxes Must Be Paid

Let every person be in subjection to the governing authorities. For there is no authority except from God, and those which exist are established by God. . . . For because of this you also pay taxes, for rulers are servants of God, devoting themselves to this very thing.
Romans 13:1, 6

Knowing the urgent business on your minds today—taxes must be paid!—let's move ahead to Romans. How well I remember all those times my husband and I have searched for a post office that stayed open until midnight on April 15. This past year the post office actually hired people to accept our "contributions" right from our car windows. We called it the "tax parade."

As a tax assessor for our county, my husband claims today's Scripture as his "life verse."

All governments are established by God. And that includes those ungodly dictators who wield their power to control and ravage their constituents. Know that they, too, are accountable to God for the way they exercised the authority that He placed in their trust.

Have you finished filling out your IRS forms? If we meet at midnight tonight, let's reassure each other that our hard-earned money isn't being thrown away. We're following Scripture. . .we're supporting a government that God has truly blessed.

Lord, let me give to the government not grudgingly but out of obedience to You. And please assist those in authority over me to direct wisely the use of these funds.

Cabbage Patch Love

The LORD said, "I have loved you."
But you ask, "How have you loved us?"
MALACHI 1:2 NCV

Mouth gaping open, Jamie stared at the array of Cabbage Patch dolls at the toy store. She examined each doll until she came to an infant boy, complete with birth certificate. "I want this one. His birthday is the same day as mine." Her mother bought the doll, and Jamie doted on it, "feeding" it with the tiny bottle and wiping its face clean. She carried the doll at all times and bragged about it to everyone she met.

Imagine if such a doll could speak. Would it say to Jamie, "You say you love me, but I don't feel loved. How do you love me?"

Sometimes we ask God the same question. "Of course we know You love us, but with everything that's happened, we don't always feel loved."

God has a ready answer: "Before I created Adam, I chose you, as I once chose Jacob instead of Esau. Not only did I choose you, I also adopted you into My family. I gave My Son to make you Mine. I am always with you."

When we examine the facts, it's obvious that God loves us. He longs for us to love Him back. Let's open our eyes—and hearts—to that perfect love.

Father, You chose us to be Your own. You love us with all the tender compassion of a doting Father. Let us rest in Your love.

Comforting Close

The LORD is close to the brokenhearted;
he rescues those whose spirits are crushed.
PSALM 34:18 NLT

Janice walked into the room full of people, still shaken from the death of her father. Her mind was filled with the memory of his laughing face; her hand yearned for his touch. Barely a day went by when she wasn't welling up with tears at some reminder of him. *When will this pain end?* she wondered.

As Janice continued across the room, she realized that everyone had stopped talking. She looked up, and the others turned away, as if they were embarrassed, not knowing what to say or do.

Janice longed for someone to say something, anything. To act normal whether she smiled or cried. She needed so much comfort. To whom could she turn? Then Janice heard a voice. "*Turn to Me, child. I am here. I am always here. Take My hand. I long to comfort you.*"

When others turn away from us, we know we can always rely on our eternal Father, the One who will never leave or forsake us. He is close to us in the best and the worst of times. He rescues us when we are crushed. Take His hand. Rest in His arms. Let Him love you.

God, thank You for always being there. Heal my broken heart, my crushed spirit. Hold my hand in Yours. With every breath I take, may I know You are right here beside me, loving me. Amen.

No Worries

"So don't worry about tomorrow, for tomorrow will bring its own worries. Today's trouble is enough for today."
Matthew 6:34 NLT

What thoughts keep you up at night? Finances? Relationships? Work? Health or family concerns? We women are worriers by nature, but living in a constant state of dread isn't what God wants for us, His beloved daughters.

If we're honest with ourselves, we admit we sometimes hold on to our worries, thinking that keeping them close somehow keeps us in control of the situation. In reality, most of our worries concern things completely out of our hands.

Instead, Jesus offers us freedom from our chains of worry. "Trust Me instead of relying on yourself. Give Me the things that you fret over and stress about," He says. "How can you doubt that I'll take care of you when you mean so much to Me?"

Today, trust Jesus' assurance that He will take care of you. Ask Him to help you let go of your worrying nature and replace it with a spirit of praise and thanksgiving. It won't happen overnight, but soon you'll feel the true freedom from worry that only Jesus can supply.

Jesus, You know the toll my worries take on my heart and mind. I don't want to hold on to these negative thoughts, but it's hard to let go of them! Help me to place all my concerns in Your capable hands so that I can be free to praise You as You deserve!

Chosen

Before I formed you in the womb I knew [and] approved of you [as My chosen instrument], and before you were born I separated and set you apart, consecrating you.
JEREMIAH 1:5 AMP

What an awesome thought! God said that before He formed Jeremiah in his mother's womb, He knew him. He *chose* Jeremiah. God separated him from everyone else to perform a specific task, and He consecrated him for that purpose. Wow!

We can be sure that if God did that for Jeremiah, He did it for each one of us. In fact, the apostle Paul said, "He chose us in Him before the foundation of the world, that we would be holy and blameless before Him. In love He predestined us to adoption as sons through Jesus Christ to Himself, according to the kind intention of His will, to the praise of the glory of His grace, which He freely bestowed on us in the Beloved" (Ephesians 1:4–6).

Nothing about us or our circumstances surprises God. He knew about everything before we were born. And He ordained that we should walk in those ways because we are uniquely qualified by Him to do so. He approved us, because He chose us for our specific situation. And He equipped us for every trial and difficulty we will ever face in life. What an awesome God we serve!

Father, the thought that You chose me before the foundation of the world and set me apart for a specific calling is humbling. You are so good. May I go forward with a renewed purpose in life.

Encounter at the Well

So He came to a city of Samaria, called Sychar. Jesus therefore, being wearied from His journey, was sitting thus by the well. It was about the sixth hour. There came a woman of Samaria to draw water. Jesus said to her, "Give Me a drink."
John 4:5–7

Here lived a woman of ill repute. Gathering water was a task customarily performed by the village women early in the day. Her presence at the well late in the afternoon was an acknowledgment that she didn't fit in. She was shunned by those who led wholesome lives. After all, she had had five husbands and now lived with a man.

Although men didn't speak to women in public, Jesus asked this woman for a drink of water. Shocked, the woman responded, " 'How is it that You, being a Jew, ask me for a drink since I am a Samaritan woman?' " (John 4:9) No self-respecting Jew would stoop to address pagans.

Jesus Christ goes right to the heart of her problem. " 'If you knew the gift of God, and who it is who says to you, "'Give Me a drink,'" you would have asked Him, and He would have given you living water' " (John 4:10). And when she asked where to get this living water, He explained the process of eternal life to her.

Transformed, she ran back to town relating her amazing news: " 'Come, see a man who told me all the things that I have done; this is not the Christ, is it?' " (John 4:29)

Father, help me to seek out those who for whatever reason are shunned and despised. They need You so much.

The Forever Word

"The grass withers and the flowers fall,
but the word of our God stands forever."
ISAIAH 40:8 NIV

There is nothing more powerful, more honest, more lasting, or more truthful than God's Word. Nothing else in our world stays the same. Nothing else holds such honest, hopeful power. Grass withers in the summer heat, flowers die and fall to the ground at their season's end. Even our precious children grow up, eventually leaving the nest to venture into the world without us.

The one thing that never changes—that's consistently the same yesterday, today, and for all eternity—is the Word of our God. We have it printed between worn black leather covers, or inside a slick contemporary hardback, or even on our computer. Wherever we keep God's Word—on fragile onion-skinned paper or in some hard-to-understand electronic world—we find life. We find the God-inspired guidance, understanding, and wisdom we need to raise our children well. God's Word is more powerful than any storm life can bring, sharper than any double-edged sword, and brighter than all the stars in the heavens.

When we study God's Word wholeheartedly, He will illuminate it, giving us an understanding that brings perfect peace. While everything around us changes, we can rest in the one thing that stands forever—the true, unchanging Word of God.

Lord Jesus, I thank You for Your Word. I pray that You would teach me more and more how to obtain its nourishment and wisdom for my spirit. I ask You to bless me with great understanding.

One Day at a Time

Blessed be the Lord, who daily loadeth us with benefits, even the God of our salvation.
Psalm 68:19 KJV

There's a reason why the Lord's Prayer teaches us to ask for daily bread. We tend to forget about yesterday's provision in the crunch of today's needs. God calls us to a childlike faith, one that basks in the provisions of the moment and forgets yesterday's disappointments and tomorrow's worries.

Think about small children. A toddler may cry when another child knocks him down and takes away his ball. The tears disappear when his mother hugs him and gives him a kiss. His joy in the expression of his mother's love obliterates his disappointment about the toy. Later he returns to the ball with fresh enthusiasm. He lives in the moment.

God always provides for us. Benefits overflow the shopping carts of our lives every single day. But He only gives us what we need for today, not for tomorrow. He knows that we need those benefits like a daily vitamin. By tomorrow, even later today, we may forget all that God has done for us. The Bible verse that spoke to us this morning feels empty by afternoon.

God gives us blessings every day so that we still have what we need after we have spent ourselves on life's disappointments.

Father, You give us bread daily. We praise You for Your constant care and ask that You will train our eyes to focus on Your blessings, not on our failings. Amen.

Turn Your Ear to Wisdom

For the LORD gives wisdom; from His mouth come knowledge and understanding. He stores up sound wisdom for the upright; He is a shield to those who walk in integrity, Guarding the paths of justice, and He preserves the way of His godly ones.
PROVERBS 2:6–8

Every family has at least one relative who cannot get his act together. (Meanwhile the rest of us scratch our heads and wonder how he can miss the obvious, every single time.) It's as though these people have to fall in every pothole in the street because it never occurs to them to go down a different road.

Are you smiling yet? Is someone in particular coming clearly into focus? Now, hold that thought.

God's Word says wisdom is truly a gift since it comes from the mouth of God, from the very words He speaks. And all God's Words have been written down for us, through the inspiration of the Holy Spirit. Therefore, those who refuse to accept God's guidance, who refuse to ask for His wisdom—those hapless relatives, perhaps—will never see the light of reality.

Know that if you hold fast to the precepts contained in the Bible, you will walk in integrity. Instead of gravitating toward potholes, your feet will be planted on the straight and narrow road.

Lord, I can't change my relatives but I can change myself. So, if my head is the one peeking out of the pothole, please pull me out!

A Little Time with God

*"I thank You and praise You, O God of my fathers;
You have given me wisdom and might."*
Daniel 2:23 NKJV

Susan headed out of her house in the same way she always did—in a hurry, guiding two children before her, double-checking their backpacks as she went and reminding them of chores and practices scheduled for that afternoon. "Remember, 3:30 is ballet; 4:00 is soccer. I'll pick you up school, but I have to go back to work, so—"

She stopped as her coat snagged on a bush. "What—" She looked down to find her hem caught firmly by a cluster of thorns. As she stooped to untangle the cloth, the stem bent suddenly, and Susan found herself nose-to-petal with a rose. It smelled glorious, and she paused, laughing.

When Susan had planted the bush, a friend had asked why. "You never stop long enough to enjoy even what God drops in front of you. What makes you think you'll care about a rose?"

Susan glanced up toward the sky. "Thanks for grabbing me. I guess I should spend a little more time with You."

God blesses us every day in both great and simple ways. Children, friends, work, faith—all these things form a bountiful buffet of gifts, and caring for them isn't always enough. We need to spend a little time with the One who has granted us the blessings.

Father God, You have given us so much to be grateful for. Show me a way to spend more time with You, and help me to grow closer and know You better. Amen.

Healed Miraculously

Now there is in Jerusalem by the sheep gate a pool. . .having five porticoes. In these lay a multitude of those who were sick, blind, lame, and withered, (waiting for the moving of the waters; for an angel of the Lord went down at certain seasons into the pool, and stirred up the water; whoever then first, after the stirring up of the water, stepped in was made well from whatever disease with which he was afflicted.)

John 5:2–4

So many times when we cry out to the Lord for healing, He seems to be asking us the same question He posed to the man who had been sitting at this gate for thirty-eight years waiting for healing: " 'Do you wish to get well?' " (John 5:6)

In other words, do you honestly desire to rid yourself of the things that debilitate? For true healing of our souls requires a change of direction.

Evidently, this man had never asked for assistance in reaching the restorative waters. Instead, he just lay there day after day, on the fringe of what "could have been." A few verses later Jesus zeroes in on the core of the man's problem. " 'Do not sin anymore' " (John 5:14).

Now everyone who is sick is not necessarily guilty of sin. Later, Christ is asked by the disciples whether or not a man sinned. Jesus answered, " 'It was neither that this man sinned, nor his parents; but it was in order that the works of God might be displayed in him' " (John 9:3). Only God knows the content of one's heart.

Lord, if sin is at the root of my infirmity, then bring me to swift repentance. But if my suffering is to point others toward Your glory, quench my thirst with Your living water.

Friday
April 26
Arbor Day

Lend a Hand

"What do you think? Which of the three became a neighbor to the man attacked by robbers?" "The one who treated him kindly," the religion scholar responded. Jesus said, "Go and do the same."
Luke 10:36–37 msg

The woman pushed the button on her garage door opener and drove her car inside. Before she climbed out, she closed the garage door, intent on getting inside for her evening meal. She never noticed the bicycle lying in the grass or the boy who had tumbled onto the asphalt. Enveloped in the cocoon of her own home, she went about her business.

Too often, we follow a similar pattern. Our lives are busy—work, church, exercise, entertainment—and we never even meet our neighbors, much less get to know them.

While it's good to be cautious, the parable of the Good Samaritan tells us to help one another. Not only does becoming involved provide someone needed assistance, it expands our heart-reach. We become Jesus to others, spreading love and kindness, increasing our witness.

Let's keep our eyes peeled for occasions when we might help a neighbor. We want to be wise, select carefully, and love openly.

Father, thank You for Your loving-kindness.
Give me an opening to share
Your love with others. Amen.

Sleep on It

It is of the Lord's mercies that we are not consumed, because his compassions fail not. They are new every morning: great is thy faithfulness.
Lamentations 3:22–23 KJV

"Sleep on it." Researchers have found that to be sound advice. They believe that sleep helps people sort through facts, thoughts, and memories, providing a clearer look at the big picture upon waking. Sleep also separates reality from emotions like fear and worry, which can cloud our thinking and interfere with rational decision-making.

Scientifically speaking, sleep is good medicine. For Christians, the biological effects of sleep are outweighed by the spiritual benefits of the new day God gives us. At the end of an exhausting day, after the worries and the pressures of life have piled high, we may lie down, feeling as though we can't take another moment of stress. But God's Word tells us that His great mercy will keep our worries and problems from consuming us.

Through the never-ending compassion of God, His faithfulness is revealed afresh each morning. We can rise with renewed vigor. We can eagerly anticipate the new day, leaving behind the concerns of yesterday.

Heavenly Father, thank You for giving me a new measure of Your mercy and compassion each day so that my concerns don't consume me. I rest in You and I lay my burdens at Your feet.

Our Refuge in Time of Pain

Be gracious to me, O God. . .for my soul takes refuge in You.
Psalm 57:1 NASB

The voice on the other end of the phone told Jill that a dear friend had been killed in a freak accident. Jill shook her head in disbelief and began to wail.

When her tears were exhausted, her eyes fell on a family Bible on the coffee table. She reached for it, and the pages opened to Psalm 57. Haltingly, Jill read the verses out loud. They comforted her soul as she mourned the loss of her childhood pal.

When death takes someone dear, the world's very foundation seems to shake. The color of the air around us looks different, and we wonder why everyone else is going about their everyday lives as if nothing had changed. We question God, asking why He couldn't stop the situation causing our pain.

His Word doesn't always answer our questions, but it is a place we can run to for comfort. Though the books of the Bible are ancient, they are timeless. Just as the psalmists poured out their anguish, joys, doubts, and fears to God, so can we. And as we commune with God—not holding anything back—He tends to us gently, giving us the scriptures we need at just the right time.

When the world around you breaks loose, don't lose your hold on God. And rest assured, He won't let go of you.

Father, thank You for Your words of comfort when I am racked with grief and pain. Help me to never forget that You are there for me.

Unremarkable Lives

Then Jephthah the Gileadite died and was buried in one of the cities of Gilead. Now Ibzan of Bethlehem judged Israel after him. And he had thirty sons, and thirty daughters whom he gave in marriage outside the family, and he brought in thirty daughters from outside for his sons. And he judged Israel seven years. Then Ibzan died and was buried in Bethlehem.
Judges 12:7–10

What do you want etched into your own tombstone? Personally, I'd like to be remembered this way: "Studied the Word of God diligently and cared about bringing it to others."

But no such accolades are recorded for the four judges Jephthah, Ibzan, Elon, and Abdon. Jephthah is known mainly for his "rash vow," while Ibzan's claim to fame is a large family, whom he married off to the pagans dwelling in that area. That's the route that led to unbelief and pagan idolatry over and over during the time in which the judges ruled Israel. Nothing is learned about Abdon except that "he had forty sons and thirty grandsons who rode on seventy donkeys" (Judges 12:14). What other tangible effects of his presence on earth did he leave behind?

How can we discern the will of God for our lives? Daily prayer is definitely the main source. And this involves not only relating our needs to God, but also listening for His directions. For He never meant for us to traverse through this maze called life without the road maps He would supply.

*Lord, remind me to linger in prayer,
listening for Your voice.*

The Blazing Furnace

"If we are thrown into the blazing furnace, the God we serve is able to save us from it, and he will rescue us from your hand, O king."
Daniel 3:17 NIV

God wouldn't actually let these three godly men, Shadrach, Meshach, and Abednego, be thrown into the furnace, would He? Their bold declaration surely was just an act of defiance to King Nebuchadnezzar's tyrannical order to worship his golden statue. Surely God would provide a way of escape.

But He didn't. Or at least not in the way they had probably hoped—by avoiding that furnace. Imagine their thoughts as Nebuchadnezzar's fury was unleashed and he ordered the furnace to be heated seven times hotter than usual. Imagine how they felt as they were bound, in highly flammable clothing, and carried to the furnace. Imagine the terror they felt as the guards who were ordered to throw them into the furnace perished from its heat!

Had God abandoned Shadrach, Meshach, and Abednego? Hardly!

Nebuchadnezzar looked into the furnace and found the three men walking around, unbound and unharmed, along with a fourth man. Scholars believe this was Jesus, preincarnate.

Too often we think that our faith should keep us out of the furnace: a health crisis, financial worries, troubling situations with our kids. But being in the furnace doesn't mean that God has abandoned us. As promised in Hebrews 13:5 (NKJV), "I will never leave you nor forsake you." He will be right there in the furnace with you.

Lord God, thank You that I can count on You to be with me in every circumstance. Though evil threatens, You hold me in Your loving hands. Amen.

It's Not My Fault

Someone who lives on milk is still an infant
and doesn't know how to do what is right.
HEBREWS 5:13 NLT

When Sara was a little girl, she found the perfect alibi for her every crime. Whether she unrolled a brand-new roll of toilet paper throughout the house or wrote her name in crayon on the wall, Sara's imaginary friend, Ella, took the blame.

"Sara, who spilled orange juice all over the floor?" her mother would ask.

"Ella did it," Sara would always reply.

Sara never outgrew her penchant for blaming others. As an adult, whether she bounced a check or showed up late for work, she always found a way to pin her failures on others.

This pattern started in Eden. When Adam ate the fruit, he blamed Eve. Then Eve blamed Satan. When we fail to take responsibility for our choices, we tend to make the same bad ones over and over again. Accepting responsibility for our actions tells God that we want to learn from our mistakes so they don't happen again. It also tells Him that we are willing to do what it takes to make them right.

Are you using the shortcomings of someone else to justify your own actions? Take a moment to ask God to examine your heart in this important area.

Lord, as hard as it is to admit when I am wrong, teach
me to humbly accept responsibility for my choices.
I pray for growth and maturity
in my Christian walk. Amen.

THURSDAY
MAY 2
NATIONAL DAY OF PRAYER

Anna, the Prophetess

And there was a prophetess, Anna the daughter of Phanuel, of the tribe of Asher. . . . And she never left the temple, serving night and day with fastings and prayer. And at that very moment she came up and began giving thanks to God, and continued to speak of Him to all those who were looking for the redemption of Jerusalem.
LUKE 2:36–38

This year, as the National Day of Prayer approached, one woman in my church did her best to evoke an enthusiastic response from members of a daytime Bible study. I watched as many offered her incredulous stares that silently stated, *What planet are you on? What do you mean, meet for prayer?*

Call a prayer meeting at your own church and you'll know what I mean. Only a handful of people bother to attend and it's always the same group. However, if we fail to pray consistently, it is little wonder we are without guidance for our leadership.

Anna had faithfully served in the temple her entire life. And despite her advanced age, she remained there even after others had gone home for the evening. She was a prophetess; she foretold the truths of God to the people. No wonder He used her life.

God had promised Anna that she would see the Messiah before she died. She waited eighty-four years, biding her time in service to the Lord. And He kept His Word. Let us strive to follow Anna's prayerful example, and we, too, will be blessed by God.

Lord, call my heart to faithfulness and prayer.
May I serve as an example to encourage others.

Time for Praise

And a voice came from the throne, saying, "Give praise to our God, all you His bond-servants, you who fear Him, the small and the great."
REVELATION 19:5

A kindergarten teacher wanted to infuse her school day with opportunities to praise God. She realized that she walked into her storage room numerous times during the day collecting such things as art supplies, kick balls for recess, and tissues for runny noses, and so she decided that in these brief moments she would lift up an offering of praise to God.

"Thank You, Lord, for giving me wisdom today," she would whisper right after the bell rang in the morning.

"Great is the Lord and greatly to be praised!" she said as she put on her sweater to go outside.

"Your loving-kindness is better than life," she would hum as she grabbed an extra box of chalk later in the day.

What a wonderful idea this teacher had! We can follow her example, examining our daily routines for snippets of time in which to offer up praises to the Almighty. A stay-at-home mom might praise the Lord at traffic lights as she is running her errands. An office worker might find her moments of praise in the break room. The more we praise God, the more we will feel the joy of His presence in the ordinary moments of our day-to-day lives.

Jesus, You are worthy to be praised; help me to making praising Your name a lifelong habit. Amen.

God in the Details

"When we heard of it, our hearts melted and everyone's courage failed because of you, for the LORD your God is God in heaven above and on the earth below."
JOSHUA 2:11 NIV

The people of Jericho had reason to be worried. They had seen evidence of God's strength and support of His children—and knew that Joshua planned to conquer Canaan. As residents of the key military fortress in the land, they understood that Joshua would soon be at their gates.

Yet only Rahab seemed to recognize the right course of action: to embrace the Lord and open her home to Joshua's agents. In return, they made sure she and her family survived the attack. Because of her courage and faith, Rahab became an ancestress of Jesus.

Sometimes, when our own lives seem to be under siege from the demands of work, bills, family, whatever—finding the work of God amid the strife can be difficult. Even though we acknowledge His power, we may overlook the gentle touches, the small ways in which He makes every day a little easier. Just as the Lord cares for the tiniest bird (Matthew 10:29–31), so He seeks to be a part of every detail in your life. Look for Him there.

Father God, I know You are by my side every day, good or bad, and that You love and care for me. Help me to see Your work in my life and in the lives of my friends and family.

Appreciate What You Have

"You shall not covet your neighbor's house; you shall not covet your neighbor's wife, nor his male servant, nor his female servant, nor his ox, nor his donkey, nor anything that is your neighbor's."
EXODUS 20:17 NKJV

The dictionary defines the word *covet* as "having a strong desire to possess something that belongs to somebody else."

It is okay to want something. The danger comes when we want *what someone else has*. You probably don't struggle with coveting a neighbor's donkey, ox, or servant as the commandment suggests. But could it be a friend's husband that you wish were your own? A neighbor's swimming pool? A sibling's talent? A star's fame?

When God tells us that we "shall not," we must pay attention. His commandments are for our good. Catch yourself when you sense a desire for that which is not yours. Appreciate your own gifts, blessings, and belongings. An even higher calling is to be happy for others in their accomplishments and as they acquire possessions.

God, You have poured out so many blessings on me. Protect my heart from desiring that which belongs to others. Amen.

Search for Happiness

I said to myself, "Come now, I will test you with pleasure. So enjoy yourself." And behold, it too was futility. I explored with my mind how to stimulate my body with wine while my mind was guiding me wisely, and how to take hold of folly, until I could see what good there is for the sons of men to do under heaven the few years of their lives.
ECCLESIASTES 2:1–3

Ah, the endless search for happiness. Remember when you thought that new dress or outfit would bring you happiness? And it did until you wore it again and again. Then you moved on to bigger and better things, like a brand-new car or a twenty-five-hundred-square-foot house or a summer home. . . .

Solomon explored with his mind how to stimulate his body. Then he enlarged his empire, built houses, planted vineyards, made gardens and parks, engineered ponds of water to irrigate a forest, bought male and female slaves, flocks, and herds, and collected silver and gold. All that his eyes desired he achieved. But did any of this bring him true happiness?

"Thus I considered all my activities which my hands had done and the labor which I had exerted, and behold all was vanity and striving after wind and there was no profit under the sun" (Ecclesiastes 2:11). It finally occurred to Solomon that in the end he would die and leave it all to others who followed him.

Lord, help me not to be drawn away from You by the endless pursuit of things. Instead, I desire Your presence, guidance, and wisdom.

So, Talk!

No one is able to come to Me unless the Father Who sent Me attracts and draws him and gives him the desire to come to Me.
John 6:44 amp

In some of the psalms, the writers seem to shake their fists at God, shouting, "Where are You, Lord? Why are You so slow? Are You sleeping? Wake up and help me!"

Interestingly, the psalmists never doubted God's existence, only His methods. They loved Him, they believed He would triumph over enemies, and they knew He was the One True God. But they had some strong opinions about the way He went about His business. And they had no qualms about telling Him!

Fortunately for us human beings, God isn't easily offended. He is deeply committed to holding up His end of our relationship, and He doesn't want us to hide anything from Him. He already knows every thought we have, anyway. Why not talk to Him about those thoughts?

Every concern we have, every little thing that's good, bad, or ugly.

Our Father always wants to talk. In fact, the very impulse to pray originates in God. In his book *The Pursuit of God*, author A. W. Tozer wrote, "We pursue God because, and only because, He has first put an urge within us that spurs us to the pursuit."

So, talk!

Lord God, it boggles my mind that You want to hear from me! And often! Your Word says that I can call out Your name with confidence. That You will answer me! Today, Lord, I give You praise, honor, and glory—and my heart's deepest longings.

Practicality vs. Passion

Leaving her water jar, the woman went back to the town and said to the people, "Come, see a man who told me everything I ever did. Could this be the Christ?"
John 4:28–29 niv

"Leaving her water jar. . ." One might overlook the phrase; nevertheless, the act was important enough to be included in John's Gospel.

Fetching water was part of the Samaritan woman's daily routine. What caused her to abandon the task, lay down her jar, and run into town?

We don't know much about this woman. We do know, like many women today, that she was searching for fulfillment in all the wrong places. She had had five husbands and was living with a man to whom she was not married. But everything changed the day she met a man at the well and He asked her for a drink of water. Then, although they had never met before, He told her everything she had ever done. He offered her living water that would never run dry.

Practicality gave way to passion! She knew this man was the Messiah, and sharing that good news became a priority. The woman tossed aside her water jar. She took an extreme measure, for she was responding to an extreme interruption in her lost existence. She had met Jesus.

Do you live with such passion, or do you cling to your water jar? Has an encounter with Christ made an impact that cannot be denied in your life?

Lord, help me to lay down anything that stifles my passion for sharing the Good News with others. Amen.

Remembering

Behold, I have engraved you on the palms of my hands;
your walls are continually before me.
Isaiah 49:16 esv

A phone number, a homework assignment, an item to pick up at the grocery store—we might jot any of these reminders on our hand if a piece of paper isn't available. We know if we write something on our hand we will see it. How can we not? We use our hands all day, every day. They are always in front of us.

When the Lord said He has engraved us on the palm of His hands, He was telling us that He remembers us. All day, every day, He remembers us. We are of utmost importance to Him. We cannot be forgotten. When He submitted Himself to Calvary's cross and allowed nails to be driven through His hands, He was remembering us. Our names are in those scars.

Romans 8:34 (niv) says, "Christ Jesus, who died—more than that, who was raised to life—is at the right hand of God and is also interceding for us." Jesus is remembering us in constant prayer to the Father. His eyes never close and His memory never fails. God remembers us.

Father, thank You that through Christ You have brought
me to Yourself, You reign over my life,
and You always remember me.

Jesus, Bread of Life

"As the living Father sent Me, and I live because of the Father, so he who eats Me, he also shall live because of Me. This is the bread which came down out of heaven; not as the fathers ate, and died, he who eats this bread shall live forever."
JOHN 6:57–58

Have you ever sat in a large lecture hall, listening to an intellectual speaker who extended your mind past the breaking point? Well, this is how the Jews of this day reacted to Christ as He spoke these words to them. They hadn't the vaguest notion as to how they might apply this information. If their minds had been file drawers, they'd have been in a quandary as to which file category to place it all under.

These listeners knew what the Scriptures said and yet they had no real comprehension that these God-breathed words were being fulfilled before their very eyes. So, they applied human understanding to Christ's words.

Some said that Jesus' teachings were too difficult to even bother with, while others stated that Christ was speaking about cannibalism. But the majority just walked away, refusing to follow Christ anymore. To continue following Him required faith and commitment.

To truly partake of Christ is to accept Him as He is, fully God and fully man, sent from God, recognizing our need for Him. He came first to the Jews, but they refused the message. What is your response?

Lord, when I don't understand the Scriptures, Your Holy Spirit will provide me with comprehension.

Timely Words

The LORD God gives me the right words to encourage the weary.
ISAIAH 50:4 CEV

Jean felt lower than she had in years. The job she had coveted, fought for, and won had disappeared. After initial success, her second project failed to meet expectations. The company downgraded her job responsibilities, and once again she was relegated to entry-level duties.

Across the country in another state, Helen didn't know about Jean's job situation, but God prodded her. *Write to Jean. Tell her how much you appreciate her and what a good job you think she did when you worked together.* Helen obeyed. It didn't take much time to send a few brief sentences through cyberspace.

Helen's timely words arrived at the time Jean most needed encouragement. Many of us can testify to similar experiences.

God has given us tongues and fingers to communicate timely words to the weary around us. Perhaps it is a simple matter of complimenting someone on a new blouse. Perhaps it is time to send a card through the mail or to pick up the phone and call a friend you haven't seen for a while. Perhaps you need to set aside your plans for the evening and visit a friend in the hospital.

When God prompts us to speak, we become part of His answer.

Lord God, You have given us gifts that can lift up the weary when they most need it. Teach us to listen for Your instructions. Amen.

Samuel Is Born

And it came about in due time, after Hannah had conceived, that she gave birth to a son; and she named him Samuel, saying, "Because I have asked him of the LORD."
1 SAMUEL 1:20

Hannah, a woman of real faith, wanted to keep her promise to God. After Samuel was born and she had weaned him, she took him promptly to the temple. There she said to Eli, " 'Oh, my lord! As your soul lives, my lord, I am the woman who stood here beside you, praying to the LORD. For this boy I prayed, and the LORD has given me my petition which I asked of Him. So I have dedicated him to the LORD; as long as he lives he is dedicated to the LORD' " (1 Samuel 1:26–28).

Every year Hannah and Elkanah returned for their sacrifice at the temple, and every year Hannah brought Samuel a new robe to wear. For her faithfulness, God blessed Hannah with three more sons and two daughters (1 Samuel 2:21).

God was now training Samuel to take over as judge of Israel, as Eli's own sons had no regard for the Lord. As Samuel continued to grow "in favor with the LORD" (1 Samuel 2:26), the Lord declared, " 'Those who honor me I will honor, but those who despise me will be disdained' " (1 Samuel 2:30 NIV).

Lord, if You should give me a child, guide me as You guided Hannah—to sincere faithfulness.

God in Disguise

"For I was hungry, and you fed me. I was thirsty, and you gave me a drink. I was a stranger, and you invited me into your home. . . . And the King will say, 'I tell you the truth, when you did it to one of the least of these my brothers and sisters, you were doing it to me!' "
Matthew 25:35, 40 NLT

What does it mean to be a missionary? Wholehearted service to God. A heart for others. A desire to lead people to a relationship with Jesus.

A missionary can be a mother, a teacher, an office worker, an emergency medical technician, or a salesperson. God instructs His followers to "go into the world"—across borders—to tell people about Him. But "go" can also mean walking across the street or driving down the road to visit another person.

What is keeping you from your mission field? The details and to-do lists of day-to-day life easily take away time for daily service to others. Sometimes we can become so concerned with serving God that we forget that God is served *when* we serve people. Just as it is possible to have head knowledge *about* God without having a relationship *with* God, so can people interact with others without ever meeting a person's real need.

Jesus met people's immediate needs, but He didn't stop there. He fed and healed people, but He also invited them to accept Him and follow Him. It's all too easy to overlook people. Sometimes they don't even look like they need help. Although we cannot force someone to accept our help, we can make a point to offer it.

Lord, open my eyes to see those who need care. Amen.

Rock of Ages

You will guard him and keep him in perfect and constant peace whose mind [both its inclination and its character] is stayed on You, because he commits himself to You, leans on You, and hopes confidently in You. So trust in the Lord (commit yourself to Him, lean on Him, hope confidently in Him) forever; for the Lord God is an everlasting Rock [the Rock of Ages].

Isaiah 26:3–4 amp

You and I can have peace. Authentic peace. God-breathed peace. Not because we live in some make-believe world, repeating positive-thinking statements in an attempt to alter reality. Not because we've been able to avoid adversity or opposition. No, we can have peace simply and only because we trust our heavenly Father.

It's not our incredible faith or extraordinary, over-the-top godly lives that brings us peace. God simply wants our complete trust. He calls us to lean confidently on Him and His faithfulness, rather than fretting over, and focusing on, our circumstances.

This doesn't imply that we'll live without difficulties. All women have those! But when we make the commitment to trust our heavenly Father, come what may, He guards us and keeps us in His peace.

No matter what we see with our eyes, no matter what the hardship, God is our solid rock. . .our Rock of Ages.

Father God, grant me the ability to trust You, come what may.

Not Even His Brothers Believed

Now the feast of the Jews, the Feast of Tabernacles, was at hand. His brothers therefore said to Him, "Depart from here, and go into Judea, that Your disciples also may behold Your works which You are doing. For no one does anything in secret, when he himself seeks to be known publicly. If You do these things, show Yourself to the world." For not even His brothers were believing in Him.

John 7:2–5

One of the most difficult challenges any believer faces is reaching her family with Christ's message. Although Jesus' own brothers had daily viewed His sinless life, they were as blind as the Pharisees to who He really was.

Surely these siblings, Christ's earthly half-brothers (Matthew 13:55–56, Mark 6:1–6), knew that the Jews were seeking to kill Him (John 7:1). But they were headed for Jerusalem to attend the Feast of Booths, as required by God. Jesus' brothers were embarking on a journey to a religious feast and yet rejecting their own Messiah.

Their unbelief had been prophesied in Psalm 69:8: "I have become estranged from my brothers, and an alien to my mother's sons."

Christ's half-brothers were completely in tune with the world, and not with God. Jesus tells them, " 'My time is not yet at hand, but your time is always opportune. . . . Go up to the feast yourselves; I do not go up to this feast because My time has not yet fully come' " (John 7:6–8). After His brothers left, Christ went secretly to the feast.

Thank You, Jesus, for reminding me to wait for God's timing in my life, especially when the pressure applied by others would have me rush on ahead.

The Gift of Receiving

"In everything I did, I showed you that by this kind of hard work we must help the weak, remembering the words the Lord Jesus himself said: 'It is more blessed to give than to receive.' "

Acts 20:35 niv

You probably already know that, like Jesus said, it is better to give to others than to receive for yourself. But what if everyone gave and no one received? That would be impossible, actually. In order for some to give, others have to receive. God designed it perfectly so that the body of Christ would work together and help each other.

Have you ever turned down help of any kind—tangible goods like money or groceries, or intangible things like babysitting or wise counsel—out of pride? Are you trying to keep a stiff upper lip to show the world how strong you are? Maybe you are fully capable of succeeding with no outside help. But in doing so, you might rob others of the joy of giving.

Next time someone offers help, consider graciously accepting the extended hand. By your willingness to receive, others might enjoy the blessings of giving.

Lord, thank You for the times that You have sent help my way. Please give me the wisdom and the grace to know when to accept help from others—and even the courage to ask for it when I need it.

Church

And let us not neglect our meeting together, as some people do, but encourage one another, especially now that the day of his return is drawing near.
HEBREWS 10:25 NLT

Do you ever find yourself making excuses to skip church? "I stayed up too late Saturday night. . . . The weather is bad. . . . I don't have anyone to sit with." The list of excuses is endless. We rationalize our decision by saying we're going to watch a TV sermon or worship the Lord by being in nature.

Attending church every Sunday takes effort. That's why the writer of Hebrews reminds us of the importance of meeting together. But why is corporate worship so necessary?

Believers are strengthened as we focus on the Lord together. Praising the Lord with one voice in song is powerful. Being reminded of God's truth is crucial. Fellowship encourages us in our spiritual walk. We've each been given at least one spiritual gift to benefit the church body, and that gift is exercised as we are connected to each other.

Church worship gives us a glimpse of what heaven will be like—believers of every nationality and background worshipping the Lord together. We will acknowledge His holiness. We will bow before Him in adoration. Why wait until heaven? Go to church this week. The blessings will be yours!

Dear Lord, I need to worship You with other believers. Help me to be consistent in church attendance. Amen.

Burden-Bearing

"For I satisfy the weary ones and refresh everyone who languishes."
Jeremiah 31:25

What kind of burdens are you carrying today? Finances, health, work, family cares, children—they're all burdens we take on, thinking we have to work out all the problems and find the solutions.

Jesus tells us, "If you are tired from carrying heavy burdens, come to me and I will give you rest. Take the yoke I give you. Put it on your shoulders and learn from me. I am gentle and humble, and you will find rest. This yoke is easy to bear, and this burden is light" (Matthew 11:28–30 cev). While these verses primarily refer to the burden of guilt and shame over sin and our inability to release that burden on our own, a secondary meaning applies to the burdens we take on ourselves—by not trusting God's sovereignty in every area of our lives.

Several times in scripture, we humans are compared to sheep. Sheep are not burden-bearing animals. You don't see shepherds loading them up like mules, camels, and horses. Neither are we required to take on burdens. The fact is that many times in God's Word we're encouraged to roll every burden onto *Him*.

The promised result is God's rest—His peace, His refreshing of our spirits—in spite of any problem we face. When we submit to His yoke, we find that the burden truly is light and easy to bear. No longer languishing, we find ourselves refreshed, walking forward in His strength.

Father God, may we heed Jesus' invitation today, knowing that Your desire is to do all things for our good and Your glory.

Thy Will Be Done

"Your kingdom come, your will be done on earth as it is in heaven."
Matthew 6:10 NIV

We pray it. We say it. But do we really mean that we want God's will to be done on earth as it is in heaven? Submitting to God's will is difficult. Jesus struggled with submission in the Garden of Gethsemane. We wrestle with it most days. Unfortunately, most of us assume that we know best. We want to call the shots and be in control. But following God's path requires trusting Him, not ourselves.

Many times submitting to God's will requires letting go of something we covet. We may be called to walk away from a relationship, a job, or a material possession. At other times God may ask us to journey down a path we would not have chosen. Venturing out of our comfort zone or experiencing hardship is not our desire.

Embracing God's love enables us to submit to His will. God not only loves us immensely, but He desires to bless us abundantly. However, from our human perspective, those spiritual blessings may be disguised. That is why we must cling to truth. We must trust that God's ways are higher than ours. We must believe that His will is perfect. We must hold fast to His love. As we do, He imparts peace to our hearts, and we are able to say with conviction, "Your will be done."

Dear Lord, may I rest secure in Your unconditional love. Enable me to trust You more. May I desire that Your will be done in my life. Amen.

A Time to Mourn

There is an appointed time for everything. And there is a time for every event under heaven. . . . A time to weep, and a time to laugh; a time to mourn, and a time to dance.
Ecclesiastes 3:1, 4

Once we've finally accepted that God truly loves us, it's hard to face the first discouraging episode or tragedy that follows. One young family had received a strong call from the Lord to the mission field. At the beginning of a fund-raising trip they were involved in an accident that totaled their van. What would they do? They transferred their focus away from the problem and to their faithful Lord who never disappoints.

Somehow we reach the faulty conclusion that if God loves us all negative incidents are nixed. Do we doubt that the Father loved the Son and yet allowed the Son to suffer a cruel death on the cross? The penalty for sin was death, a penalty that had to be paid by someone absolutely sinless in order for us to be forgiven. Only Jesus Christ could fill that role.

If Christ Himself suffered, then why should we be immune from all maladies?

Occasionally a time of mourning enters our lives, sometimes stealing in almost silently, sometimes brashly breaking down the door to our well-constructed sense of security. Neither path reflects nor distorts the fact that God loves us. But tragedy and mourning are both part of the ebb and flow or "rhythm of life."

Lord, through my veil of tears help me to view Your rescuing hand, that I might reach out to grasp You more firmly.

Keeping On

Blessed is the man who perseveres.
James 1:12 NIV

A child played with an inflatable superhero toy. When he punched the towering figure, it flopped over, then bounced back upright on its round base. Despite constant pummeling, nothing the child did could keep the superhero flat on its back.

We can feel like the superhero toy: We get knocked down by situations we cannot control. We're off balance, our breath thumped out of us. At these times, we need to adopt our own ability to bounce back.

The Book of James encourages us to persevere so we might attain "the crown of life that God has promised to those who love him" (James 1:12 NIV). He reminds us that God is with us. When Satan attacks, finds our Achilles' heel, and knocks us over, we need to dig deep into reservoirs of faith, tap in to God's Word, and pop back up, fighting the fight He's put before us. We can't be passive, or we will be demolished.

Perseverance means staying in the fight and refusing to give up. This attitude empowers us and makes the victim mentality dissipate. It builds confidence, one fight at a time. Keep on keeping on—it's a powerful life tool.

Lord, give me the strength to get up from the mat and continue. I choose to believe in Your promises. Amen.

But Even If

"If we are thrown into the blazing furnace, the God whom we serve is able to save us. He will rescue us from your power, Your Majesty. But even if he doesn't, we want to make it clear to you, Your Majesty, that we will never serve your gods or worship the gold statue you have set up."

DANIEL 3:17–18 NLT

Shadrach, Meshach, and Abednego were men of faith who stood on their belief in God's power. They trusted God to take care of them, no matter what King Nebuchadnezzar did.

These three faithful men said, "But even if he doesn't [rescue us], it wouldn't make a bit of difference" (Daniel 3:18 MSG). Even in the face of earthly consequences—like a blazing furnace—they were committed to obeying God.

Every day, our faith is tested by fiery furnaces of one sort or another. We want a new coat; do we tithe? The boss gave us cash; do we report it as income and pay the tax?

We need to be so grounded in the Word of God that we know His truth and trust Him above all else. Regardless of the circumstances or the temptations to disobey, we can stand firm in our faith in God's ability to rescue us from all situations. That's a faith that says, "But even if God doesn't rescue me, I'll obey Him no matter what."

Is our faith like that of Shadrach, Meshach, and Abednego?

Heavenly Father, I trust You no matter what and will obey Your Word. Help me stand in faith and face any fiery furnace that comes my way. Please give me total confidence in You.

Marvelous Plans

O LORD, you are my God; I will exalt you and praise your name,
for in perfect faithfulness you have done marvelous things,
things planned long ago.
ISAIAH 25:1 NIV

God had marvelous plans for the children of Israel, and they were blessed by God. God sent bread from heaven each morning in the form of manna while Israel wandered in the wilderness. When the people complained they had no meat, God sent quail. When the people complained they had no water, God gave water from a rock.

Amazingly, everything the people needed, God provided in the wilderness over and over again. Yet when they came to the Promised Land, only Joshua and Caleb believed that God would help them conquer the land. Everyone else was afraid and complained—again. Because of their faith, Joshua and Caleb were the only ones God allowed to move into the Promised Land.

God has a "promised land" for us all—a marvelous plan for our lives. Recount and record His faithfulness in your life in the past, because God has already demonstrated His marvelous plans to you in so many ways. Then prayerfully anticipate the future journey with Him. Keep a record of God's marvelous plans in a journal as He unfolds them day by day. You will find God to be faithful in the smallest aspects of your life and oh so worthy of your trust.

Oh Lord, help me to recount Your faithfulness, record Your faithfulness, and trust Your faithfulness in the future. For You are my God, and You have done marvelous things, planned long ago. Amen.

The Well-Stocked Purse

We can make our plans, but the Lord determines our steps.
Proverbs 16:9 NLT

Have you ever noticed how a woman will carry a purse, a diaper bag, a work satchel, a beach bag, and other totes appropriate for the occasion while men go empty-handed? She'll stuff everything from snacks to sewing kit to toilet paper in her bag. He'll shove his wallet in his pocket and is good to go.

Women want to be prepared for any and every crisis that may arise, while most men figure they will find, make, or otherwise produce whatever they need should an emergency cross their path. Women don't understand what seems to be neglect on the part of men, but that is just the way it is.

We women can plan every move we are going to make, but all the planning we do will not keep trouble away. We can horde all the things on our persons, in our cars, and in our houses that we think will make a problem manageable, but they cannot dam up the flood of emotions that come with a crisis.

Only God knows what tomorrow brings, and only He knows the tools we will need to get through any given situation. No packet of tissues or pocket-size scissors are going to be more useful than a spirit that is calm and trusts in the Lord.

Lord, help me to carry a peace-filled spirit with me at all times, and I will trust You to guide me and to provide for my needs along any path You may take me.

Beans or Steak?

Each of you must bring a gift in proportion to the way the LORD your God has blessed you.
DEUTERONOMY 16:17 NIV

At the harvest celebration, every Jew was to thank God with a sacrifice according to the blessings He'd been given. God's Word assumes that every believer would receive a blessing of some sort. At the very least, His people were alive because He provided food for them. Those who didn't have much more than that would bring a small but heartfelt offering. Others, blessed with physical abundance, brought a generous offering of much greater value.

Our blessings may not be the kind we'd like: We may look for extra money to pay off bills while God sends us spiritual strength. But just as God provided for His Old Testament people even in the years of lean harvests, He provides for us.

We may be eating more beans and rice than steak and lobster, but isn't the former better for us in the long run? While we're looking for the good life, God's looking at what's good for us. Sometimes that means physical blessing—but other times it's a spiritual challenge.

No matter what our circumstances, God is blessing us—if we're following Him with steadfastness. Let's bless Him in return with our thanksgiving.

Lord, I thank You for the many blessings You give. In exchange, I offer You the gift of my heart and life.

Where Did Sunday Go?

By the seventh day God had finished the work he had been doing; so on the seventh day he rested from his work. And God blessed the seventh day and made it holy, because on it he rested from all the work of creating that he had done.

Genesis 2:2–3 niv

Kate remembered that when she was growing up stores were closed on Sunday. It was as if the whole country held that day as sacred. Sunday even felt different, a day set apart.

But now? Kate lamented one afternoon, while trying to find a parking spot at the mall, that Sunday felt like any other day. Overscheduled, overcommitted, running from church (if sporting events didn't preclude it) to the grocery store. Too often she woke up tired on Monday mornings—not tired from lack of sleep but from a relentless pace.

"And God blessed the seventh day and made it holy," the Bible says. *If God rested on that day, shouldn't I?* Kate wondered. And if it was meant to be a blessed day, was Kate missing something God had in store for her?

From that afternoon on, Kate didn't go to stores on Sunday. By planning ahead, she could have Sunday's meals taken care of and at least be prepared for Monday school lunches. She noticed that she started the week feeling renewed and refreshed, just the way the Lord intended a Sabbath to be: a blessed day.

Lord, You gave us an example of Sabbath rest
for our good—spiritually and physically.
May we faithfully set aside Your day
for worship and rest. Amen.

Tears

Jesus wept.
JOHN 11:35 NIV

Jesus wept. He cried when he heard the news of the death of His good friend, Lazarus. Jesus knew He would bring Lazarus back to life, yet His heart still broke with sadness. Jesus experienced sorrow Himself, and He knows the depth of our pain when we lose someone or something important to us.

Grief is an intense emotion. Knowing that Jesus cried helps us to accept our own weeping—especially when our loss is still fresh.

Sometimes we're embarrassed that our tears stream from a seemingly bottomless well. Yet tears are so precious to God that He records and stores each one. The psalm writer said, "You keep track of all my sorrows. You have collected all my tears in your bottle. You have recorded each one in your book" (Psalm 56:8 NLT).

Jesus' tears demonstrate God's empathy as we go through the grieving process. God cares deeply about our situation. He desires to gather us in His arms. He understands the sorrow and turmoil we feel when we experience serious heartache.

Crying is a natural response to deep pain and loss. Our tears form wordless prayers connecting us with God. He knows the depth of our sorrow. He comforts us with His love and His tears.

Loving Lord, You know my tears. You value each of my tears so much that You gather them in Your bottle and write them in Your book. Thank You for understanding me.

The Days of Your Youth

Remember also your Creator in the days of your youth, before the evil days come and the years draw near when you will say, "I have no delight in them." Fear God and keep His commandments, because this applies to every person. God will bring every act to judgment, everything which is hidden, whether it is good or evil.
ECCLESIASTES 12:1, 13–14

Most of us have encountered women who freely share biblical truths "handed down to them" from their grandmothers or mothers. Is the faith being displayed in their lives?

The Book of Ecclesiastes concludes with the admonition not only to remember our Creator when we are young, but to continue following His precepts throughout our time on earth. For nothing is sadder than to see those who began the race of life with so much vigor and potential now sitting on the sidelines watching the parade pass by.

High school reunions are great places to witness such scenes. Those girls whose faces glowed with extraordinary promise at eighteen may now display ones that appear more like a map of New York City. They've been betrayed, besieged, and bewildered by people promising much and delivering little.

Have you forgotten the God of your youth? Have His principles been compromised away by the pressures of a world that teaches the Ten Commandments are optional? With the Lord's help, it's not too late to turn it all around.

Lord, if I look back and see a trail of regret,
please give me the courage to change the view.

For His Own Good

And we know that all things work together for good to them that love God, to them who are the called according to his purpose.
ROMANS 8:28 KJV

One day, as Jesus walked down the dusty roads of Jerusalem, He came upon a blind man. Jesus spat in the dust, made a clay paste, and rubbed it on the man's eyes. When the man washed the mud from his eyes, he could see!

Many people thought the sightless man was blind because of sin in his parents' lives. In response, Jesus said, "Neither this man nor his parents sinned. . .but this happened so that the work of God might be displayed in his life" (John 9:3 NIV).

It wasn't the dirt that held the healing power—we never find healing in the dirt of our lives. The miracle was in how Jesus used the dirt. And so it is in our own lives. The dirt and pain of life are simply tools that God uses.

Sometimes life's circumstances cause us to cry out, "Why, Lord? Why?" And God's response is always the same: so that His good work might be displayed in our lives. And like the blind man's story, our stories—our testimonies of God's involvement in our lives—could be the light that points someone else to true faith.

Father, help me to trust You more. Help me to see Your hand at work and to let go of my desire for control. May Your glory be displayed in my life for all to see.

Present Help

"For I, the LORD your God, hold your right hand; it is I who say to you, 'Fear not, I am the one who helps you.' "
ISAIAH 41:13 ESV

We shake hands to greet each other; it's a sign of welcome. We reach for the hand of a child when we're walking in a crowd or near a street; it helps protect and comfort the child. In times of great emotion or anticipation, we grab the hand of a nearby friend or family member; it says, "I am with you." By a hospital bed, we clasp the hand of a sick loved one; our hand tells them we are present, suffering with them. With every gripping of another's hand, we are bearing witness to God.

He holds your hand. He welcomes you into His kingdom. He protects you. He comforts you. He is with you in your most anxious moments and in your darkest hours. With the clasp of His hand comes courage for any situation. He tells you not to fear, for He is your ever-present help in times of trouble. He has a hold of you.

Almighty God, I am grateful that You hold my hand. Forgive me for the times I have forgotten this and let fear reign in my life. Help me to remember I am never alone. Grant me the courage that comes from knowing You as my helper.

Beauty of the Beholder

So God created human beings in his own image. In the image of God he created them; male and female he created them. . . . Then God looked over all he had made, and he saw that it was very good!
GENESIS 1:27, 31 NLT

Janet looked in the mirror and winced. *I shouldn't have eaten that extra piece of cake,* she thought as she pinched a bit of fat around her waist.

Janet's not alone. Women tend to find something wrong with themselves, no matter how they actually look. Our noses have bumps. Our hips are too large. Our eyes are too small for our face. We've got wrinkles where smooth skin used to be.

Though there's nothing wrong with presenting ourselves in the best light, we should always remember one important fact: God created us in His image. We don't have to look like the models in a women's magazine to be beautiful. The One who created us loves us exactly as we are!

Those little things we see as imperfections are actually attractive to God. Just as we see our own kids as the most adorable things, God sees us as His lovely children.

When it comes to self-image, let's not view our own perceived flaws as negatives. Let's see ourselves through God's eyes, remembering that His creation is always good.

Dear Lord, when I look in the mirror, remind me that I was created in Your image and that, although I may not always see myself as beautiful, You think I look very good.

Jesus, the Good Shepherd

*"He who enters by the door is a shepherd of the sheep.
To him the doorkeeper opens, and the sheep hear his voice,
and he calls his own sheep by name, and leads them out."*
John 10:2–3

Sheep just aren't very bright. They need constant overseeing, tender treatment, and strict boundaries. The shepherd took them to the best pastures, found safe lodging for them during the night, and then led them out again in the morning. He was the ultimate caregiver!

In fact, the shepherd would stretch his own body out across the opening to the sheep pen. What a graphic picture of protection this provides as we consider that Christ considers Himself our Shepherd.

As the world screams out for us to follow every wind of doctrine, Christ's voice calls us back to obedience: " 'When he puts forth all his own, he goes before them, and the sheep follow him because they know his voice' " (John 10:4). His voice will never call us to rebellion, sinful pleasures, or departure from His Word.

In our day we hear those who defend heinous acts by saying, "Voices told me to do it." Certainly the one they chose to listen to was not the voice of Jesus Christ, for He cannot contradict Himself. True sheep listen only for the voice of their Shepherd.

God calls us by name, just as the shepherd has pet names for his sheep. Someday, when the King of kings, our Good Shepherd, calls us home to heaven, we'll hear the name He calls us.

*Lord, guide me to safe pastures today.
Never leave me.*

God's Mirror

Charm is deceptive, and beauty does not last;
but a woman who fears the LORD will be greatly praised.
PROVERBS 31:30 NLT

A woman admitted that she spent much of her attention on how she looked and who was looking at her. She even watched her reflection in store windows to see how passersby reacted as she walked down the street.

Her overwhelming focus on appearance was driven by a fear of being alone. The woman was afraid that if she wasn't outwardly attractive, she might not be loved. But she misunderstood what really determined her value.

Proverbs 31:30 shares a very important truth about charm and beauty: They fade. If a woman relates to men primarily on the basis of physical beauty, the couple will eventually be left wanting. Much more fulfilling is the woman's spiritual focus.

May our minds be focused on the qualities that last: honesty, faithfulness, loyalty, and spiritual growth. Mr. Right defines beauty as God does—and will value good personal qualities above physical perfection.

Today, gaze into the mirror of scripture. Allow your true beauty to be that inner beauty of soul—a reflection of Christ—that never fades.

Father, thank You for the beauty that You reflect from my soul. Help me to place less importance on my outward appearance and more value on the inner qualities that You are developing in me.

Perfect Guidance

May the Lord direct your hearts into the love of God and into the steadfastness of Christ.
2 Thessalonians 3:5 nasb

A woman recalls the day she passed her driver's test many years ago. "My dad handed me the car keys and kissed me on the cheek. I said, 'What was that for?' He laughed and said, 'Because, as bad as your sense of direction is, I'll probably never see you again!' "

This is our predicament when we try to operate without the Spirit of God. It's like trying to drive our car to an unfamiliar destination without a map or GPS. We end up making wrong turns and poor decisions. We drive around and around in circles, and we don't bother to stop to ask for directions.

Even before Jesus sent His Holy Spirit to indwell believers, God used a variety of means to guide His people. He spoke to Israel through the prophets. He gave certain individuals dreams and visions. God even gave the Israelites a pillar of clouds by day and a pillar of fire by night in which God's Spirit dwelled to lead them out of Egypt into the Promised Land.

Thanks to GPS technology in our automobiles, we need never be lost on the road. Praise be to God for giving us His Spirit, who resides in us so that we need never lose our direction as we navigate our way through life.

Thank You, Jesus, for sending Your Holy Spirit to lead me in the right direction. Amen.

When God Redecorates

God is the builder of everything.
Hebrews 3:4 niv

While planning to renovate the living room, a husband and wife most wanted to change two large rectangular posts that stood floor-to-ceiling in the middle of the room.

But the couple's cautious contractor didn't remove the posts. He explained that, without the posts as support, the room's ceiling could come crashing down.

Unlike that contractor, God—the renovator of hearts—doesn't work cautiously. When He begins renovations, He removes (or allows the removal of) all existing supports. Maybe that "support" is health—ours or a loved one's. Maybe it's our savings. Maybe it's something else. Our lives, as we know them, crash. We hurt. We don't know how we can go on.

But God knows. If we let Him, He'll replace the temporary supports we'd relied on—health, independence, ability, you name it—with eternal spiritual supports like faith, surrender, and prayer. Those supports enable us to live a life of true freedom, one abounding with spiritual blessing.

Lord, I am tempted to cling to the supports I've erected.
When my life crashes, I'm tempted to despair.
Please help me to be still and place my trust in You,
the great builder of all lives.

Isaiah, a Major Prophet

The vision of Isaiah the son of Amoz, concerning Judah and Jerusalem which he saw during the reigns of Uzziah, Jotham, Ahaz, and Hezekiah, kings of Judah. Listen, O heavens, and hear, O earth; for the Lord speaks, "Sons I have reared and brought up, But they have revolted against Me. My people do not understand."
Isaiah 1:1–3

Had the word *clueless* been coined during Isaiah's lifetime, he would probably have used it to describe the people of Israel who foolishly continued to abandon the Lord. However, through the prophet Isaiah, God provides extraordinary clues to His character. This prophet was surely named appropriately, for *Isaiah* means "Jehovah saves" or "salvation of Jehovah."

Isaiah's very lifeblood would be poured out as he brought this message of hope to Israel, for it is written that he was sawed in two by Manasseh, the king of Judah who reigned after Hezekiah (2 Kings 21:16).

Reading Isaiah provides a necessary heart check. Like Israel, if we fail to turn from our defiant ways, we must ask, "Where will you be stricken again, as you continue in your rebellion? The whole head is sick, and the whole heart is faint. From the sole of the foot even to the head there is nothing sound in it, only bruises, welts, and raw wounds, not pressed out or bandaged, nor softened with oil" (Isaiah 1:5–6).

Lord, this book of prophecy displays Your promises and prophecies. Open my mind to receive Your truth. And keep me from confusion, that I might know You as both Messiah and Lord.

Sowing the Wind

"They sow the wind and they reap the whirlwind."
HOSEA 8:7 NASB

Admit it. Sometimes our jam-packed days leave us feeling as if we're running around like chickens with our heads cut off. From the first drop of morning coffee to the last sip of evening tea, our days reel by in fast motion. The next thing we know, a year has passed. Then two, then three. And what have we done? Where are we?

And why are we running? Why are we constantly moving at warp speed, our feet barely touching the ground as the world around us becomes a blur amid the busyness?

What is the point of our days? Are we chasing after foreign idols, proudly wearing a badge of busyness, worshipping the almighty dollar, determined to keep one step ahead of the Joneses?

That's what the Israelites were doing when Hosea wrote, "They sow the wind and they reap the whirlwind." In sowing the wind, nothing of everlasting value is produced, and we end up with arms filled with temporal nothings.

As followers of Christ, we are to reap righteousness, keeping our eyes on Jesus, for He is our ultimate prize—not that new car, new house, or new wardrobe.

Don't lust for earthly idols that keep you from sowing the right seeds—those of righteousness. Take a deep breath. Take a long walk. Depart from the rat race. Relax in God's arms. Keep your eyes on Christ instead of worldly goods, and you will reap not the earthly whirlwind but heavenly treasure.

God, keep my eyes on the right prize—Your Son, Jesus Christ. Help me to slow down, walk in Your will, and become a blessing in this world, always looking toward the next. Amen.

Rachel's Saddlebags

Rachel had taken the household gods and put them inside her camel's saddlebag and was sitting on them. Laban searched through everything in the tent, but found nothing.
GENESIS 31:34 TNIV

Why did Rachel feel a compulsion to steal her father's household idols and hide them in her saddlebags? The idols were probably little statues of gods common to the time and culture. She risked the wrath of the true God and jeopardized the safety of her family. Didn't she know better, as the wife of Jacob—the great patriarch of God's nation of Israel?

From our twenty-first-century vantage point, it's easy to wag a finger at Rachel. Living in a western culture, we find such idols, of sexualized bulls and multi-breasted women, to be grotesque. But in Rachel's day, those little idols were pervasive, part of the culture. She didn't dismiss Jacob's God—she just added to Him. Naive, ignorant, or sinful, she allowed idols to replace God's primary position in her life.

Household idols probably don't tempt us. But we can all identify with Rachel. Think of the importance we place on material things, financial security, our achievements—those ambitions can easily consume us! They can occupy our thought life, fill our spare time, and become our life's focus.

Let's take care to keep God exactly where He belongs, in first place.

Lord, clean my house! Open my eyes to the worthless idols in my life. Teach me to desire only You.

What Are Your Gifts?

There are different kinds of gifts, but the same Spirit.
There are different kinds of service, but the same Lord.
1 Corinthians 12:4–5 niv

A woman felt called by God to help out at her church, but she couldn't figure out which ministry best suited her. While some people were clearly Bible teachers, she was not. And while some could sing, she didn't feel that was her gifting. After spending time praying and seeking the Lord, she finally opted to work in children's ministry. She'd always done well with children, and she realized she could bless the little ones and fulfill her calling, all at the same time.

Maybe you know what it's like to search for your place. Perhaps you've tried different ministries and still haven't figured out your best place of service. Be patient. God has placed specific gifts within you, and you are needed in the body of Christ. Although your gifts may be different from someone else's, they are all from the same Spirit.

Today, thank the Lord for entrusting you with spiritual gifts. If you're struggling to know where you fit, ask Him to give you opportunities to minister in different areas until you find just the right spot.

Lord, thank You for pouring out Your Spirit on me,
and thank You for the gifts You've placed within me.
I want to reach others for You, so place me in the
very spot where I can be most effective.

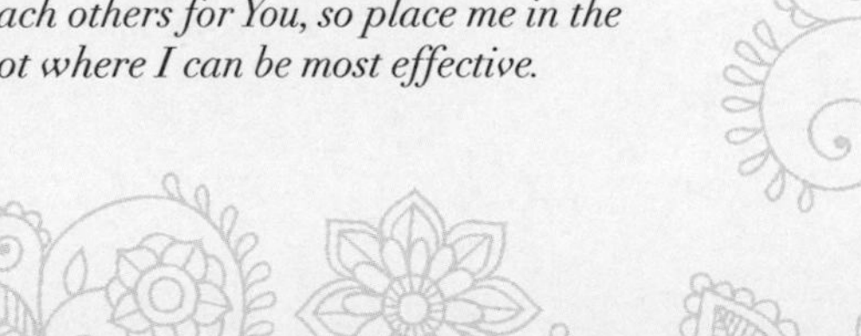

Life Preservers

My comfort in my suffering is this: your promise preserves my life.
PSALM 119:50 NIV

It's the law for boaters in many states: Always wear your life preserver. The purpose is simple. A life preserver keeps people afloat—and their heads above water—should they accidentally fall overboard. The device's buoyancy can even keep an unconscious person afloat in a face-up position as long as it's worn properly.

In the difficulties of life, God is our life preserver. When we are battered by the waves of trouble, we can expect God to understand and to comfort us in our distress. His Word, like a buoyant life preserver, holds us up in the bad times.

But the life preserver only works if you put it on *before* your boat sinks. To get into God's life jacket, put your arms into the sleeves of prayer and tie the vest with biblical words. God will surround you with His love and protection—even if you're unconscious of His presence. He promises to keep our heads above water in the storms of living.

Preserving God, I cling to You as my life preserver. Keep my head above the turbulent water of caregiving so I don't drown. Bring me safely to the shore.

An Invitation to Dine

"The Kingdom of heaven may be compared to a king, who gave a wedding feast for his son. And he sent out his slaves to call those who had been invited to the wedding feast, and they were unwilling to come."
Matthew 22:2–3

Have you ever given a dinner party only to have your guests cancel at the last minute? Perhaps they didn't even offer a decent excuse. You're seething inside. You've worked all day long to prepare your home for these "ungrateful people," who will surely never be invited again.

When God sent His Son to earth, He invited all men and women to a wedding feast. Those who accept the invitation become part of the Church. And the Church is the bride of Christ. But there are many who have offered feeble excuses for their lack of faith.

The Son is the Bridegroom for whom the wedding feast is prepared. God Himself has laid the groundwork in the hearts that will respond to His Son, Jesus Christ.

There will be an appointed hour in the future when the guests will come to the banquet. And Christ will call them forth to be His Church when all is made ready, after His Resurrection and Ascension and the coming of the Holy Spirit at Pentecost.

Also, those in attendance receive "wedding clothes." Jesus Christ now clothes them in His righteousness. Those not wearing these garments are cast out because they refused Christ's invitation, and in so doing, have rejected His salvation.

Lord, You've invited me to dine with You. Let me graciously accept my "wedding clothes."

A Shadow of the Past

"Only Rahab the prostitute and all who are with her in her house shall be spared, because she hid the spies we sent."
Joshua 6:17 TNIV

Rahab lived in the city of Jericho. When Israelite spies came to her home, she hid them under flax on the roof until they could make a fast getaway. In return, they promised her safety during the coming siege of the city. True to their word, the spies saved Rahab and her family from Jericho's doom. Rahab apparently converted to Judaism, married an Israelite, and became part of the lineage of King David—and, eventually, of Jesus Christ.

And Rahab had been a prostitute in Jericho.

That fact was part of her story. But Rahab wasn't trapped by her past. Her past didn't hold her back. It may have hurt her, but it didn't shape her. She was used by God. Her name has come down to us centuries later because of her bold faith.

We all have to deal with a past. All of us! Disappointments, poor choices, dysfunctional families, parents who failed us, husbands who harmed us. God is able to bring good from even those years that were painful. By the grace and power of God we can make choices in the present that can affect our future.

There is transforming power with God. We have hope, no matter what lies behind us.

Holy Spirit, You are always at work. Don't ever stop! Show me a new way, Lord. Help me to make healthier choices for myself and my family. Thank You for Your renewing presence in my life.

Toss Those Boxing Gloves!

Avoiding a fight is a mark of honor; only fools insist on quarreling.
Proverbs 20:3 NLT

A woman struggled in her relationship with a particular friend. Though they'd known each other for years, they often found themselves disagreeing on things, sometimes even arguing. Whenever they got together, their quiet conversations evolved into heated discussions. Their personalities were vastly different, and they both tended to be a little stubborn. Neither wanted to give in, even though the things they argued about were sometimes silly. Would they ever just get along without all the quarreling?

Maybe you're in a complicated relationship with a friend. Perhaps she brings out the worst in you. She gets you stirred up. And yet, you love her. You don't want to see the friendship come to an end. What can be done to salvage it?

As with any relational issue, you approach it with a servant's heart. You've got to follow the golden rule—doing unto others as you would have them do unto you. And you've got to love others as you would love yourself. This is tough to do when you're arguing. But just how important is it to prove your point—in the grand scheme of things? Important enough to sacrifice a friendship? Surely not.

Lord, I ask You today to be at the center of my friendships, especially the difficult ones. Show me what to say and what not to say to avoid strife. Give me Your heart toward my friends.

Do We Need to Do It All?

I have glorified thee on the earth:
I have finished the work which thou gavest me to do.
John 17:4 KJV

On the night before Jesus was crucified, He offered a bold prayer to the heavenly Father. He prayed for Himself, His disciples, and us. In that prayer, He declared that He had finished the work the Father gave Him to do, and in so doing, He glorified the Father.

Although Jesus did all the Father required, did Jesus do it all?

No.

Jesus did not heal every crippled, blind, or demon-possessed person He encountered. Nor did He save everyone who came to Him. More than once the unbelieving departed, and He let them go.

Early in Jesus' ministry, He explained His method: He could do nothing of Himself; He worked where He saw the Father working. He never went rashly ahead of the Father.

This should be our pattern.

We women often think that because we *can* do something, we *should* do it. We listen to the world's chant that we "can do it all."

Simply because we can do all things through Christ doesn't mean He is calling us to do everything.

If we would be like Jesus, we will do only the work the Father gives us, not all the work we can do.

Dear Father, give me eyes to see where You are working so that I may work with You. Help me rebuff the world's temporal demands so that I can focus on heavenly duties that bring eternal rewards. Amen.

In God We Trust

Moses summoned all the Israelites and said to them, "You have seen with your own eyes everything the LORD did. . . . For forty years I led you through the wilderness, yet your clothes and sandals did not wear out. . . so you would know that he is the LORD your God."
DEUTERONOMY 29:2–6 NLT

Each election season, political candidates tickle the ears of listeners by vowing to take care of their constituents. One promises to cut taxes. Another promises to fix health care and give the middle class relief.

But there is a graveyard where political promises typically go to die. When in office, many politicians get distracted by lobbyists or their party's leaders. And we are disappointed once again.

Still, it's our duty and privilege as citizens to vote. But whether we line up with the conservative or liberal side of politics, we must not trust in government—or any politician—to save us. Jesus Christ is the only Savior. And He never breaks any of His promises.

When the children of Israel suffered under their Egyptian oppressors, God freed them with signs and wonders. Then for forty years they wandered in the desert, and each day they had just enough food and water to sustain them.

God will do the same for us. He will clothe, feed, shelter, and rescue us from those who try to oppress us. What government can't—or won't—do, God will. Put your trust in Him.

Lord, thank You that You promise to take care of us. Help us not to put too much trust in men or agencies.

Jesus Raises Lazarus

Now a certain man was sick, Lazarus of Bethany. . . . The sisters therefore sent to Him, saying, "Lord, behold, he whom You love is sick."
JOHN 11:1, 3

When we hear that a good friend is critically ill we run to his side. Why then does Jesus tarry? "But when Jesus heard it, He said, 'This sickness is not unto death, but for the glory of God, that the Son of God may be glorified by it' " (John 1:4).

Obviously, this remark puzzled His disciples. They had honestly laid out the situation for Him. Lazarus was about to breathe his last. And yet Christ seemed to be denying the gravity of the situation. We can almost picture Mary and Martha wringing their hands and consoling each other that soon Jesus would be there and everything would be all right again.

Instead, Jesus took His time getting there, four days as a matter of fact. And when He did arrive, Lazarus had been buried! Now Christ was only a few miles away from Bethany. It took all the human restraint He possessed not to run to Lazarus's aid. But Jesus has, as always, a greater purpose.

At the tomb of His friend Jesus called: " 'Lazarus, come forth' " (John 11:43). And Lazarus arose from the tomb and walked out, his grave clothes dangling from his body. Have you allowed Christ to exercise His authority to bring you forth to new life?

Lord, strengthen my faith so that when tragedy strikes, I know that You are the Resurrection and the Life.

Daughter of the King

You are all sons of God through faith in Christ Jesus.
GALATIANS 3:26 NIV

Galatians 3:26–29 is packed with statements about who you are as a Christian. You are Abraham's seed. You are an heir according to God's promise. And best of all, you are a *child of God*. Galatians reminds us that there is no male or female, race, or social status in the Lord's eyes. Believers are truly *one in Christ*.

You may have had a wonderful upbringing with loving parents. Or you may not have been as fortunate. You may have spent years in the foster system or had abusive parents.

Whether your childhood reflected love or abandonment, there is good news! As a Christian, you are a daughter of the King of kings, the Lord of lords, the sovereign God. He is the One who hung the stars in the sky, and yet He knows the number of hairs on your head. You are not just God's friend or distant relative. You are His *daughter*!

If you have a child of your own, consider the unconditional love you feel for him or her. As intense as that love is, because you are human, you are limited in your ability to love. In contrast, God loves us in a way we will not fully understand until we reach heaven. He is our *Abba Father*, our "Daddy."

Thank You, Father, for adopting me through Christ as Your daughter. Teach me to live as a reflection of my Father's love. Amen.

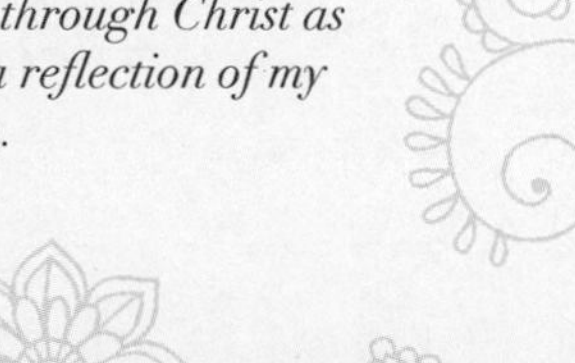

I've Fallen and I Can't Get Up

The godly may trip seven times, but they will get up again.
PROVERBS 24:16 NLT

Years ago, a famous television commercial depicted an elderly woman who had fallen, but, try as she might, she just couldn't get back up. Thankfully, she wore a device that connected her to an outside source of help. All she had to do was push the button! The dear grandma was just one click away from rescue.

In our lives, too, there are times when we fall down—not physically, but emotionally, spiritually, and relationally. We fall in our attempts to parent; we fall in our struggle with particular temptations. We may fall as we try to climb the ladder of success or in our effort to lead a consistently godly life.

But in whatever area we wrestle, however many times we fall, our heavenly Father never gives up on us. He never leaves us to ourselves, to stagger to our feet alone. God is always present with us, encouraging us to keep trying—regardless of past failures—picking us up, dusting us off, and setting us on our way again.

He is better than any button we could ever push!

Heavenly Father, it's such a comfort to know You will never leave me or forsake me. You are closer than the clothes I wear. I love You, Lord.

Expect Trouble

These things I have spoken unto you, that in me ye might have peace. In the world ye shall have tribulation: but be of good cheer; I have overcome the world.
John 16:33 KJV

Why do bad things happen to good people? It is an age-old question. Sometimes we expect God to surround us with an invisible shield that keeps us from all harm and disease, all hurt and disappointment. As nice as this might sound, it is simply not how life works. Christians are not exempt from trials.

In the Gospel of John, we read that Christ told his followers to *expect* trouble in this world. The good news is that we do not have to face it alone. When trials come, remember that Jesus has overcome this world. Through Him, we, too, are overcomers. Draw upon the promise that through Christ you can do all things. The children's song says it this way: "Jesus loves me, this I know, for the Bible tells me so. Little ones to Him belong. They are weak, but He is strong."

Expect trouble, but refuse to let it defeat you. Trials strengthen our faith and our character. No one gets excited about a trial, yet we can be assured that God is still in control even when trouble comes our way.

Lord Jesus, be my strength as I face trouble in this life. Walk with me. Hold my hand. Assure me that in my weakness, You are strong. Amen.

A Counselor for the Troubled

"In My Father's house are many dwelling places."
JOHN 14:2

Jesus Christ has promised to prepare a place for us in heaven. Does it get any better than that? The only problem is that we have to wait down here until He's got our mansion ready for us. There are days when it's so hard to stay tied to earth, especially with the realization that a perfect place exists.

My father-in-law is now in the last stages of emphysema and each breath is excruciating for him. Consequently, we've talked about his true future elsewhere. "What if I don't like it there?" he posed during one of our conversations. I responded, "How can you possibly think you won't?"

Heaven is truly the place where God exists. John, the gospel writer, was given a vision of heaven so that we might know what it looks like. God's Spirit inspired him to record it in the Book of Revelation.

"Behold, a throne was standing in heaven, and One sitting on the throne. And He who was sitting was like a jasper stone and a sardius in appearance; and there was a rainbow around the throne, like an emerald in appearance. . . . And from the throne proceed flashes of lightning and sounds and peals of thunder" (Revelation 4:2–3, 5).

Entertainers use special effects to hold the attention of their audiences. But God has the ultimate performance already prepared for us.

Lord, thank You for the Holy Spirit,
who brings us peace and comfort until
we can be united with You in heaven.

The Waiting Game

I wait for you, O LORD; you will answer, O Lord my God.
PSALM 38:15 NIV

Some researchers have estimated that Americans spend as much as two to three years of their lives waiting in line. We wait at the bank, the supermarket, the theater, and the airport. We wait for our paychecks, for Friday, and for vacation. It seems we are always waiting for something.

Waiting on God is just as hard. What are you waiting for today? Perhaps it's for financial deliverance, for a spouse, to finish school, or for your next big break. Perhaps you're waiting for the results of a medical test or news from your loved one in the military. Waiting can be downright agonizing. But God's Word tells us to wait patiently—with peace. Easier said than done, right? Rather than sighing with impatience, try praying, reading scripture, and making your waiting time productive and meaningful.

God's timing is certainly not ours. But as we wait on Him, we can be confident that He is never too early and never too late. Wait patiently and with confidence. God *will* come through.

Heavenly Father, when the waiting seems unbearable,
remind me that Your timing
is always perfect. Amen.

Friday
June 21
First Day of Summer

Charm Bracelet

But the fruit of the Spirit is love, joy, peace, patience, kindness, goodness, faithfulness, gentleness, self-control; against such things there is no law.
Galatians 5:22–23 NASB

A charm bracelet is a beautiful way to commemorate milestones or special events. A dangling baby bootie, a tiny graduation cap, a pair of wedding bells, or a palm tree from Cancun are all commonly treasured trinkets. Each tiny charm signifies a huge achievement.

We are told in Galatians that the marks of the Holy Spirit are love, joy, peace, patience, kindness, goodness, faithfulness, gentleness, and self-control. It takes constant growth, through a consistent pursuit of godliness, to acquire these character traits. It is a struggle to walk consistently in patience, always showing love and kindness to people. Self-control is another struggle all its own. These things do not come easily to most of us, and they require concentrated effort.

Consider your spiritual charm bracelet. If you had a charm to represent your growth in each of those traits, how many would you feel comfortable attaching to your bracelet in representation of that achievement? Ask your Father which areas in your Christian walk need the most growth. Do you need to develop those traits more strongly before you feel comfortable donning your bracelet?

Lord, please show me which milestones of Christian living I need to focus on in order to have the full markings of the Holy Spirit in my life. Please help me to grow into the Christian woman You call me to be. Amen.

Attitude Is Everything

A cheerful disposition is good for your health;
gloom and doom leave you bone-tired.
Proverbs 17:22 msg

A large banner hung in the classroom where Andrea was substitute teaching. In bold red letters, the banner read: Attitude is a little thing that makes a BIG difference! Andrea stood in the doorway as the middle school students filed into the English class. Just before the bell rang, the last student entered the classroom. She was in a motorized wheelchair, and Andrea could not help but notice that the girl had no legs.

"Good morning," the teenager said with a broad smile across her face. "I'm Jenny. Are you subbing for Mrs. Browning today?" She was the only student who had greeted Andrea.

Have you ever noticed that many people with serious hardships in life choose to make lemonade from the lemons life has dealt them? Scientific studies of terminal patients indicate that a positive attitude influences the quantity and quality of their final days. Many books have been written on the power of positive thinking. The Bible was around long before any of these books, and this proverb still rings true today.

Sometimes we have to fake it till we feel it. Experiment with this strategy today. Put a smile on your face when you feel discouraged over a setback or frustrated about an inconvenience. A cheerful heart is good medicine.

Father, thank You for this day You have given me.
Create in me a happy heart. Amen.

Aiding the Enemy

Would God my lord were with the prophet that is in Samaria! for he would recover him of his leprosy.
2 KINGS 5:3 KJV

The young girl screamed as the burly Syrian soldier hauled her onto his shoulder like a sack of grain, far away from the only home she had known. She never saw her parents or baby brother again.

Still, the girl prayed every night to the God of Israel, as her parents taught her. She found herself a slave in the household of Naaman, the scary captain of the soldiers who kidnapped her. But his lovely wife talked to her kindly. Little by little, the girl's fears subsided. She even pitied her master. Despite his great victories, Naaman suffered from leprosy, a sad fact that dimmed her mistress's smile.

"Elisha, the prophet in Israel, could make him well!" the girl told her.

Naaman's wife gave him her maid's strange advice; the desperate soldier traveled to see Elisha, who told him to wash in the Jordan River. After Naaman swallowed his initial stubbornness, he found, to his amazement, that the God of Israel had healed him.

The Lord did not forget the young girl, alone in a difficult world. And the lessons her parents had taught her made a difference not only in her life, but also in the lives of unbelievers around her.

Father, I do not know the paths I will take, whether happy or sad. But please let the truths You have taught me glorify You.

An Intimate Conversation

"And this is eternal life, that they may know Thee, the only true God, and Jesus Christ whom Thou has sent. I glorified Thee on earth, having accomplished the work which Thou hast given Me to do. And now, glorify Thou Me together with Thyself, Father, with the glory which I had with Thee before the world was."
JOHN 17:3–5

Have you ever unwittingly overheard an intimate conversation? Well, that's exactly what this chapter of John is like. We are privileged to overhear Jesus as He speaks to the Father.

Christ was with the Father before the world was. That makes Him not only eternal but equal with the Father. These are the claims Jesus made to the Pharisees who constantly confronted Him concerning His origin.

Christ's prayer to the Father also includes concern for whom the Father has given to Him. " 'I manifested Thy name to the men whom Thou gavest Me out of the world; Thine they were, and Thou gavest them to Me, and they have kept Thy Word' " (John 17:6). Notice that these are the people who respond to God's message and keep His Word.

Then Jesus also asks the Father to keep us in His name. " 'Holy Father, keep them in Thy name, the name which Thou has given Me, that they may be one, even as We are' " (John 17:11). Christ prayed that God's power would keep us from being swayed by the world and the evil one (John 17:15).

Lord Jesus Christ, I acknowledge
You as God and Savior.

Faithful One

*Let us hold unswervingly to the hope we profess,
for he who promised is faithful. And let us consider how we
may spur one another on toward love and good deeds.*
Hebrews 10:23–24 niv

When we have painful questions, therapists and counselors often have answers. Their offices overflow with hurting people looking for those answers.

But the people who offer the most practical and beneficial advice are those who have walked in our shoes—and who kept walking even when their soles wore through.

Such people have helped us—and we, in turn, can help others. We may feel as if we have nothing to offer, but that's simply not so. As women who have traveled the potholed road of life, we can be a blessing to others just lacing up their sneakers for the journey.

By holding tightly to the hope we have, we can benefit those around us who are struggling to find hope of their own. We can spur another hurting woman on to love and goodness and, in so doing, help ourselves better understand the God in whom our hope lies.

*Dear Jesus, I know You are faithful—but I often
forget that. Sometimes I wander in a direction
that does not encourage others to love or do good.
Please forgive me and help me to hold tighter
to that which I know is true. Show me how to
live every minute today to spur others
toward Your love tomorrow.*

God Has Left the Building

And the curtain of the temple was torn in two.
LUKE 23:45 NIV

On the day of Christ's death on the cross, all of creation was affected as the earth shook and the skies turned black. Inside the Jerusalem temple, the thick curtain separating the people from the inner room was split in two by a power unknown to man.

God, who had dwelled in the temple, the holy of holies, and had talked to Zechariah there (Luke 1), left the building when the curtain ripped on crucifixion day. He left a man-made structure to go and make a new home inside each individual who would invite Him in.

No longer did people have to physically move to Him to offer sacrifices and pray. Now God came to each individual on a personal level that was never known before. He made Himself accessible to anyone in any country on any continent.

God is an unchanging God who seeks relationship with us just as He did throughout biblical history. But we no longer have to walk the streets of Jerusalem to find God's Spirit. He comes to us and finds us just where we are.

Holy God, I invite You to make Your temple within me. I pledge that all I do will show honor to You and give You praise.

Slipped Moorings

But Jonah ran away from the Lord. . . . He went down to Joppa, where he found a ship bound for that port. After paying the fare, he went aboard and sailed for Tarshish to flee from the Lord.
Jonah 1:3 niv

Has God ever made it clear that He wants you to head in a certain direction—one you just balk at? Maybe fear fills your heart as you think of a move, or doubts weigh heavily on you as you consider your future prospects.

You may not run down to Joppa and find a ship, but you do find yourself slipping away from the center of His will. Maybe Bible study becomes harder or you think of things to do that don't involve the church. New, unbelieving friends may begin to attract you.

Though you have never gone aboard ship, you are heading for Tarshish. As your spiritual ship slips its moorings, you are sailing in a dangerous direction.

Before you leave port, consider your course and head back to shore. For, like Jonah, you can't evade God. Wherever you go, He'll be there already, calling you back to Himself. But the adventure you face first may be no more pleasant than Jonah's visit in a whale's belly.

You can walk away from God, but you can't escape Him. Even if you did, you would find yourself in a very lonely spot. A huge piece of your heart, God's piece, would be missing.

Turn my heart always to You, Lord.
I never want to leave You. Amen.

Well of Salvation

With joy you will draw water from the wells of salvation.
Isaiah 12:3 esv

In biblical times, wells were of great importance. Digging a well meant you planned to stay at a place. Owning a well meant your family possessed the surrounding countryside. Wells were gathering places and landmarks. People went to the well daily to get water for drinking, cooking, and cleaning. A well was essential to life for man and beast.

Our salvation is also a well. In it is not only our eternal life, but also our abundant life while we live on earth. Christ is the living water, continually refreshing and nourishing us, giving life to our bodies and souls. He is strength when we are weak, wisdom when we are foolish, hope when we are despondent, and life when we are dying.

Just as a bucket is lowered into a deep well, what begins as a descent into unknown darkness and depth becomes the means by which we draw up the water of life. Colossians 2:12 (cev) says, "When you were baptized, it was the same as being buried with Christ. Then you were raised to life because you had faith in the power of God, who raised Christ from death." We have died with Christ and now we live, but daily we need to go the well of our salvation, remembering our need for Jesus' life, and drawing out the living water with joy.

Lord, thank You for saving me. Thank You for being the living water, my continual source of peace, comfort, strength, and joy. Cause me to remember that my life is hidden in Yours.

Question the Witnesses

The high priest therefore questioned Jesus about His disciples, and about His teaching. Jesus answered him, "I have spoken openly to the world; I always taught in synagogues, and in the temple, where all the Jews come together; and I spoke nothing in secret. Why do you question Me? Question those who have heard what I spoke to them; behold, these know what I said."
John 18:19–21

In our courts of law the jury is instructed to listen carefully and then weigh the testimony in order to make a proper judgment. Christ calls the high priest to do the same.

How do we respond to the truth of Christ's testimony? How we treat His messengers is, in effect, a measure of our acceptance of Him.

Jesus Christ didn't come for a few souls; He presented the Gospel message openly for all to hear. Teaching in the Jewish temple, which was frequented not only by those who sought knowledge but also those in search of an explanation of the truth, Jesus provided both.

As we go out into a world that is hostile to the Gospel message, there are those who listen to our testimony and then draw near to its refreshing waters. Others sit on the riverbanks, vowing that nothing will force them to make a life change. And then there are those who deny the metamorphosis has even taken place. Their hearts are closed to receive the truth.

Lord, break down my walls of stubbornness that prevent me from hearing, seeing, and rallying to Your message.

Sabbath Queen

"Observe the Sabbath day, to keep it holy."
EXODUS 20:8 MSG

Weekends are a time to catch up on chores. A time to get some sunshine and to work in the yard. A time to sort laundry and wash clothes. A time to grocery shop and plan menus. A time to sort paperwork and pay bills.

For Sharon, weekends are also a time to do a little extra work for her job, to get ahead by responding to work e-mails and phone calls, to sort through papers, set goals, and prepare presentations.

But something has gone wrong. Sharon is worn out. Joy has been wrung from her soul. Her forty-hour workweek has grown to sixty—and she is burned out.

What happened to the Sabbath?

Nan Fink, in *Stranger in the Midst*, wrote, "Shabbat is like nothing else. Time as we know it does not exist for these twenty-four hours, and the worries of the week soon fall away. A feeling of joy appears. The smallest object, a leaf or a spoon, shimmers in a soft light, and the heart opens. Shabbat is a meditation of unbelievable beauty."

Lauren F. Winner, a messianic Jew and author of *Mudhouse Sabbath*, wrote, "We spoke of the day as *Shabbat ha-Malka*, the Sabbath Queen, and we sang hymns of praise on Friday night that welcomed the Sabbath as a bride."

Shabbat. Quiet. Holy. Worship.

Welcome the Sabbath Queen to your home this week.

Lord, help me practice a rhythm of rest and restoration, weekly welcoming the Sabbath, restoring order and worship to my weary soul. Amen.

Shake It Off

Then [Paul simply] shook off the small creature into the fire and suffered no evil effects.
ACTS 28:5 AMP

How many times do we make a mistake and confess it to the Lord, then continue to punish ourselves with guilt and condemnation? Psalm 103:12 tells us that God will remove our transgressions as far as the east is from the west.

When we make a mistake—and we all do—we should be like the apostle Paul. Immediately shake it off. Don't worry about it or allow guilt to grow. God removed the sin and no longer thinks about it. Why should we?

By immediately shaking a snake off his hand, Paul avoided harm. The viper's intentions were to infect Paul with poison and make him ill. Paul recognized the danger and immediately went into action, shaking it off. Afterward, he didn't worry over it. Instead, he went about helping the people on the island of Malta.

Don't allow your mistakes to so worry or condemn you that you can't be helpful to others around you. The poison of stress and worry will harm us if we allow it to penetrate our hearts and minds. Follow Paul's example: Shake it off.

Dear Lord, thank You for cleansing me of my sins. I will not worry or feel condemned any longer. Thank You, Lord, for helping me to shake things off and suffer no evil effects.

You Are What You Cling To

Hate what is evil; cling to what is good.
ROMANS 12:9 NIV

The invention of superglue was revolutionary, because the glue has the ability to bond immediately with a variety of materials. That is wonderful news if your grandmother's porcelain vase breaks in half. But superglue must be used with extreme caution. Accidents can happen in a split second. If the tiniest drop falls in the wrong place, two items will unintentionally and permanently bond.

What are we cemented to? Bonding takes place as we draw close to something. Choose to cling to what is good and avoid evil at all costs. We should not even flirt with sin, because it can quickly get a foothold in our lives. Like superglue in the wrong place, we could unintentionally find ourselves in bondage by embracing temptation. What may seem innocent at the time could destroy us.

Beware of your temptations. Know your areas of vulnerability and avoid them. If you struggle with unhealthy eating habits, do not buy tempting foods. If gossip is a temptation, avoid the company of friends that enjoy passing on tidbits about others. If overspending is an issue, stay away from the mall. Instead, draw close to the Lord. Allow Him to satisfy your deepest longings. When we cling to good, evil loses its grip.

Dear Lord, help me avoid temptation. May I draw close to You so I can cling to good and avoid evil in my life. Amen.

Quick and Slow

My dear brothers, take note of this: Everyone should be quick to listen, slow to speak and slow to become angry, for man's anger does not bring about the righteous life that God desires.
James 1:19–20 niv

Kindergartners learning traffic signals know that yellow means "slow down." James 1:19–20 also is a yellow light!

Have you wished, after a conversation with a friend, that you had not given that unsolicited advice? Your friend needed a listening ear, but you attempted to fix her problem instead.

Have you raced through a hectic day, only to end it by taking out your frustrations on family members or friends? Or perhaps you have borne the brunt of someone else's anger and reacted in the same manner, thus escalating the situation. Later, when tempers calmed, you found yourself regretting the angry outburst.

Too often words escape before we know what we are saying. Like toothpaste that cannot be put back in the tube, once words are spoken it is impossible to take them back. Words, whether positive or negative, have a lasting impact.

Practice being quick and slow today—quick to listen, slow to speak, slow to become angry.

God, grant me the patience, wisdom, and grace I need to be a good listener. Remind me also, Father, to use my words today to lift others up rather than to tear them down. Amen.

Dependence Day

"Then the glory of the Lord will be revealed, and all flesh will see it together; for the mouth of the Lord has spoken."
Isaiah 40:5

No, today's title is not misspelled, and no, I'm not thinking of Independence Day. Only when we are totally dependent on our Redeemer are we are truly free!

Carefully woven throughout chapters forty to sixty-six of Isaiah are specific portraits of Christ, presented by the names He called Himself throughout His ministry on earth. "Like a shepherd He will tend His flock, in His arm He will gather the lambs, and carry them in His bosom; He will gently lead the nursing ewes" (Isaiah 40:11).

Then we see Him as the Counselor. "Who has directed the Spirit of the Lord, or as His counselor has informed Him?" (Isaiah 40:13).

We can know Him as Creator. "Do you not know? Have you not heard? The Everlasting God, the Lord, the Creator of the ends of the earth does not become weary or tired. His understanding is inscrutable" (Isaiah 40:28).

Jesus is the First and the Last. " 'Who has performed and accomplished it, calling forth the generations from the beginning? I, the Lord, am the first, and with the last. I am He' " (Isaiah 41:4). Christ clarifies this further in Revelation 1:8: " 'I am the Alpha and Omega,' says the Lord God, 'who is and who was and who is to come, the Almighty.' "

Lord Jesus, I rejoice in the words from Isaiah 53: 4-6, that You came to be my Redeemer. Hallelujah! Amen!

The Heart Test

You have tested my heart; You have visited me in the night; You have tried me and have found nothing; I have purposed that my mouth shall not transgress.
Psalm 17:3 NKJV

You've probably heard a voice on television announce, "This is a test. For the next sixty seconds, this station will be conducting a test of the emergency broadcast system." Then the screen would go black and a high-pitched tone would come over the airways. Well, life conducts its own tests, sometimes. Some we pass; others we struggle through.

If you're in a season of emotional testing—of heartbreak or disappointment—don't allow your heart to become hardened. Don't allow bitterness to creep in. Do your best to pass the test, even if it's a hard one.

Let God do the work He wants to do in you—purging, purifying, and penetrating. Listen to His *This is a test* whisper, then stand firm. Don't yield to the temptation to give up or to say it's not worth it.

Take another look at today's encouraging scripture. How amazing to realize you really can come through the trials of life transgression-free. What a wonderful—and realistic—goal.

Lord, sometimes I feel like my heart is being tested by circumstances, relationships, or even by You. I want to make it through the testing period without falling apart. Help me to stand strong in what I know to be true.

Board God's Boat

Then, because so many people were coming and going that they did not even have a chance to eat, he said to them, "Come with me by yourselves to a quiet place and get some rest."
MARK 6:31–32 NIV

Are you "missing the boat" to a quieter place of rest with God? You mean to slow down, but your church, work, and family responsibilities pile higher than a stack of recyclable newspapers. Just when you think a free moment is yours, the phone rings, a needy friend stops by, or your child announces she needs you to bake cookies for tomorrow's school fund-raiser.

The apostles ministered tirelessly—so much so, they had little time to eat. As they gathered around Jesus to report their activities, the Lord noticed that they had neglected to take time for themselves. Sensitive to their needs, the Savior instructed them to retreat by boat with Him to a solitary place of rest where He was able to minister to them.

Often we allow the hectic pace of daily life to drain us physically and spiritually, and in the process, we deny ourselves time alone to pray and read God's Word. Meanwhile, God patiently waits.

So perhaps it's time to board God's boat to a quieter place and not jump ship!

Heavenly Father, in my hectic life I've neglected time apart with You. Help me to board Your boat and stay afloat through spending time in Your Word and in prayer. Amen.

Ideal Place

For consider your calling, brethren, that there were not many wise according to the flesh, not many mighty, not many noble; but God has chosen the foolish things of the world.
1 Corinthians 1:26–27

Once my life is running smoothly. . .

If I didn't have toddlers underfoot. . .
As soon as I get this anger problem under control. . .
When I get enough money. . .
As soon as I (fill in the blank). . .then I can be used by God.

We are *where* we are, *when* we are, because our Father chose us for such a time as this. Our steps are ordered by Him. Whether He has called us to teach a Sunday school class, pray with other women, lead a Bible study, or sing in the choir—we need not wait for the ideal time and place to serve Him. The only "ideal" is where you are right now.

God delights in using His people—right in the middle of all that appears crazy and wrong and hopeless. *Now* is the time to serve God, not next week or next year or when things get better. He wants our cheerful, obedient service right in the midst of—even in spite of—our difficult circumstances.

Father, help me see that there is no "ideal" place or circumstance to serve You. You can, and will, use me right where I am. Thank You that I do not have to have it all together to be used by You.

Fear of the Lord

The fear of the LORD *leads to life:*
Then one rests content, untouched by trouble.
PROVERBS 19:23 NIV

Eight-year-old Elizabeth had a healthy fear of her father. Oh, she loved him, called him "Daddy," and climbed up into his lap for hugs and kisses each day when he came home from work. But she also knew that when Daddy said to do something, he meant business.

Once, when playing in the front yard, Elizabeth lost her ball. It went bouncing into the street, and she ran after it. Just then, her father yelled out, "Stop!" Because of training and discipline her parents had poured into Elizabeth from a very young age, she heeded the warning and stopped at the curb just as a car sped by.

A healthy fear of their earthly parents is good for children. This type of fear might also be considered honor or respect.

To fear the Lord is to respect Him and acknowledge that His ways are best for us. Our Abba Father, a gracious and loving God, is also a just and mighty God who is saddened, and even angered, by continuous, deliberate sin.

Proverbs sums it up in one verse: "Fear the Lord. Live. Rest content, untouched by trouble." Consider the alternative. Which will you choose?

Lord, I respect You. Help me to acknowledge that You are God, You know best, and You have given me guidelines by which to live. Amen.

Jonathan, Faithful to the End

Now the Philistines were fighting against Israel, and the men of Israel fled from before the Philistines and fell slain on Mount Gilboa. And the Philistines overtook Saul and his sons; and the Philistines killed Jonathan and Abinadab and Malachi-shua the sons of Saul.
1 Samuel 31:1–2

Who has faithfully stood beside you through life's triumphs and tragedies? For David this person was Jonathan.

Jonathan walked a tightrope, remaining faithful to God, to Saul, his father, and to David. Considering Saul's obsession with killing David, this task took on monstrous proportions.

Their friendship began shortly after David killed the giant Goliath. Jonathan even gave David his "armor, including his sword and bow and belt" (1 Samuel 18:4). And how quickly David would need these weapons! David's accomplishments in battle became the stuff of legend and song, and this, of course, enraged Saul.

From then on Jonathan's time was spent trying to help David keep one step ahead of Saul. "So Jonathan told David saying, 'Saul my father is seeking to put you to death. Now therefore, please be on guard in the morning, and stay in a secret place and hide yourself. And I will go out and stand beside my father in the field where you are, and I will speak with my father about you; if I find out anything, then I shall tell you' " (1 Samuel 19:2–3).

Father, help me to be a faithful, loving, and unforgettable friend.

Mountain-Moving Company

*"If you have faith as small as a mustard seed,
you can say to this mountain, 'Move from here to there,'
and it will move. Nothing will be impossible for you."*
MATTHEW 17:20 NIV

We've all made the lament at some point, "If only I had enough faith. . ."

". . .my parent/child/friend/husband wouldn't have died."

". . .I would have received that job offer."

". . .I would have enough money for everything in my budget and more besides."

Any of those laments for greater faith pale when compared to faith to move a mountain. After all, doesn't Jesus say that all we need is faith the size of a tiny seed?

The problem with that line of thought is that we put the emphasis on ourselves. If *we* have faith, our problems will go away.

Jesus isn't prodding us to show more faith. He is pointing us to the object of our faith—God. However small our faith, God can move mountains. When we drop the seed of our faith into the ground of His will, He will move the mountains out of our way. He will show us the direction He wants us to take. He may move the mountain; or He may carry us over, around, or through it.

The next time a mountain looms ahead, God wants us to apply to His moving company. He will take us to the right destination.

*Lord God, You are the God of the impossible.
We trust You to move the mountains of our
lives and to move us through them. Amen.*

Meat or Mush?

Anyone who runs ahead and does not continue in the teaching of Christ does not have God; whoever continues in the teaching has both the Father and the Son.
2 JOHN 1:9 NIV

Have you had to contend with "smorgasbord Christianity"? Suddenly, your minister leaves, and as your congregation seeks a new leader, a succession of preachers fills the pulpit week after week. And every week you're being fed a different kind of spiritual food.

Don't relax and figure you're on a spiritual vacation. This is the time to listen very carefully. You have no idea where these people come from theologically, and it might be easy to be led astray by a deep, mellow voice or empty but high-sounding words.

Spiritual ideas abound, but not all are sound. Sometimes it's easy to assume you're getting good meat when you're actually being served mushy, rotten vegetables.

How can you tell meat from mush? Compare the message to Christ's words. Is the preacher avoiding the Bible's tough commands, preaching ideas that are not biblical, or appealing to non-Christian ideas? Better beware.

Jesus gave us strong doctrines and good teaching to lead us into His truth. Faithful expositors cling to His Word. They offer meat and milk but no rotten teachings.

Eat well!

Keep me aware of Your truth, Lord.
I want to live on it, not on mush. Amen.

Still Waters

"They will lie down on good grazing ground and feed in rich pasture. . . . I will feed My flock and I will lead them to rest," declares the LORD God.

EZEKIEL 34:14–15

"I have to get this house clean." "The last load of laundry has to be done before I go to bed." "If I miss that meeting at work, how will I ever get that promotion?" "I can't forget the kids' school play—they've had enough disappointment." "We have to be at church by 10:00." "I need to get the oil changed soon." "Where's that dry cleaning?" Whew. . .one gets tired just reading a woman's to-do list.

How do we rest? By simply stopping. The laundry can wait. The house doesn't have to be squeaky clean. You can push the oil change out to 6,000 miles. Maybe we can ask a friend to help with the dry cleaning, or go to an occasional Sunday evening service so we can sleep in.

When do we rest? It won't find us, so we'll have to pursue it. Schedule it, pencil it in, do what needs to be done—just get some rest. Physical, mental, and emotional rest is paramount. If we miss it, we'll burn out, stress out, or just plain give out.

God promises to lead us to lush, green pastures, while restoring our soul. Let's take Him up on the offer!

Heavenly Father, I need to learn to simply rest and relax. I see so much to do and have so much responsibility—so please enable me to lie down in the pastures You have provided.

Keep Running

Let us run with perseverance the race marked out for us.
HEBREWS 12:1 NIV

Karen began the marathon filled with confidence. She had been training for months. She knew the course well and trusted her body. The weather was perfect. But ninety minutes later, she was overcome with a fatigue like none she had ever known. Not only was she exhausted, she was nauseated. Her feet and legs screamed for mercy. She paused at a water station and considered giving up completely. She was about to step off the course and call it a day when a seasoned runner approached her. "Looks like you're having a hard time," she said cheerfully. Karen mustered a weak smile.

"Come on—I'll run with you for a while. See that sign up ahead? Think you can make it at least that far?" Karen willed her body to continue. For the next few miles, her companion slowed her own race to keep pace with Karen's. Every half mile or so she pointed out a goal to reach—mailboxes, stoplights, street signs. Thirty minutes later, Karen felt her strength return, buoyed by her new friend who clearly knew the value of a traveling companion. Finally Karen made it to the finish line. She was exhausted and overwhelmed, but grateful. Grateful she had endured and grateful for a friend who helped her along the way.

Father, when the race is too much for me, give me strength for the journey. Thank You for the friends I have along the way. Help me to finish with confidence. Amen.

Ezekiel's Call

While I was by the river Chebar among the exiles, the heavens were opened and I saw visions of God. (On the fifth of the month in the fifth year of King Jehoiachin's exile, the word of the LORD came expressly to Ezekiel the priest, son of Buzi, in the land of the Chaldeans by the river Chebar; and there the hand of the LORD came upon him.)

EZEKIEL 1:1–3

Sometimes God's plans are so different from what we expect to be doing with our lives that it's really astonishing.

Although he was only eighteen years old when some of the nobles and princes were captured by King Nebuchadnezzar and taken from Judah to Babylon, Ezekiel had already been groomed for the priesthood.

Ezekiel's life plan became forever altered ten years later, in 597 B.C., when he was among those taken in Nebuchadnezzar's second siege against Jerusalem. Never again would he view the temple where he had hoped to serve God. However, when he was thirty years old the Lord gave him a vision of a new temple and another Jerusalem. His call was to prophesy concerning Judah and Jerusalem, Israel's coming restoration, and the temple.

Ezekiel's visions parallel those of John recorded in the Book of Revelation. These dreams show that no matter how bleak Israel's present situation might be, their future would be bright.

Lord, despite my own problems and challenges I can keep going forward as long as You show me a vision of hope. As I read the prophecies of Ezekiel, fill me with expectation!

Laying Down Your Life

*Greater love hath no man than this,
that a man lay down his life for his friends.*
JOHN 15:13 KJV

God-breathed love is sacrificial. It continues to give even under the most difficult of circumstances, never keeping track of the cost. As indicated in today's scripture, the ultimate expression of love is one's willingness to lay down his or her life for another.

We wonder if such love is really possible—and if we have it in ourselves to love so sacrificially. Does this scripture refer only to literal death, or is there a deeper message?

Sacrifice, by its very definition, is the ability to place another's needs before your own—to continue pouring out, even when you're tapped out. Every instance you give of your time, energy, or resources to care for a loved one in need, you demonstrate your willingness to lay down your life. You're expressing the heart of God.

Your ability to continue giving day in and day out pleases the heart of your heavenly Father, who perfectly understands the principle of "laying down" one's life. After all, that's what He did for us at Calvary.

Dear Lord, please create a caregiver's heart within me—a heart ready to give sacrificially no matter the cost. When I feel I'm "given out," remind me of Your great sacrifice on the cross for me.

A Child in Need

"For all those things My hand has made, and all those things exist," says the LORD. "But on this one will I look: on him who is poor and of a contrite spirit, and who trembles at My word."
ISAIAH 66:2 NKJV

When a teacher looks across a room full of students working quietly at their desks, which one gets her attention? The one with a raised hand—the one with an immediate need.

Like the student, a humble child of God with a need catches His eye. Though He is always watching over all of us, He is drawn to a child who needs Him. We may need forgiveness, wisdom, courage, endurance, patience, health, protection, or even love. God promises to come to our aid when He sees us with a hand up, reaching for His assistance. He will not ignore a contrite heart and spirit. God's grace rushes to one who cries out for mercy, and He offers restoration to the repentant heart.

What needs do you have in your life today? Raise your hand in prayer to God. He'll take care of your needs and then some—blessing your life in ways you can't even imagine!

Father, thank You for caring about the needs of Your children. Help me to remember to always seek You first.

Look Up, Not Around

We're not, understand, putting ourselves in a league with those who boast that they're our superiors. We wouldn't dare do that. But in all this comparing and grading and competing, they quite miss the point.
2 Corinthians 10:12 msg

Humans tend to be competitive. It's a part of our nature that shows up at work, on the ball field, even at church. Human competition is also seen throughout the Bible, from Cain and Abel, Jacob and Esau, David and Saul, all the way through the apostles (Luke 22:24). Women are not immune to the pull of competition either (Luke 10:41–42), and often the busier we are, the harder we compete with those around us, as if the very act of winning will make our lives easier.

Nowhere does scripture condemn the drive to achieve a worthy goal. Ambition, in itself, is not a problem. It is how ambition manifests itself that Paul warns the Corinthians about. Are we striving to better ourselves for God, for our families, for our employers? Or has the goal become winning, looking better than others? Are we looking for worldly admiration only?

If we strive toward our goals in a way that causes other believers to stumble or violates the values God has set forth for us, then perhaps we should take a step back. After all, our final victory has little to do with what the world thinks about us.

Father God, Your standards are what I need to hold before me. Grant me the wisdom to keep Your values in mind as I aim for any higher goal. Amen.

Lacking Nothing

Consider it pure joy, my brothers, whenever you face trials of many kinds, because you know that the testing of your faith develops perseverance. Perseverance must finish its work so that you may be mature and complete, not lacking anything.
JAMES 1:2–4 NIV

Trials are never fun. Nor are they pain-free. But they're still necessary.

When people speak of trials, they might mean anything from sleep deprivation to the loss of a loved one—or anything in between. How can we "consider it pure joy" when we face such trials? It's not the trial itself that we celebrate, but the personal growth and expansion of our faith that can lead to joy. Unfortunately, our attitude in the midst of the trial often leaves us empty and hurting.

Trials don't get easier from one to the next. But when we get through one—battered but not broken—we can look back to see growth and strength, which we can take into the next. We have become better equipped to face the next trial with perseverance, comfort, and hope. And we can walk straight ahead, knowing that in the end we will be mature and complete, lacking absolutely nothing in Christ Jesus.

Abba Father, I know You go with me through these trials. I know that any perseverance or strength I have is only because of You and Your faithfulness to me. Increase my joy through these trials and help me remember the purpose of them—that I may not lack any good thing.

Ezekiel Speaks to the Lost

Then He said to me, "Son of man, go to the house of Israel and speak with My words to them."
EZEKIEL 3:4

How did you become a Christian? By hearing the Word of God? That's the way I came to know Him as Savior. We respond to the message of truth that is given to us. The powerful Word of God convicts our hearts of sin and turns us toward the Lord.

Knowing this, the apostle Paul wrote, "For I am not ashamed of the gospel, for it is the power of God for salvation to everyone who believes, to the Jew first and also to the Greek. For in it the righteousness of God is revealed from faith to faith" (Romans 1:16–17). The same power that resurrected Christ can be with us today!

Did you wonder why the Gospel should be given "to the Jew first and also to the Greek"? All through history God has desired to communicate salvation to His chosen people, so that they could then bring this hope to the Gentiles. But when they refused to respond, He brought the message to all the unbelieving nations. And now we who are Gentiles are bringing the message back to the Jews. The Word is coming full circle.

At times we are unwilling to risk presenting the Gospel message because of personal rejection. However, the outcome isn't our problem, it's God's. And He says the same thing to us that He did to Ezekiel: " 'But you shall speak My words to them whether they listen or not, for they are rebellious' " (Ezekiel 2:7).

Lord, help me depend on Your Word to accomplish all You intend, by Your powerful Spirit.

The Secret of Serendipity

A happy heart makes the face cheerful.
Proverbs 15:13 niv

Can you remember the last time you laughed in wild abandon? Better yet, when was the last time you did something fun, outrageous, or out of the ordinary? Perhaps it is an activity you haven't done since you were a child, like slip down a waterslide, strap on a pair of ice skates, or pitch a tent and camp overnight.

Women often become trapped in the cycle of routine, and soon we lose our spontaneity. Children, on the other hand, are innately spontaneous. Giggling, they splash barefoot in rain puddles. Wide-eyed, they watch a kite soar toward the treetops. They make silly faces without inhibition; they see animal shapes in rock formations. In essence, they possess the secret of serendipity.

A happy heart turns life's situations into opportunities for fun. For instance, if a storm snuffs out the electricity, light a candle and play games, tell stories, or just enjoy the quiet. When we seek innocent pleasures, we glean the benefits of a happy heart.

Jesus said, "I am come that they might have life, and that they might have it more abundantly" (John 10:10 kjv). God wants us to enjoy life, and when we do, it lightens our load and changes our countenance.

So try a bit of whimsy just for fun. And rediscover the secret of serendipity.

Dear Lord, because of You, I have a happy heart. Lead me to do something fun and spontaneous today! Amen.

Core Strength

He gives strength to the weary and increases the power of the weak.
Isaiah 40:29 niv

A regular exercise program is essential to keep our bodies functioning the way God designed them to. One of the components of an effective exercise regime is the development of core strength. These muscles—the abdomen, trunk, and back—are responsible for strength, stabilization, and balance. Strong core muscles protect our spines, enable us to stand and move gracefully, and prevent the development of chronic pain. Investing the time and energy in developing and maintaining core muscles pays enormous dividends.

The same is true for our spiritual core muscles. Our spiritual core consists of foundational elements from which our lives move. It can include core beliefs—about who God is and the role of the Father, Son, and Holy Spirit in our daily lives.

Another spiritual core muscle can be principles on which we build our lives—what is our purpose on earth? What is our motivation for working, living, and interacting with others? Who are we in Christ? We can exercise our spiritual core by reading God's Word every day, praying about everything, and spending time in fellowship with other believers.

A strong spiritual core will help ensure that you remain stable and secure in a changing world. That you are able to keep from falling and that you are able to move and live gracefully. As you exercise your physical body, also make a commitment to regularly exercise your spiritual core as well.

Father, help me to return again and again to the core foundations of my spiritual health. Amen.

The Father's Voice

What use is it, my brethren, if someone says he has faith but he has no works? Can that faith save him?
JAMES 2:14 NASB

A young family set out on a three-day hike. The mother and father were avid hikers and were excited to share the experience of the mountain trails and campsites with their young son and daughter. The children marveled at the sights and sounds of the wilderness. At nightfall they sat around the fire after their meal. The young son explored the edges of the campsite, and his father warned him not to step outside of the light.

Curious, the boy traced the shadows on the trees and followed a night crawler to its hiding place under a rock. Suddenly, the son had lost sight of the campfire and of his family. He cried out in panic, "Daddy, I'm lost!" The father responded calmly, "As long as you can hear me, you're not lost." The father called out to him over and over again until the son had followed the sound of his voice safely back to the campsite.

Perhaps you've felt like that small boy, lost with darkness all around you. Your heavenly Father is always listening, and as long as you follow His voice, He will guide you back to safety and into His loving arms.

God, help me to listen for Your voice and follow Your direction. Amen.

David's Family Tree

Now when evening came David arose from his bed and walked around on the roof of the king's house, and from the roof he saw a woman bathing; and the woman was very beautiful in appearance. So David sent and inquired about the woman. And one said, "Is this not Bathsheba, the daughter of Eliam, the wife of Uriah the Hittite?" And David. . .lay with her; and when she had purified herself from her uncleanness, she returned to her house. And the woman conceived; and she sent and told David, and said, "I am pregnant."

2 Samuel 11:2–5

The Bible presents the true account of man's record on this earth, warts and all! Although David should have accompanied his men into battle against the sons of Ammon, he instead stayed home. And there was beautiful Bathsheba, washing herself on her rooftop in the warmth of the evening. At any rate, David succumbed to temptation, and Bathsheba later realized she was with child.

David knew Bathsheba was Uriah's wife but he seduced her anyway. But an even greater sin occurred as David tried to cover his tracks. He sent for Uriah and told him to go home, hoping that Uriah would then sleep with Bathsheba and all would appear fine. However, Uriah decided instead to deny himself the comforts that his soldiers on the battlefront were also lacking and instead he "slept at the door of the king's house with all the servants of his lord. . ." (2 Samuel 11:9).

David then implemented "plan B" and had Uriah sent to the front lines where he was killed. After a period of mourning David took Bathsheba to be his wife.

Lord, help me to be accountable to You.

A Very Important Phrase

And it came to pass. . .
Found More Than 400 Times in the King James Bible

What tremendous words of encouragement! Headaches, toothaches, car troubles, clogged drains, personality conflicts—all come only *to pass.* We can focus on the Lord, and He will bring us through.

There are times in life when we think we can't bear one more day, one more hour, one more minute. But let's not get down—for no matter how bad things seem at the time, they are temporary. The situation will pass; life will go on. Tomorrow will be another day with new victories and challenges—but always also with new grace.

What's really important is how we handle the opportunities before us today, whether we let our trials defeat us or look for the hand of God in everything. He's giving us more chances to glorify Him in the daily events of our lives.

Every day, week, and year are made up of things that "come to pass"—so even if we fail, we needn't be disheartened. Other opportunities—better days—will come. Let's look past those hard things today and glorify the name of the Lord.

Lord Jesus, how awesome it is that You send or allow these little things that will pass. May we recognize Your hand in them today and praise You for them.

The Bar Is Too High!

She gets up while it is still dark; she provides food for her family. . . .
Her lamp does not go out at night.
Proverbs 31:15, 18 niv

The Proverbs 31 woman puts Wonder Woman to shame. Up before dawn, late to bed, caring for her household, negotiating business contracts down at the city gate. She gives to the poor, plans for her household to run smoothly, anticipates future needs, such as snowy weather. Even her arms are buff! "She sets about her work vigorously; her arms are strong for her tasks" (Proverbs 31:17 niv).

She is highly energetic, an efficiency expert, *and* gifted in relationships. "Her children arise and call her blessed; her husband also, and he praises her" (v. 28). This woman is downright intimidating!

So how do we benefit by reading about the Proverbs 31 woman? Reading about her day makes us feel overwhelmed, discouraged by our inadequacies. That bar is too high!

God doesn't place the bar so high that we live in its shadow. He wired each of us with different gifts, different energy levels, different responsibilities. Proverbs 31 casts a floodlight on *all* women—those gifted in business, in home life, as caregivers. This chapter displays how women undergird their families and their communities.

Remember, the book of Proverbs was written in the tenth century BC, when women were considered chattel. But not in God's eyes. He has always esteemed women and the many roles we fulfill in society.

Father, thank You for the important women in my life. You made each one of us with gifts and abilities. May we be used to glorify You. Amen.

The White Knight

Then I will rejoice in the LORD. I will be glad because he rescues me.
PSALM 35:9 NLT

Ever since she was a little girl, Alex had dreamed of someday playing the part of a damsel in distress who is heroically rescued by a white knight.

Reality soon set in.

"How long am I supposed to wait for him?" she lamented to a friend over lattes. "My white knight apparently has a problem with punctuality."

We're all waiting for someone to rescue us. Maybe you're waiting for a soul mate to fill a void in your heart. Or perhaps you're waiting for a friend to come through in your time of need. It could be that you're waiting for your mom to finally treat you like an adult or for a prospective employer to call back with a job offer. We wait and wait and wait for a rescuer to come.

The truth is, God doesn't want you to exist in a perpetual state of waiting. Live your life—your whole life—by seeking daily joy in the Savior of your soul, Jesus Christ. And here's the best news of all: He's already done the rescuing by dying on the cross for our sins! He's the *true* white knight who secured your eternity in heaven.

Stop waiting; seek His face today!

Jesus, I praise You because You are the rescuer of my soul. Remind me of this fact when I'm looking for relief in other people and places. You take care of my present and eternal needs, and for that I am grateful. Amen.

Is Anyone Listening?

And I will ask the Father, and He will give you another Comforter (Counselor, Helper, Intercessor, Advocate, Strengthener, and Standby), that He may remain with you forever.
John 14:16 amp

Christians have the assurance that God will hear them when they call. In turn, we can hear God's voice of love when *we* listen.

People who love each other spend time together. They share their dreams and hopes. So it is with our heavenly Father, who wants to hear from us. He cares so much that He sent the Holy Spirit to be our Counselor, our Comforter.

The Greek translation for "comfort" is *paraklesis* or "calling near." When we are called near to someone, we are able to hear his or her whisper. It is this very picture scripture paints when it speaks of the Holy Spirit. God sent the Spirit to whisper to us and to offer encouragement and guidance, to be our strength when all else fails. When we pray—when we tell God our needs and give Him praise—He listens. Then He directs the Spirit within us to speak to our hearts and give us reassurance.

Our world is filled with noise and distractions. Look for a place where you can be undisturbed for a few minutes. Take a deep breath, lift your prayers, and listen. God will speak—and your heart will hear.

Dear Lord, I thank You for Your care. Help me to recognize Your voice and to listen well.

A Comfortable Place

Don't you realize that your body is the temple of the Holy Spirit,
who lives in you and was given to you by God?
You do not belong to yourself.
1 CORINTHIANS 6:19 NLT

Sandra spent the day picking up her apartment. She purchased a new bedspread for her guest room. On the coffee table, she placed a vase of fresh wildflowers. She got a magazine and set herself to work finding some new recipes for dinner.

Why did she take the time to do all these things?

Sandra's friend from out of state was coming to stay the weekend. She knew that her home was a reflection of herself. The effort that she took in preparing it for her guest would show that she cared enough to make her friend feel at home.

We take the time to make our homes comfortable and beautiful when we know visitors are coming. In the same way, we ought to prepare our hearts for the Holy Spirit who lives inside of us. We should daily ask God to help us clean up the junk in our hearts. We should take special care to tune up our bodies through exercise, eating healthful foods, and dressing attractively and modestly.

Our bodies belong to God. They are a reflection to others of Him. Taking care of ourselves shows others that we honor God enough to respect and use wisely what He has given us.

Dear Lord, thank You for letting me belong to You.
May my body be a comfortable place for You. Amen.

Saul and Stephen

And they went on stoning Stephen as he called upon the Lord and said, "Lord Jesus, receive my spirit!" And falling on his knees, he cried out with a loud voice, "Lord, do not hold this sin against them!" And having said this, he fell asleep. And Saul was in hearty agreement with putting him to death. And on that day a great persecution arose against the church in Jerusalem.

Acts 7:59–60; 8:1

Have you ever committed an action so despicable that you can't imagine God could ever forgive you? Saul—who would soon be acclaimed as the fearless apostle Paul—had been persuaded by his own pious intentions to stamp out the Gospel's heresy. After the stoning of Stephen, Saul entered home after home and dragged Christians off to prison.

And then the powerful hand of the Lord God intervened.

"Suddenly a light from heaven flashed around him; and he fell to the ground, and heard a voice saying to him, 'Saul, Saul, why are you persecuting Me?' And he said, 'Who art Thou, Lord?' And He said, 'I am Jesus whom you are persecuting, but rise, and enter the city, and it shall be told you what you must do' " (Acts 9:3–6).

Blinded for three days by God's incredible power, Saul had to be led into the city of Damascus. There, a disciple named Ananias, to whom God gave a message, would intervene.

Thank You, God, for changing Saul into Paul!

Complicated Relationships

And David said unto him, Fear not: for I will surely shew thee kindness for Jonathan thy father's sake, and will restore thee all the land of Saul thy father; and thou shalt eat bread at my table continually.
2 Samuel 9:7 KJV

Like people today, Old Testament characters struggled with personal relationships. David's wife Michal turned against him. Her father, King Saul, hunted David like an animal, though the younger man ultimately triumphed and was crowned king.

Most rulers executed their opponents—and their families. But King David, in a major risk-taking move, not only returned Saul's estate to his grandson Mephibosheth but also offered him financial support and a place at the king's table.

David's advisors probably thought him crazy. That is, unless they knew Mephibosheth's father, Jonathan. In the midst of family turmoil, he and David were fast friends. Jonathan even offered to step down as Saul's heir and support David's kingship. When his father threatened to kill David, Jonathan risked his own life by defending his friend. Later Jonathan died with Saul on the battlefield.

David's love for his late friend extended to Jonathan's children. When he summoned Mephibosheth, the terrified man probably thought David was planning to kill him. Instead, the king treated Mephibosheth like a son, welcoming him with open arms.

In our own difficult relationships, loyalty and kindness may also seem an unwise response. But God wants our actions to always reflect His readiness to bless amid heartache and hurt.

Father, when forgiveness seems impossible, help me act in accordance with Your unconditional love.

Judged!

A woman who had lived a sinful life. . .brought an alabaster jar of perfume, and as she stood behind him at his feet weeping, she began to wet his feet with her tears. Then she wiped them with her hair, kissed them and poured perfume on them.
Luke 7:37–38 niv

What a beautiful story of repentance. Though we don't know her name, we relate to this woman's loving testimony. How we would like to be able to anoint Jesus with our love.

Had it been up to the Pharisee who shares the story with her, we probably wouldn't know about the sinful woman. This man who had invited Jesus to dinner missed the point of her actions and began judging her and the Master who accepted her loving gift. *Surely*, assumed the Pharisee, *a prophet would know this woman is a sinner.*

This first-century Jew isn't alone in leaping to judgment. Many churchgoers fall into the same trap. A new person comes to our church and doesn't follow the rules. Maybe she doesn't dress like everyone else or doesn't use the right spiritual jargon. In an instant, we doubt her salvation.

But if she doesn't know Jesus, isn't this the right place for her to be? Standing near Him, an unbeliever may come to faith—if the people in God's congregation are loving and nurturing.

We need not judge a casual acquaintance's spiritual life—God can do that. All we need to do is love, and He will bring blessings.

Thank You, Lord, that Your first reaction to me was love, not condemnation. Turn my heart in love to all who don't yet know You. Amen.

Antichrist, the Ruler to Come

"And in his place a despicable person will arise, on whom the honor of kingship has not been conferred, but he will come in a time of tranquility and seize the kingdom by intrigue. And the overflowing forces will be flooded away before him and shattered, and also the prince of the covenant. And after an alliance is made with him he will practice deception, and he will go up and gain power with a small force of people. In a time of tranquility he will enter the richest parts of the realm, and he will accomplish what his fathers never did, nor his ancestors; he will distribute plunder, booty, and possessions among them, and he will devise his schemes against strongholds, but only for a time."

Daniel 11:21–24

The antichrist is a real person who will one day deviously slither onto the scene right on cue. He will appear indispensable at a time of worldwide, unsolvable chaos. His allies will be the foes of God.

His deception will be so great that people will fail to see his face of evil until "the abomination of desolation" takes place (Matthew 24:15). Three and one-half years after he comes on the scene, the antichrist will enter the rebuilt temple in Jerusalem, declare himself god, and demand worship and allegiance from the world. Jesus Himself warned the Jews about this diabolical person, telling them that when they saw him to " 'let those who are in Judea flee to the mountains' " (Mark 13:14).

Lord, compel me with new urgency to study Your powerful Word, that I might bring it to others.

One Thing Is Needed

"Martha, Martha," the Lord answered, "you are worried and upset about many things, but only one thing is needed."
Luke 10:41–42 NIV

We are each given twenty-four hours in a day. Einstein and Edison were given no more than Joseph and Jeremiah of the Old Testament. The president and the paratrooper are all given an equal share. Even Mother Teresa and plain ol' women are peers when it comes to time.

Time—we can't buy it, save it, or get a greater share no matter what we do. Its value is beyond measure. So we should learn to use it carefully. Do we tackle the laundry now or help the kids read *If You Give a Mouse a Cookie* one more time? Do we stay up late, cleaning the living room, or slip into bed early, knowing we need the rest? Do we fuss over our hair and makeup or find a moment to kneel before our Father?

Since God has blessed each of us with twenty-four hours, let's seek His direction on how to spend this invaluable commodity wisely—giving more to people than things, spending more time on relationships than the rat race. In Luke, our Lord reminded dear, dogged, drained Martha that only one thing is needed—Him.

Father God, oftentimes, I get caught up in the minutia of life. The piled laundry can appear more important than the precious little ones You've given me. Help me to use my time wisely. Open my eyes to see what is truly important.

Confident Persistence

"Don't be afraid. Just stand still and watch the LORD rescue you today. The Egyptians you see today will never be seen again."
EXODUS 14:13 NLT

Sharon was confused. Doubts and fears assailed her mind. *Lord, I think I've bitten off more than I can chew. Now I'm out here, in the middle of nowhere, ready to give up.*

Her confidence waning, Sharon cried out to God. Then, reaching for her Bible, she opened to where she'd last left off reading in Exodus, where the Israelites were running from Pharaoh.

The hard-hearted pharaoh thought he had a good chance to bring his slaves back to him. He figured that the Israelites, hemmed in by the desert, would be wandering around the land in confusion.

Indeed, the Israelites had gone out of Egypt with boldness. Yet when trapped by the sea, they became discouraged and frightened. But while at a literal standstill, they called out to God and He became a shield for them, using a cloud in front and behind them and the walls of the sea on either side. And after going through the sea on dry land, God's people never saw those Egyptians again.

When you become bewildered and petrified with fear, "don't be afraid. Just stand still and watch the LORD rescue you today," because the problems, frustrations, and barriers you see today will never be seen again. Be persistent, and God will see you through.

Lord, be my shield. Surround me with Your presence. Help me to keep still in this situation and watch You see me through it. And I will praise You forever and ever, in Jesus' name. Amen.

Answered Knee-Mail

The prayer of a righteous man is powerful and effective.
James 5:16 niv

We communicate with others in our cyberspace world at lightning speed—an e-mail, instant message, text messaging—all of these provide quick results. But prayer is even faster than the digital world. We have God's attention the moment we focus on Him.

The concept of the power of prayer is familiar, but sometimes we forget what it means. Prayer is a powerful tool for communicating with God, an opportunity to commune with the Creator of the universe. Prayer is not something to be taken lightly or used infrequently. Yet, in the rush of daily life, we often lose sight of God's presence. Instead of turning to Him for guidance and comfort, we depend on our own resources.

But prayer isn't just a way to seek protection and guidance; it's how we develop a deeper relationship with our heavenly Father. We can access this power anywhere. We don't need a wi-fi hotspot or a high-speed modem. We just need to look up. He's connected and waiting.

Father, thank You for being at my side all the time.
Help me to turn to You instantly,
in need and in praise. Amen.

Who Helps the Helper?

The LORD is my strength and my shield; my heart trusted in him, and I am helped: therefore my heart greatly rejoiceth; and with my song will I praise him.
PSALM 28:7 KJV

Women tend to be helpers. They can't help it.

God made them that way. From the foundation of the earth, their primary job has been to help.

It is a woman's nature to assist, to nurture, to render care. Even in these days of more "equitable" roles, it is typically the woman who is found feeding the baby at 2 a.m., cheering the young soccer players, counseling the college student by long-distance phone calls, holding a shaky hand in a hospital room, and comforting the bereaved at a funeral.

Helping can be exhausting. The needs of young children, teens, grandchildren, aging parents, our neighbors, and fellow church members—the list is never-ending—can stretch us until we're ready to snap. And then we find that *we* need help.

Who helps the helper?

The Lord does. When we are weak, He is strong. When we are vulnerable, He is our shield. When we can no longer trust in our own resources, we can trust in Him.

And we can trust Him before we snap. He is always there, ready to help. Rejoice in Him, praise His name, and you will find the strength to go on.

Father, I'm worn out. I can't care for all the people and needs You bring into my life by myself. I need Your strength. Thank You for being my helper and my shield.

Magnifying Life

My soul makes its boast in the Lord; let the humble hear and be glad. Oh, magnify the Lord with me, and let us exalt his name together!
Psalm 34:2–3 ESV

To magnify is to make larger, more visible, more easily seen. When the angel of the Lord appeared to Mary telling her she would be the mother of the Messiah, her response was to quote the psalm, "Oh, magnify the Lord with me." Mary knew she was the object of God's favor and mercy. That knowledge produced humility. It is the humble soul that desires that God be glorified instead of self.

Try as we might, we can't produce this humility in ourselves. It is our natural tendency to be self-promoters, to manage the impressions others have of us, and to better our own reputations. We need the help of the Spirit to remind us that God has favored each of us with His presence. He did not have to come to us in Christ, but He did. He has chosen to set His love on us. His life redeemed ours, and He sanctifies us. We are recipients of the action of His grace.

Does your soul make its boast in the Lord? Does your life make Christ larger and easier for others to see? Maybe you can't honestly say you desire this. Start there. Confess that. Ask Him to remind you of His favor and to work humility into your life, to help you pray like Mary did.

Christ Jesus, help me to remember what You have done for me and desire for others to see and know You.

But What about the Jews?

For if Abraham was justified by works, he has something to boast about; but not before God. For what does the Scripture say? "And Abraham believed God, and it was reckoned to him as righteousness."
ROMANS 4:2–3

Our work ethic is as old as the Garden of Eden. Because of sin Adam's free ride was over and he would now have to earn a living. But God said, " 'Because you have listened to the voice of your wife, and have eaten from the tree about which I commanded you, saying, "You shall not eat from it"; cursed is the ground because of you; in toil you shall eat of it all the days of your life' " (Genesis 3:17).

Somehow men and women have transferred this attitude about working for things to salvation. However, salvation is not based on our "goodness," but rather on Christ's. For no matter how diligently we try to keep those Ten Commandments, we're going to fail.

God made Abraham, the one the Jews claim as their father, a promise and he believed God.

His belief wasn't merely an intellectual assent. The "Supreme God of the Universe," who made absolutely everything that Abraham now saw in his world, had deigned not only to speak to him, but He promised him an heir. The reason that Abraham could place his trust in God was because God kept His promises. No matter how impossible the situation looks, God always comes through.

I thank You that I worship a God whose Word can be trusted. I know Jesus will always be there for me.

No More Sting

O death, where is thy sting? O grave, where is thy victory?
1 Corinthians 15:55 kjv

Two female golfers were driving from one hole to the next when a huge bumblebee flew into the cart. The passenger panicked. Attempting to avoid the bee, she overreacted, lost her balance, and fell out of the cart. Later she sheepishly remarked to friends, "I was frightened for nothing. That kind of bee doesn't even sting!"

We have so many fears that names have been given to identify our phobias. *Arachnophobia*: the fear of spiders. *Claustrophobia*: the fear of being in closed spaces. *Acrophobia:* the fear of heights. What are you afraid of? Do we make situations even worse by overreacting? Perhaps our fears are unfounded in the first place.

We have a choice to make. We can either live life in fear or live life by faith. Fear and faith cannot coexist. Jesus Christ has conquered our greatest fear—death. He rose victorious and has given us eternal life through faith. Knowing this truth enables us to courageously face our fears. There is no fear that cannot be conquered by faith. Let's not panic but trust the Lord instead. Let's live by faith and experience the victory that has been given to us through Jesus Christ, our Lord.

Lord, You alone know my fears. Help me to trust You more. May I walk in the victory that You have purchased for me. Amen.

Understand. . .Then Act

Make the most of every opportunity in these evil days. Don't act thoughtlessly; but understand what the Lord wants you to do.
EPHESIANS 5:16–17 NLT

An older woman found herself acting on impulse—a lot. When things would go wrong, she'd react, and not always in a good way. She would blurt out things she didn't really mean. Sometimes she even made issues out of nonissues. Then later—in the quiet times—she would wonder why. If she'd just taken the time to think before speaking, so many problems could have been avoided.

Can you relate to this woman? Do you ever act or speak without thinking first? If so, you are certainly not alone. Women are emotional creatures and often knee-jerk, based on emotions. We're especially vulnerable when our feelings are hurt. We don't always take the time to understand what the Lord wants us to do before implementing our own plan of action.

Are you an actor or a reactor? Are you a thinker or a knee-jerker? The Lord longs for us to think before we act or speak—to act on His behalf. To react takes little or no thought, but to live a life that reflects the image of Christ takes lots of work!

Lord, I don't want to be a reactor. I want to be an actor—reflecting You in my life. Today, I give You my knee-jerking tendencies. Guard my words and actions, Father. Help me to think before I speak.

Well Watered

"The Lord will guide you always; he will satisfy your needs in a sun-scorched land and will strengthen your frame. You will be like a well-watered garden, like a spring whose waters never fail."
Isaiah 58:11 NIV

The county restrictions allowed for watering only twice a week. It just wasn't enough. Her carefully tended acre—once lush, green, and profuse with color and variety—was now brown and crunchy underfoot. The blooms hung limp, pale, and dehydrated. She couldn't ignore the living word picture this was to her own spiritual life. For months now, she'd actually only watered her spirit with Sunday morning sermons. She, too, felt lifeless and dried up from the stresses that weighed on her—too many demands, the urgent bumping out the important, a frenzied sprint from place to place, poor nutrition from grabbing unhealthy foods on the run, no margin to properly rest or enjoy life.

She needed a downpour of God's Word and the Holy Spirit's presence in her parched spirit. Not an occasional sprinkle but a soul soaking to replenish her frazzled body and weary mind. She knew this soaking came from consistent Bible study, the necessary pruning of confessed sin, and prayer time. These produce a well-watered garden, fruitful and lush, mirroring God's beauty, creating a life to which others are drawn to come and linger in His refreshing presence.

Eternal Father, strengthen my frame, guide my paths, and satisfy my needs as only You can. Make my life a well-watered garden, fruitful for You and Your purposes. Amen.

What Is Your Request?

And pray in the Spirit on all occasions with all kinds of prayers and requests. With this in mind, be alert and always keep on praying.
EPHESIANS 6:18 NIV

What burdens your heart today? Is there a trial that engulfs you or someone you love? Present your request to your heavenly Father with the assurance that He will act on your behalf—either by changing your circumstances or by changing you. He is always concerned for you.

But be patient. What we may view as a non-answer may simply be God saying, "Wait" or "I have something better for you." He *will* answer. Keep in mind that His ways are not our ways, nor are His thoughts our thoughts.

God knows what He's doing, even when He allows trials in our lives. We might think that saving a loved one from difficulty is a great idea—but God, in His wisdom, may decide that would be keeping them (or us) from an opportunity for spiritual growth. Since we don't know all of God's plans, we must simply lay our requests before Him and trust Him to do what is right. He will never fail us!

Father God, here are my needs. I lay them at Your feet, walking away unburdened and assured that You have it all under control. Thank You!

Peace Despite Our Trials

Therefore having been justified by faith, we have peace with God through our Lord Jesus Christ, through whom also we have obtained our introduction by faith into this grace in which we stand; and we exult in hope of the glory of God. . . . For while we were still helpless, at the right time Christ died for the ungodly.
Romans 5:1–2, 6

People have scoured every nook and cranny of the globe in search of peace. From yoga and transcendental meditation to new age tranquility tapes and self-empowerment courses, people will try just about anything. But do these methods work?

Of course not! Instead, each new road eventually leads to the dead ends of dissatisfaction and emptiness. "I have seen all the works which have been done under the sun, and behold, all is vanity and striving after the wind" (Ecclesiastes 1:14). The promises of peace that this world has to offer are nothing more than vapors of an expensive fragrance.

Enduring tranquility cannot be found outside a relationship with Christ. So why can't we just believe it's that simple?

Maybe we're simply afraid to end the search. Before I became a Christian I can recall thinking of God as my "ace in the hole." If all else failed, I'd try religion. And when all the other inlets I traveled led to dry lake beds, I did reach out for religion. However, this, too, was but an attempt on my part to "be good enough for God." Human effort doesn't bring peace.

Lord, I know the only true and lasting peace comes from Jesus Christ.

A Better Offer

"So in everything, do to others what you would have them do to you."
MATTHEW 7:12 NIV

"I need to cancel plans on Friday because I have the opportunity to go out of town with friends," Anne said. Marsha felt rejected, unloved, and inconsequential again as Anne canceled their weekly prayer and Bible study time because a better offer came along.

At least, Marsha thought, *she didn't cancel on me this time because she needed to get her nails done*.

How do you treat friends, colleagues, and acquaintances? Do you remain committed to your responsibilities? What are your priorities? Do you take on more than you can handle? Do you not give 100 percent to a task or relationship?

Jesus took responsibilities, commitments, and obligations seriously. In fact, Jesus said, "Simply let your 'Yes' be 'Yes,' and your 'No,' 'No'; anything beyond this comes from the evil one" (Matthew 5:37 NIV). Satan desires for us to be stressed out, overcommitted, and not able to do anything well. Satan delights when we treat others in an unkind, offensive manner. However, God, upon request, will help us prioritize our commitments so that our "yes" is "yes" and our "no" is "no." Then in everything we do, we are liberated to do to others as we would have them do to us.

Lord, please prioritize my commitments to enable me in everything to do to others as I would desire for them to do to me. Amen.

Anxieties

Casting the whole of your care [all your anxieties, all your worries, all your concerns, once and for all] on Him, for He cares for you affectionately and cares about you watchfully.
1 PETER 5:7 AMP

Because He cares for you. Not because you have to. Not because it's the "right" thing to do. Not because it's what you're supposed to do. No. Read it again. . . Because He cares for you. That's right, He cares for you!

Our Father isn't standing there with His hand on His hip, saying, "All right, spit it out, I don't have all day," or worse. . .holding His hands to His ears, saying, "Enough! You have way too many problems."

The Amplified Bible puts it this way: "Casting the whole of your care [all your anxieties, all your worries, all your concerns, once and for all] on Him, for He cares for you affectionately and cares about you watchfully" (1 Peter 5:7).

Because He cares for you. How humbling and emotionally overwhelming it is to realize that our Lord and God, Jesus Christ, actually wants us to unburden our hearts to Him. Not just because He knows that's what's best for us but simply because He cares. To know He isn't just informing us of one more requirement we have to meet. No. He asks each one of us to cast all our cares and anxieties on Him because He cares for us.

Father, I am overjoyed at Your concern for me. Thank You! Please teach me to cast my cares into Your arms. . .and leave them there.

Put On a Happy Face

He restoreth my soul: he leadeth me in the paths of righteousness for his name's sake.
PSALM 23:3 KJV

Sometimes we become discouraged with the direction of our lives. Circumstances are not of our choosing, not the plan we laid out. God's timetable isn't meshing with ours. But to keep others around us pacified, we paste on a smile and trudge through the murky waters.

Be encouraged. The Lord has promised He hears our pleas and knows our situations. He will never leave us. Our God is not a God of negativity, but of possibility. He will guide us through our difficulties and beyond them. In *Streams in the Desert*, Mrs. Charles E. Cowman states, "Every misfortune, every failure, every loss may be transformed. God has the power to transform all misfortunes into 'God-sends.' "

Today we should turn our thoughts and prayers toward Him. Focus on a hymn or a praise song and play it in your mind. Praise chases away the doldrums and tips our lips up in a smile. With a renewed spirit of optimism and hope we can thank the Giver of all things good. Thankfulness to the Father can turn our plastic smiles into real ones, and as the psalm states, our souls will be restored.

Father, I'm down in the dumps today. You are my unending source of strength. Gather me in Your arms for always. Amen.

Hold On!

Let us not become weary in doing good, for at the proper time we will reap a harvest if we do not give up.
GALATIANS 6:9 NIV

Have you ever felt that God abandoned you? Have the difficulties in your life pressed you to physical and mental exhaustion? Do you feel your labor is in vain and no one appreciates the sacrifices you have made?

When Elijah fled for his life in fear of Jezebel's wrath, depression and discouragement tormented him. Exhausted, he prayed for God to take his life, and then he fell asleep. When he awoke, God sent an angel with provisions to strengthen his weakened body. Only then was he able to hear God's revelation that provided the direction and assistance he needed.

God hears our pleas even when He seems silent. The problem is that we cannot hear Him because of physical and mental exhaustion. Rest is key to our restoration.

Just when the prophet thought he could go on no longer, God provided the strength, peace, and encouragement to continue. He does the same for us today. When we come to the end of our rope, God ties a knot. And like Elijah, God will do great things in and through us, if we will just hold on.

Dear Lord, help me when I can no longer help myself. Banish my discouragement and give me the rest and restoration I need so that I might hear Your voice. Amen.

Safety Net

There is therefore now no condemnation for those who are in Christ Jesus. For the law of the Spirit of life in Christ Jesus has set you free from the law of sin and death. For what the Law could not do, weak as it was through the flesh, God did: sending His own Son in the likeness of sinful flesh and as an offering for sin, He condemned sin in the flesh, in order that the requirement of the Law might be fulfilled in us, who do not walk according to the flesh, but according to the Spirit.

Romans 8:1–4

Now that our children are older, my husband and I look back on some of their episodes of outright disobedience with a different perspective. We can see that even as they responded to our discipline with absolute hostility, these incidents became turning points in their lives.

With reckless abandon their flesh cried out with insolence, "Don't tell me what to do!" Fifteen or twenty years earlier we wanted to say the same things to our parents.

The "Law" Paul speaks of here is God's law, given to Moses and the Israelites in the entirety of what has been recorded in the Bible. It's the law that requires that we "love our enemies and do good to those who hate us." And it's also the law that says, "'Come to me, all who are heavy laden and I will give you rest.'" To be out of control is such a weighty burden, one that we were never meant to carry.

God's rules provide for us a huge safety net. When we bounce against its sides, we become aware of the need to change our direction.

I rejoice that I am a child of God and heir to the kingdom! Hallelujah!

Sunday
August 18

Be Still, My Soul

Be still in the presence of the Lord, and wait patiently for him to act.
Psalm 37:7 NLT

When life doesn't go the way we planned, it's easy to become upset, discontented, even distrustful. As women, we're pulled in so many directions. Inevitably, parents get older and need care. Husbands require much of our time and energy. Children may have birth defects or illnesses or behavioral problems.

And anxious thoughts beset us. Our dreams and plans are put on hold. We may wish we could be somewhere else. It can all add up to a restless soul, as we chafe at the unfairness of life.

But God asks us to quiet our spirits before Him, to submit to His will for us. As people of God, we wait expectantly for Him to work all things for our good and His glory (Romans 8:28). Let's follow the advice of the hymn writer Katharina von Schlegel, who wrote the great "Be Still, My Soul":

Be still, my soul: the Lord is on thy side;
Bear patiently the cross of grief or pain;
Leave to thy God to order and provide;
In every change He faithful will remain.

Father, may I quiet my soul before You today.
Help me to see Your loving hand in every difficulty
I face, knowing that You are accomplishing
Your purposes in me.

One Step at a Time

With your help I can advance against a troop;
with my God I can scale a wall.
Psalm 18:29 NIV

Sandi returned home from the doctor feeling discouraged and defeated. She knew she had put on a few pounds since her last visit, but was shocked when she saw the number on the scale. Her shock turned to humiliation when the doctor frankly addressed it. "Sandi, your health is on the line. If you don't lose at least seventy-five pounds, the next time I see you you'll be in a hospital bed. Your heart simply cannot take th e strain of the excess weight you're carrying."

Seventy-five pounds! It seemed like an insurmountable goal. But a year later, when Sandi returned to the doctor for her annual check-up, she beamed when he looked at her chart. "Congratulations on your weight loss," he said. "How did you do it?"

Sandi smiled, "One pound at a time."

We often become discouraged when we face a mountain-sized task. Whether it's weight loss or a graduate degree or our income taxes, some things just seem impossible. And they often *can't* be done—not all at once. Tasks like these are best faced one step at a time. One pound at a time. Chipping away instead of moving the whole mountain at once. With patience, perseverance, and God's help, your goals may be more attainable than you think.

Dear Father, the task before me seems impossible.
However, I know I can do it with Your help. I pray that
I will trust You every step of the way. Amen.

Peace through Prayer

Be anxious for nothing, but in everything by prayer and supplication, with thanksgiving, let your requests be made known to God; and the peace of God, which surpasses all understanding, will guard your hearts and minds through Christ Jesus.
Philippians 4:6–7 NKJV

Some days it is easy to be thankful. We nearly bubble over with thanksgiving. These are mountaintop days—a graduation day, a wedding, or a reunion with old friends. The day comes to a close, and we whisper a prayer. It flows easily off the tongue. "Thank You, God," we say, "for a perfect day."

There are days when thankfulness is not as natural, not as easy. These are valley days—in the hospital room, at the graveside, or when we are distraught about a relationship or work issue. It is in these times that the Father wants us to give Him our burdens through prayer. It seems impossible to be thankful for the pain, the confusion, or the longings in our lives. We can be thankful, though, that we have a loving heavenly Father who stands ready to help.

The peace of God cannot be explained. It cannot be bought. The world cannot give it to us. But when we release our cares to the Lord in prayer, His peace washes over us and fills our hearts and minds. What a comfort is the peace of God when we find ourselves in the valley.

Sovereign God, You are the same yesterday, today, and tomorrow. You are with me through the good and the bad. Draw near to me and replace my worry with Your peace. Amen.

Silence

He was oppressed, and he was afflicted, yet he opened not his mouth; like a lamb that is led to the slaughter, and like a sheep that before its shearers is silent, so he opened not his mouth.
Isaiah 53:7 esv

Jesus fulfilled Isaiah's prophecy by remaining silent before His accusers prior to His crucifixion. This fact is surprising to read because it goes against everything in us as humans—we can't imagine being falsely accused and not seeking to vindicate ourselves.

Jesus' silence can teach us important lessons. Underneath His silence was an implicit trust in His Father and His purposes. Christ knew who He was and what He had come to do.

Perhaps He was praying silently as He stood before Pilate. It is often in the stillness of our lives that we hear God best. When we take time to think, meditate on scripture, pray, and reflect, we find that we can indeed hear the still, small voice. Many of us avoid quiet and solitude with constant noise and busyness. But important things happen in the silence. The Father can speak; we can listen. We can speak, knowing He is listening. Trust is built in silence, and confidence strengthens in silence.

Lord Jesus, help me to learn from Your silence. Help me to trust You more so that I don't feel the need to explain myself. Give me the desire and the courage to be alone with You and learn to hear Your voice.

Paul's Prayer for the Jews

Brethren, my heart's desire and my prayer
to God for them is for their salvation.
ROMANS 10:1

Is the deepest concern of your heart that those whom you love will share heaven with Christ? The deepest longing of Paul's soul was that the Jews might know their Messiah.

Paul longed for the Israelites, "to whom belongs the adoption as sons and the glory and the covenants and the giving of the Law and the temple service and the promises," to understand that Christ had come to save them (Romans 9:4–5).

The Jews couldn't truly be God's children until they partook of the light of truth. "For the Scripture says, 'Whoever believes in Him will not be disappointed.' For there is no distinction between Jew and Greek; for the same Lord is Lord of all, abounding in riches for all who call upon Him; for 'Whoever will call upon the name of the Lord will be saved' " (Romans 10:11–13).

Paul presents the simple process by which they can become cleansed of their sins. "But what does it say? 'The word is near you, in your mouth and in your heart'—that is, the word of faith which we are preaching, that if you confess with your mouth Jesus as Lord, and believe in your heart that God raised Him from the dead, you shall be saved; for with the heart man believes, resulting in righteousness, and with the mouth he confesses, resulting in salvation" (Romans 10:8–10).

Lord, clarify Your Word,
that women may yield in faith.

A Fresh Perspective

"Listen now to me and I will give you some advice, and may God be with you."
Exodus 18:19 NIV

Moses was doing too much.

Exodus 18:2–3 tells us that the great leader of Israel sent away his wife, Zipporah, and their sons. Though the Bible doesn't elaborate, it appears that Moses was working too hard—possibly even neglecting his family. Maybe he sent them away because he couldn't work as hard as he was working and care for the family at the same time. Whatever the reason, his father-in-law, Jethro, decided to visit.

The next morning as usual, Moses got up to go to work. After observing Moses' exhausting routine, Jethro sat down with his son-in-law. "Why are you doing all the work yourself?" he asked. "You need to start delegating."

Moses was working so hard that he had lost his objectivity. Jethro provided him with a different—and helpful—perspective.

It's easy to get caught up in the "tyranny of the urgent" and lose perspective. When we take a step back and look at our lives more objectively, we often see alternative ways of doing things. Such insights can come from a trusted friend or relative.

What is there about your present situation that might require perspective from someone else? Is there something you could be doing differently? Is there a task you could be delegating or an option you haven't considered? Learn from Moses—take the advice of someone who could offer you a much-needed perspective.

Heavenly Father, I thank You for the perspective that others can bring. Teach me to listen to and heed wise advice.

Lady Wisdom Gives Directions

Does not wisdom cry out, and understanding lift up her voice?
She takes her stand on the top of the high hill,
beside the way, where the paths meet.
Proverbs 8:1–2 NKJV

Wisdom. The very term sounds outdated, a concept hiding in musty, dusty caverns of the past. Has it anything to do with real life?

Many answer, "No, especially in the twenty-first century!"

But biblical wisdom, crafted by God before the earth existed, remains as fresh and powerful as its Creator. In the Book of Proverbs, God personifies wisdom as a godly woman who does not hesitate to let her voice be heard. She stands atop a high hill "where the paths meet," at busy intersections, trying to help travelers find their way. But they rush past Wisdom, most talking into cell phones glued to their ears. Business meetings must start on time. Carpools must follow schedules. Bills must be paid. The travelers hardly notice Wisdom as they scurry past her. Focused on themselves, they make their deadlines and achieve their goals. Most do not realize they are completely lost.

Wisdom longs to make a difference in their stressful existence that leads to destruction. She never stops sharing her vital message: whoever heeds God's instruction gains more than silver, gold, or rubies. His truth, His directions lead listeners to life.

Father, help us shake off the hypnotizing effects of our culture's values and listen to Your wisdom. Give us courage to share with others who desperately need Your truth. Amen.

Esther Is Chosen

Then the king's attendants, who served him said, "Let beautiful young virgins be sought for the king. And let the king appoint overseers in all the provinces of his kingdom that they may gather every beautiful young virgin to Susa the capital, to the harem, into the custody of Hegai, the king's eunuch, who was in charge of the women; and let their cosmetics be given them. Then let the young lady who pleases the king be queen in place of Vashti."

Esther 2:2–4

The search was on for "the fairest maiden of them all."

The Book of Esther is a beautiful story of a woman's absolute faith and trust in her God. God placed Esther in a position of authority—in order to save the people of Israel. Mordecai, a Jew in Susa, had returned from the Babylonian exile and was raising his orphaned niece, Esther. And she was "beautiful of form and face. . . . Esther was taken to the king's palace" (Esther 2:5–8).

Wisely, "Esther did not make known her people or her kindred" (Esther 2:10). Esther lived in the ultimate spa resort where, for over twelve months, she received beauty treatments and perfume baths.

Finally, "Esther was taken to King Ahasuerus. . . . And the king loved Esther more than all the women, and she found favor and kindness with him, so that he set the royal crown on her head and made her queen instead of Vashti" (Esther 2:16–17).

In the beginning, Esther was unaware of how God would use her life. Lord, let me be as available and obedient to You.

Mirror Image

*Behold, thou art fair, my love; behold, thou art fair;
thou hast doves' eyes.*
SONG OF SOLOMON 1:15 KJV

Getting up in the morning and looking in the mirror can be tough. The glass reflects back our exact image with all the blemishes in plain sight. In our eyes, the flaws stand out. Instead of seeing any beauty, we focus on the imperfections. The longer we consider them, the more pronounced they become. Before long, we see only ugliness in ourselves.

No matter how hard we try, when the focus is on self, we see shortcomings. Beauty treatments, plastic surgery, makeup, beautiful clothing—nothing helps. There is no way to cover the flaws we see. Our outlook even affects how others view us.

Our only hope is to see ourselves through a different mirror. We must remember that as we grow as Christians we take on the characteristics of Christ. The more we become like Him, the more beautiful we are in our own eyes and to those around us.

When God looks at us as Christians, He sees the reflection of Christ. He sees us as very beautiful. God loves to behold us when we are covered in Christ. The mirror image He sees has none of the blemishes or imperfections, only the beauty.

*Oh God, thank You for beholding me as
being fair and valuable. Help me to see
myself through Your eyes. Amen.*

Good Works Are All Around

Well reported of for good works; if [a widow] have brought up children, if she have lodged strangers, if she have washed the saints' feet, if she have relieved the afflicted, if she have diligently followed every good work.
1 TIMOTHY 5:10 KJV

Often when we read the Bible, we miss its practicality. In Ephesians 2:10, for example, Paul tells us that we are created for "good works, which God hath before ordained that we should walk in them" (KJV).

How many times do we read this and wonder, *What good works am I supposed to do for God?* We may spend hours in prayer, laboring to find God's will and discover the works we are to do.

But the Bible shows us not many pages later—and from the same pen as Ephesians—the good works of a woman and services that believers of either sex can provide. In 1 Timothy 5, we see that our good works include being faithful spouses, bringing up children, showing hospitality to strangers and fellow believers, and helping those in distress.

Good work is not a mystery that we have to meditate to find.

We just need to see the needs around us and meet them as God gives us the strength and resources to do so.

That's practical—and pure—Christianity.

Father, how often I have wondered about Your will for my life, thinking it was something grand and glorious. But Your Word says it's all around me. Help me to see and follow the good works that are within my reach.

The Martha Syndrome

But the Lord said to her, "My dear Martha, you are worried and upset over all these details! There is only one thing worth being concerned about. Mary has discovered it, and it will not be taken away from her."
LUKE 10:41–42 NLT

Mary and Martha perfectly depict the inner battle that most women fight daily. Martha busied herself with tasks in her desire to serve people. Mary, on the other hand, ignored the tasks, choosing fellowship with her Master over service to others. Martha surely felt as though she had no choice, because the people needed to be fed and someone had to do it. And, as scripture reports, she resented the lack of help that she got from Mary.

What Martha was doing was not wrong; she just had her priorities out of order. Jesus teaches her that relationship with her Lord is the highest priority. Mary was not about to give up precious moments with her Lord while she labored in a kitchen.

It's very easy to create a life jam-packed with responsibilities and commitments with no time to enjoy any of it or seek fellowship with the Father. If you find yourself worried and upset about many things, like Martha, take some time out to sort through the priorities and decide what is really important.

Jesus, I want to be like Mary, patiently and expectantly sitting at Your feet in relationship with You. Help me to sort out my duties and commitments in such a way that proves that I have discovered the one thing worthy of my concern. Amen.

Build for Today

"Build homes, and plan to stay. Plant gardens, and eat the food they produce."
JEREMIAH 29:5 NLT

Skeptics sometimes accuse Christians of being so heavenly minded that they are no earthly good. Today few of us would sell all our earthly possessions and camp out on a hilltop, waiting for the Lord's return. However, we still often live in "Tomorrowland."

Tomorrow, we think, *we will serve God more fully, after our children are grown and we have more time. Tomorrow we will give more, after we have paid off the car and saved enough for a down payment on a house. Tomorrow we will study the Bible more, after we no longer work full-time.*

Jeremiah's audience, Jews deported from their homeland to Babylon, knew all about Tomorrowland. They said, "Soon God will return us to our homes. As soon as that happens, we will serve God." They lived with their suitcases packed, ready to return.

God sent a stern message through His prophet Jeremiah. "You're going to be there a long time. Put down roots where I have sent you."

God sends the same message to us. He wants us to live for today. We can't allow dreams for tomorrow to paralyze our lives today.

God's presence enables us to live in the present.

Dear heavenly Father, You have given us the gift of today. You want us to plant gardens and make homes. Show us joy and fulfillment in the present. Amen.

Hearing God's Spirit Speak

For to us God revealed them through the Spirit; for the Spirit searches all things, even the depths of God. . . . Now we have received, not the spirit of the world, but the Spirit who is from God, that we might know the things freely given to us by God.
1 Corinthians 2:10, 12

Have you ever tried to learn a foreign language? In high school I decided to take Spanish, and although I met the class requirements, I certainly didn't display unusual proficiency. Years later, God brought many Spanish-speaking people into my life. After taking a "Speed Spanish" course at the local junior college, my skills were rejuvenated enough so I could speak on a rudimentary level. Later I took a more in-depth class, and as long as I practiced, the ability to speak and understand Spanish came fairly easily.

This is exactly how to understand the things of God. You can't rely totally on what you received in your early education.

If you came to Christ as an adult then it's probably necessary to start from the beginning, using the Bible, not your memory. Find out what you believe and know why. If you never arrive at this understanding, how on earth can you share your faith with others?

Here's an excuse heard often: "We can't try to interpret the Bible ourselves because we'll get confused." But to refuse the Holy Spirit the opportunity to instruct you, as He promised He would, is to refuse true understanding.

Lord, fill my mind and heart with true understanding.

Delightful Study

Great are the works of the LORD;
they are pondered by all who delight in them.
PSALM 111:2 NIV

An accomplished pianist and a skilled tennis player both know that the more they practice, the more enjoyment they get out of their skill. Someone who has studied furniture design can value a fine antique that another person sees as a plain brown chest. A chef can taste and enjoy flavors the average palate cannot identify.

Have you ever thanked God for the pleasure of an orderly column of numbers in a balanced ledger? Ever noticed the shelves at the pharmacy and thanked God for all the research and discovery that led to such life-saving medications? Have you picked produce from your own garden and praised God for the delight of harvesting?

Your delight in God's creation is a gift from Him and an offering of praise back to Him for what He has done. To be thankful for the interest God gives you in creation brings glory to Him and leads to knowing and appreciating Him more.

Great God of all creation, Giver of all good things, thank You for the endless beauty and wisdom in the world around me that speaks of You.

Stop and Consider

*"Listen to this, Job; stop and consider God's wonders.
Do you know how God controls the cloud and makes his
lightning flash? Do you know how the clouds hang poised,
those wonders of him who is perfect in knowledge?"*
Job 37:14–16 niv

On a late summer morning, as the sun streamed through the window, Charlotte sat at her desk and stopped for a moment. She heard a radio blasting a popular song through the hallway, muffled sounds of her daughter talking on her cell phone in her bedroom, the washing machine rumbling in the laundry room.

Today the sounds of an ordinary morning caught at her heart. Charlotte knew it wouldn't last. Change was coming. Her daughter would be leaving for college soon, and those noises would move with her. It wasn't that Charlotte couldn't accept change. It was just that for one moment she stopped, paused, and really soaked up the sweet ordinariness of family life. *Too rare, too rare.*

"Stop and consider My wonders," God told Job. Then He pointed to ordinary observations of the natural world surrounding Job—the clouds that hung poised in the sky, the flashes of lightning. "Not so very ordinary" was God's lesson. Maybe He was trying to remind us that there is no such thing as ordinary. Let's open our eyes and see the wonders around us.

*O Father, teach me to stop and consider the
ordinary moments of my life as reminders of
You. Help me not to overlook Your daily care and
provisions that surround my day. Amen.*

Jesus' Wristwatch

Look carefully then how you walk, not as unwise but as wise, making the best use of the time, because the days are evil. Therefore do not be foolish, but understand what the will of the Lord is.
EPHESIANS 5:15–17 ESV

Time is money, they say. Society preaches the value of making good use of our time—and the expense of wasting it.

In the Bible, Ephesians 5 speaks of using every opportunity wisely. But even though scripture teaches the value of time, Jesus never wore a watch. He didn't view His opportunities within the bounds of earthly time.

Have you ever ended a day with guilt and regret over the growing black hole of work yet to be completed? Or do you feel peace at the end of your day, having walked in the presence of the Lord?

Satan wants to consume you with endless lists of meaningless tasks. Fight back! Concern yourself less with the items you can cross off your to-do list, and more with those things the Lord would have you spend your time and energy on. You can strive to be a great multitasker or workhorse—but it's more important and fulfilling to be an efficient laborer for the Lord.

Father, help me to see where You are working and join You there. Let me place my list of tasks aside as I seek Your will for me today. Then give me the ability to show myself grace over the things I do not get done.

Our Bodies, God's Temple

Do you not know that you are a temple of God, and that the Spirit of God dwells in you? If any man destroys the temple of God, God will destroy him, for the temple of God is holy, and that is what you are.
1 CORINTHIANS 3:16–17

While people were living out the Old Testament times, God dwelt in His tabernacle. At first this was a traveling altar, known as the ark of the covenant, which the people carried with them from the time of Moses, through all the lands in which they wandered. When God's Son, Jesus Christ, came to earth He fulfilled God's requirements for sinful man through His death on the cross. Now God could cleanse man that He might indwell him, for God's temple is to be a holy place.

As we go about the business of life perhaps it's hard to remember that God indwells us. The apostle Paul constantly wrestled with desiring to do the right thing but having his flesh at war with his spirit. "For I know that nothing good dwells in me, that is, in my flesh; for the wishing is present in me, but the doing of the good is not. For the good that I wish, I do not do; but I practice the very evil that I do not wish" (Romans 7:18–19).

"However, you are not in the flesh but in the Spirit, if indeed the Spirit of God dwells in you. . . And if Christ is in you, though the body is dead because of sin, yet the spirit is alive because of righteousness" (Romans 8:9–10).

Lord, let me live as though I believe You are permeating my very being. Amen.

Rejoicing with Friends

"Then he calls his friends and neighbors together and says, 'Rejoice with me; I have found my lost sheep.' "
LUKE 15:6 NIV

Gathering with friends and family can be so much fun, especially when you have something to celebrate. Birthday parties, weddings, and anniversaries are a blast when you're celebrating with people you love. There's just something about being together that adds to the excitement.

God loves a good party, especially one that celebrates family togetherness. Just like the good shepherd in today's verse, He throws a pretty awesome party in heaven whenever a lost child returns to the fold. Celebrating comes naturally to Him, and—since you're created in His image—to you, too!

Think of all the reasons you have to celebrate. Are you in good health? Have you overcome a tough obstacle? Are you handling your finances without much grief? Doing well at your job? Bonding with friends or family? If so, then throw yourself a party and invite a friend. Better yet, call your friends and neighbors together, as the scripture indicates. Share your praises with people who will truly appreciate all that the Lord is doing in your life. Let the party begin!

Lord, thank You that I'm created in the image of a God who knows how to celebrate. I have so many reasons to rejoice today. Thank You for Your many blessings. And today I especially want to thank You for giving me friends to share my joys and sorrows.

Did God Say. . . ?

For we walk by faith, not by sight.
2 Corinthians 5:7

The more complex life becomes, the easier it is to lose our perspective.

Maybe we begin to feel that we weren't supposed to be in our current role after all. There must be someone else who can do a better job, who can handle all the stuff that comes up, who can do it more graciously than we can. Did God really say *we* should do this?

This is the time faith really comes into play. God *has* given us the task—and we must believe that not only has He asked us to do this job, He's also given us an abundance of mental, emotional, and physical supply. And not just once, but over and over every morning.

Rarely can we see our way clear, but we can believe that God has the situation under His perfect control. We can believe that He will work it for His glory and for the good of ourselves and those around us.

As we learn to become more and more dependent on God, we trust Him more and more. Our faith, though it may have begun as the size of a mustard seed, will grow into a mighty tree.

Lord, I thank You for choosing me to work with You. Give me the faith I need to see Your hand in everyday circumstances and to ask You for the help I need.

Persistently Presented Petitions

"O woman, great is your faith! Let it be to you as you desire."
MATTHEW 15:28 NKJV

When our loved ones are troubled—emotionally, spiritually, financially, physically, mentally—our hearts are heavy and we feel helpless. But with Christ's ear within reach of our voice, we are anything but powerless. We have an interceder, someone to whom we can continually go and present our petitions.

In Matthew 15:21–28, a Canaanite woman asked Jesus for mercy and to heal her demon-possessed daughter. At first Christ seemed not to hear her pleas. The disciples, irritated with her persistence, told Jesus to send her away.

Yet this woman had dogged determination. She *knew* that the Son of God could heal her daughter. She continued to plead, driven by love for her child and faith in Christ's power.

Her insistence was met by a reproach from Christ, who told her He did not come to help the Gentiles but the Jews. This had to have crushed her expectations. Yet even then she persisted. She did not despair but continued running after Him, worshipping Him, pleading with Him, begging for mercy.

Jesus reproached her again. But still she was undeterred. Finally, Jesus said the words we all long to hear: "Woman, great is your faith! Let it be to you as you desire."

May we live our lives as persistent in our petitions as the Canaanite woman. And may God see our faith and honor our requests as we boldly bring the needs of others before His throne!

God, I come to You, bringing the concerns of others. Lord, have mercy! Help these people in their hour of need. Amen.

God, Judge of Immorality Past and Present

For I do not want you to be unaware, brethren, that our fathers were all under the cloud, and all passed through the sea; and all were baptized into Moses in the cloud and in the sea; and all ate the same spiritual food; and all drank the same spiritual drink, for they were drinking from a spiritual rock which followed them; and the rock was Christ. Nevertheless, with most of them God was not well-pleased; for they were laid low in the wilderness. Now these things happened as examples for us, that we should not crave evil things, as they also craved. . . . Nor let us act immorally, as some of them did, and twenty-three thousand fell in one day.

1 Corinthians 10:1–6, 8

By reading the entire Bible we have the privilege of learning from God's dealings with men and women throughout recorded history so we will not fall into the same traps. Twenty-three thousand people fell by the sword in one day because they joined themselves with pagan gods in sexual rituals, refusing to obey the true God.

How can we stop ourselves from falling into sin? By remembering: "No temptation has overtaken you but such as is common to man; and God is faithful, who will not allow you to be tempted beyond what you are able, but with the temptation will provide the way of escape also, that you may be able to endure it" (1 Corinthians 10:13).

Father, help me avoid temptation by taking one step closer to You.

Desperate Faith

*And He said to her, "Daughter, your faith has made you well.
Go in peace, and be healed of your affliction."*
MARK 5:34 NKJV

When Jesus healed the woman with the hemorrhage, He commended her faith. She had exhausted all her resources on doctors to no avail. Without addressing Jesus at all, she simply got near Him in a crowd and touched His clothes. Instantly His power healed her, and He knew that she had reached out to Him in a way no one else in the pressing throng had. What was unusual about this woman's touch? Why would Jesus commend her faith?

Maybe in her touch He felt her complete emptiness and need. She had nowhere else to turn. He was the source of healing power. Her faith was an act of utter dependence; it was Jesus or nothing.

Proverbs 3:5–6 tell us to trust in the Lord with all our hearts and not lean on our understanding. This is hard to do, since we prefer to trust in the Lord along with our own understanding of how things should work out. Though we are given minds to read, think, and reason, ultimately our faith comes from abandoning hope in ourselves and risking all on Jesus.

*Lord, I am often blind to my own weakness
and my need of You. Help me to trust You
the way this sick woman did.*

Why Me?

I am Alpha and Omega, the beginning and the ending, saith the Lord, which is, and which was, and which is to come, the Almighty.
Revelation 1:8 kjv

When we find ourselves in difficult situations, what do we do?

Many people look at those circumstances selfishly and cry: "Oh God, why me? Why do these things happen to *me*?"

But we mortals have a too-narrow view of our existence. In our minds, this world at this time is all there is. Sure, God is eternal—but maybe that just means He was around before us and had some supervision that we would come into being someday.

If that's our concept of God, we need to read His Word more closely.

Jesus said He is the "Alpha and Omega." He's the beginning and the end. Jesus, like the Father, *is.* He is the ever-present One who is apart from time.

When God spoke our world into existence, He called into being a certain reality, knowing then everything that ever was to happen—and everyone who ever was to be.

That you exist now is cause for rejoicing! God made *you* to fellowship with Him! If that fellowship demands trials for a season, rejoice that God thinks you worthy to share in the sufferings of Christ—and, eventually, in His glory.

Why do these things happen to you?

Because God in His infinite wisdom, love, and grace determined them to be. Praise His holy name!

Father, I thank You for giving me this difficult time in my life. Shine through all my trials today. I want You to get the glory.

Faith, the Emotional Balancer

No man is justified by the law in the sight of God, it is evident: for, The just shall live by faith.
Galatians 3:11 KJV

Our moods often dictate our actions. For instance, we schedule lunch with a friend for Saturday afternoon, but on Saturday morning we regret having made plans. Or we strategize what to accomplish on our day off but suffer from mental anemia and physical fatigue when the day arrives. So we fail to do what we had intended to do in a more enthusiastic moment.

Emotions mislead us. One day shines with promise as we bounce out of bed in song, while the next day dims in despair and we'd prefer to hide under the bedcovers. One moment we forgive, the next we harbor resentment.

The emotional roller coaster thrusts us into mood changes and affects what we do, what we say, and the attitudes that define us.

It has been said that faith is the bird that feels the light and sings to greet the dawn while it is still dark. The Bible instructs us to live by faith—not by feelings. Faith assures us that daylight will dawn in our darkest moments, affirming God's presence so that even when we fail to pray and positive feelings fade, our moods surrender to song.

Heavenly Father, I desire for my faith, not my emotions, to dictate my life. I pray for balance in my hide-under-the-cover days, so that I might surrender to You in song. Amen.

The Holy Spirit, Our Great Gift

Therefore I make known to you, that no one speaking by the Spirit of God says, "Jesus is accursed"; and no one can say, "Jesus is Lord," except by the Holy Spirit.
1 CORINTHIANS 12:3

For twenty-nine years a desperate woman waded through the motions of life, wondering whether the Creator really cared for her at all. Her loneliness and despair seemed to confirm to her that He didn't. And then came the day when the Gospel message finally penetrated her soul with its extraordinary light and she began to call Him Lord.

I was that woman. When I heard today's Scripture the truth flew straight and sure as an arrow to the deepest part of my being.

It's no accident that despair caused me to succumb to messages of doubt concerning God's nature and character. The evil one is, after all, the author of confusion and lies. However, as I tested the spirits the truth became clear. "By this you know the Spirit of God: every spirit that confesses that Jesus Christ has come in the flesh is from God; and every spirit that does not confess Jesus is not from God; and this is the spirit of the antichrist, of which you have heard that it is coming, and now it is already in the world" (1 John 4:2–3).

Lord, I know if I'm listening to a message that makes me depressed and defeated, that's from Satan. I know the one that says I'm worth dying for is from Christ.

A Healthy Fear

To fear the Lord is to hate evil; I hate pride and arrogance, evil behavior and perverse speech.
Proverbs 8:13 niv

When we think about our fears, our minds and bodies almost always tense. Whether it's a fear of heights, spiders, public speaking, failure, or being alone, everyone has fears. In fact, it's considered perfectly natural to avoid what we fear.

Why does the Bible say we should "fear" God? In reality, to fear God is not the same as fearing the creepy-crawly spider inching up the living room wall. Instead, we fear God when we have a deep respect and reverence for Him.

Imagine that the president of the United States was paying your home a visit. The house would be extra clean, the laundry would be washed and put away, and the children would be instructed to be on their best behavior. Why? Because the visitor deserves respect.

Our lives should reflect a similar reverence for our heavenly Father every day—our souls scrubbed extra clean, sin eliminated, and love for our Creator bursting forth in joy. God wants speech and actions to match. Take time today to stand in awe of the One who deserves our greatest respect and love.

Lord, help my daily actions and speech to reflect my respect for You. Amen.

Peace, Be Still

God makes his people strong. God gives his people peace.
PSALM 29:11 MSG

At the center of life's storms, how do we find peace? If we're tossed about, struggling and hopeless, where is the peace? Don't worry—peace can be ours for the asking.

You see, *God* is our peace. He is ready to calm our storms when we call on Him. He will comfort and strengthen us each day.

The Bible tells of Peter and the other disciples, who were rowing their small boat against strong waves on the way to Capernaum. They knew Jesus was planning to join them, but they'd drifted out into the sea and left Him far behind. When they saw Jesus walking on the water, they were terrified—but He spoke and calmed their fears.

Impulsive Peter asked to meet Jesus on the water. He stepped out of the boat and, briefly, walked on the waves like his Lord. As long as Peter's eyes were on Jesus, he stayed atop the water—but the moment he looked away, he sank. Peter learned a valuable lesson.

The lesson works for believers today: Keep your eyes focused on the problems and you'll have mayhem. Focus on Jesus and you'll have peace.

Dear Lord, I thank You for Your protection.
Help me to keep my eyes on You.
Please grant me peace.

What's This Thing in My Eye?

"Why do you look at the speck of sawdust in your brother's eye and pay no attention to the plank in your own eye?"
LUKE 6:41 NIV

Whether we admit it or not, we judge others. Maybe it's how they look ("Just how many tattoos does a person need?") or their political leaning ("How can you call yourself a Christian and vote for a president from *that* party?"). Sometimes we pigeonhole others because of an accent ("What an ignorant hillbilly!") or an achievement of some kind ("Mr. Smarty Pants thinks he's better than everyone else because of his PhD.")

Our Father God urges us not to judge others in this way. After all, He doesn't look at our outward appearance. He doesn't pay attention to our political affiliation or anything else in our lives that is open to interpretation. He looks at the heart and judges by whether we have a personal relationship with Him.

In Luke 6:41, Jesus reminds us through His sawdust/plank analogy that none of us are blameless. It's important to put our own shortcomings into perspective when we face the temptation to judge others. Today, work on removing the plank from your eye and praise God for His gift of grace!

God, please forgive me for the times that I have judged others. Help me to develop a gentle spirit that can share Your love and hope in a nonjudgmental way. Amen.

What Response Does God Require?

With what shall I come to the LORD and bow myself before the God on high? . . . He has told you, O man, what is good; and what does the LORD require of you but to do justice, to love kindness, and to walk humbly with your God?
MICAH 6:6, 8

They drag themselves across the uneven pavement until their knees are bloodied and their exhausted bodies finally fall against the splintered wooden doors to the church. In this way, many in Mexico seek to do their yearly public penance for sin.

Christ has already paid the price that needed to be exacted for our sins. He took the whips, the lashes, the nailing to the cross, the verbal rebukes, and also the physical agony on our behalf. The God of this universe looked upon our futility and became a man, and then He sacrificed His life so that we who did not and could not ever deserve His mercy might obtain it. Jesus Christ did all this because He is both just and kind.

Isaiah prophesied the promise of Christ's cross. "Surely our griefs He Himself bore, and our sorrows He carried. . . . But He was pierced through for our transgressions, He was crushed for our iniquities; the chastening for our well-being fell upon Him, and by His scourging we are healed" (Isaiah 53:4–5).

Though I expend every effort, I can never rid myself of sin. You've already provided the only way in which I can be cleansed.

My Way or God's Way?

Good and upright is the LORD; therefore He instructs sinners in the way. He leads the humble in justice, and He teaches the humble His way. . . . He will instruct him in the way he should choose.
PSALM 25:8–9, 12

In today's culture, it is easy to follow "my way." We are bombarded with advertisements from TV, magazines, billboards, and the Internet that tell us "It is all about me" and "We can have it all." We have access to people, information, and products 24/7. We have the Internet, e-mail, telephone, cell phone, fax, and pager that provide us with availability and resources. In buying anything, there is an overwhelming number of options to choose from. With all these distractions, it is not surprising that we have difficulty surrendering daily to God's way.

Nevertheless, God wants us to live life His way. Our good and upright God tells us that when we come before Him as humble, meek, needy, or afflicted, He will teach us what is right and just. God will teach us His way of living. If it is a decision that needs to be made, a course of action that needs to be taken, or a word that needs to be spoken, God will instruct us in a manner consistent with who He is. Therefore, it is of the utmost importance that we intentionally fall before the throne of God seeking His way, not our own. What way will you choose today?

Good and upright God, please allow me not to be distracted in this world but to focus on You. Teach me Your way, I humbly pray. Amen.

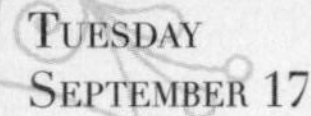

Choose Life

"The thief comes only to steal and kill and destroy; I have come that they may have life, and have it to the full."
John 10:10 NIV

Too often, it seems as if the negatives of life outweigh the positives. The bills are piling up and it's a juggling act to see who gets paid this month. Your loved one needs to have special care during the upcoming treatments. You're exhausted and lacking mental focus. Life begins to cave in around you. . . . It's just too much!

God's Word, though, shows us the lie—and the "liar"—behind those defeating thoughts. We have an enemy who delights in our believing such negative things, an enemy who wants only destruction for our souls. But Jesus came to give us life! We only have to choose it, as an act of the will blended with faith.

God is always a gentleman—He's not going to force His life on us. But when we rely on Him alone, He'll enable us to not only survive but *thrive* in our daily routine.

Each day, let's make a conscious decision to take hold of what Christ offers us—life, to the full.

Loving Lord, help me daily to choose You and the life You want to give me. Give me the eyes of faith to trust that You will enable me to serve lovingly.

Follow the Lord's Footsteps

"Come, follow me," Jesus said, "and I will make you fishers of men."
MATTHEW 4:19 NIV

The beach was empty except for one lone walker near the water's edge. With every step she took, her feet left an impression in the sand. But as the waves lapped upon the shore, her footprints quickly vanished. Following her footsteps would have been impossible unless someone were walking close behind.

Jesus asked His disciples to follow Him, and He asks us to do the same. It sounds simple, but following Jesus can be a challenge. Sometimes we become impatient, not wanting to wait upon the Lord. We run ahead of Him by taking matters into our own hands and making decisions without consulting Him first. Or perhaps we aren't diligent to keep in step with Him. We fall behind, and soon Jesus seems so far away.

Following Jesus requires staying right on His heels. We need to be close enough to hear His whisper. Stay close to His heart by opening the Bible daily. Allow His Word to speak to your heart and give you direction. Throughout the day, offer up prayers for guidance and wisdom. Keep in step with Him, and His close presence will bless you beyond measure.

*Dear Lord, grant me the desire to follow You.
Help me not to run ahead or lag behind. Amen.*

How to Know If You're in Love

If I speak with the tongues of men and of angels, but do not have love, I have become a noisy gong or a clanging cymbal.
1 Corinthians 13:1

"Although we love each other deeply, I know there will be times when we'll fail to be there for one another. That's when we'll go to the Lord to receive in abundance what we lack." These words of wisdom were spoken by a twenty-four-year-old woman who had just become engaged. If only more marriages began this way! For even though we've prayed for godly mates, and then relied on His guidance, there will still be times when our attempts to love are less than perfect.

However, if both man and woman turn back to God's blueprint, harmony can be restored. "Love is patient, love is kind, and is not jealous; love does not brag and is not arrogant, does not act unbecomingly; it does not seek its own, is not provoked, does not take into account a wrong suffered, does not rejoice in unrighteousness, but rejoices with the truth; bears all things, believes all things, hopes all things, endures all things. Love never fails" (1 Corinthians 13:4–8).

Why don't more people tap in to this resource? To truly love someone means that we will always place that person's welfare above our own. This, after all, is how God loves us.

Lord, help me exhibit true love.

Budget Breaker

Then the LORD said to Moses, "Behold, I will rain bread from heaven for you; and the people shall go out and gather a day's portion every day, that I may test them, whether or not they will walk in My instruction."
EXODUS 16:4

The month lasted longer than the paycheck. The grocery bill exceeded the budget. Medical expenses surpassed the rent. It's not an easy road to travel, yet one that many of us walk.

Isn't it interesting that we can trust God for eternal life, yet find it harder to trust Him for help with the mortgage?

In the Old Testament, God told the wandering Israelites He would feed them "manna from heaven," but with one caveat: He would only allow them to gather enough food for one day. No storing food away for the dreaded "what if 's" of tomorrow. They would simply have to trust their God to faithfully supply their needs.

They didn't always pass the "trust test"—and neither do we. But thankfully, God is faithful in spite of us! He will meet our needs when we come to Him in simple trust. Then we can bask in His faithfulness.

Father, Your Word promises to supply all my needs. I trust You in spite of the challenges I see. You are ever faithful. Thank You!

Annual or Perennial?

They are like trees planted along the riverbank, bearing fruit each season. Their leaves never wither, and they prosper in all they do.
Psalm 1:3 NLT

Emily and Lisa had a lot in common, but their gardening preference was not one of them. Every spring, Emily ran to the garden center at her local home improvement store to purchase cartloads of beautiful flowers. Soon her yard would be a riot of color—from daisies to zinnias and everything in between.

While Emily was busy at the home improvement store, Lisa patiently waited. The majority of her planting had been done in the fall and in prior years, so each spring she simply waited. Nothing inspired hope in Lisa like the little green shoots poking their heads out of ground that had been cold for far too long.

Annuals or perennials? Each has its advantages. Annuals are inexpensive, provide instant gratification, and keep boredom from setting in. Perennials require an initial investment, but when properly tended, faithfully provide beauty year after year—long after the annuals have dried up and withered away. What's more, perennials generally become fuller and more lush with each year of growth. Perennials are designed for the long haul—not just short-term enjoyment but long-term beauty.

The application to our lives is twofold. First, be a perennial—long lasting, enduring, slow growing, steady, and faithful. Second, don't be discouraged by your inevitable dormant seasons. Tend to your soul, and it will reward you with years of lush blossoms.

Father, be the gardener of my soul. Amen.

Have You Looked Up?

The heavens proclaim the glory of God. The skies display his craftsmanship. Day after day they continue to speak; night after night they make him known.
PSALM 19:1–2 NLT

One afternoon, Cathy was walking around the park near her home. Her mind whirred with concerns about work and worries about her family.

Suddenly, a man called out, "Hey lady! Have you looked up?"

She stopped and turned to see who was shouting. The voice belonged to an elderly man, seated on a bench.

"Have you looked up?" he asked her again.

She lifted her head and saw a magnificent scarlet oak tree, with leaves of crimson at the peak of their color. It was so beautiful, such a fleeting autumnal sight, that it took her breath away. She thanked the man and resumed her walk, relaxed and grateful after being reminded to "look up!"

God has placed glimpses of creation's majesty—evidence of His love—throughout our world. Sunsets, seashells, flowers, snowflakes, changing seasons, moonlit shadows. Such glories are right in front of us, every single day! But we must develop eyes to see these reminders in our daily life and not let the cares and busyness of our lives keep our heads turned down.

Have you looked up today?

Lord, open my eyes! Unstuff my ears! Teach me to see the wonders of Your creation every day and to point them out to my children.

True Environmentalists

"But now ask the beasts, and let them teach you; and the birds of the heavens, and let them tell you. Or speak to the earth, and let it teach you; and let the fish of the sea declare to you. Who among all these does not know that the hand of the Lord has done this, in whose hand is the life of every living thing, and the breath of all mankind?"
Job 12:7–10

The news media regularly report how the earth's resources and species are diminishing rapidly. Perhaps we have forgotten that God also cares about every living thing.

While I was visiting with friends recently, one asked if animals go to heaven. I reminded her man alone is made in the image and likeness of God, and also the recipient of salvation. This pat answer seemed to leave my friends very disappointed. So, I offer another verse of Scripture as comfort: "And there is no creature hidden from His sight" (Hebrews 4:13).

"For in Him all things were created, both in the heavens and on earth. . .all things have been created through Him and for Him" (Colossians 1:16). It's important to remember that Christ created animals for our enjoyment. Therefore, be grateful to the Lord.

Lord, I know that even if I didn't have Your written Word, the order and perfection of Your creation still prove Your existence!

Water's Cost

"To him who is thirsty I will give to drink without cost from the spring of the water of life."
REVELATION 21:6 NIV

Drinking an ice-cold glass of water on a hot summer day is a wonderful experience. It seems that the thirstier we are, the better water tastes and the more of it we can drink.

Imagine attending a sporting event in the heat of the day. The sun beats down on you, you sweat like crazy, your senses become dull, and an overwhelming desire for a cold bottle of water gradually becomes the only thing you can think about. The players disappear, and the hard bleachers cease to matter; you would pay any amount of money for one sip of water.

Jesus, well aware of basic human needs, likens His message to water, "the spring of the water of life." Just as we cannot live without water, we cannot live without the Word of God. We are shocked to learn that this life-giving message, one we must have at any price, and one to which we cannot assign value, costs us nothing. Jesus loves us so much that He gave up His life that we might partake of these invigorating waters. So drink up, and leave your money at home; the water of life is free.

Dear Lord, thank You for letting me drink for free from the spring of the water of life. Help me to remember Your sacrifice and Your love for me. Amen.

Wednesday
September 25
See You at the Pole

You Are an Answer to Prayer

Praise God, the Father of our Lord Jesus Christ!
The Father is a merciful God, who always gives
us comfort. He comforts us when we are in trouble,
so that we can share that same comfort with others in trouble.
2 Corinthians 1:3–4 cev

It's part of our maturing process. At some point, as Christians, we should arrive at a place where we are comfortable using our own past experiences and current circumstances as tools to reach out to others in need. A maturing believer is one who is beginning to look back on the things she has gone through with gratitude, as her purpose in the body of Christ begins to unfold.

For various reasons, it can be difficult to move past that point of being ministered to, in order to minister to others in need. But, according to the apostle Paul, one of the reasons God comforts us is so we can share that comfort with others when they need it.

We might say, "I'm just a new Christian," or "I wouldn't know what to say." But as members of the body of Christ, we are an extension of the Holy Spirit.

So when someone is praying for comfort, be ready—it might just be you God will send to minister to that hurting soul.

Jesus, please help me open my heart and eyes to see the needs around me. Give me the grace and wisdom to comfort others with the comfort You have shown me time and time again.

Faultless

To him who is able to keep you from falling and to present you before his glorious presence without fault and with great joy.
Jude 1:24 NIV

Who is at fault? Who is to blame? When something goes wrong at work, at home, or at church, someone is held accountable. People want to know who is responsible, who made a mistake. The ones pointing fingers of accusation don't always care about the truth as much as they do about making sure they aren't blamed for the transgression.

Ever since God confronted Adam and Eve in the Garden of Eden, we have been pointing fingers at someone else instead of taking responsibility for our own actions. Shame and fear make us want to deny we have done any wrong even when we have done so accidentally or by mistake. We value what God and other people think of us. When we are at odds with God or others over a transgression, we often become depressed.

Jesus loves us so much despite our shortcomings. He is the One who can keep us from falling—who can present us faultless before the Father. Because of this we can have our joy restored no matter what. Whether we have done wrong and denied it or have been falsely accused, we can come into His presence to be restored and lifted up. Let us keep our eyes on Him instead of on our need to justify ourselves to God or others.

Thank You, Jesus, for Your cleansing love and for the joy we can find in Your presence. Amen.

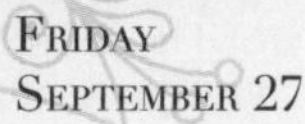

Reflecting God in Our Work

Whatever you do, work at it with all your heart, as working for the Lord, not for men.
COLOSSIANS 3:23 NIV

Parents often tell their children to do their best in school or to behave well when they visit friends' homes. Children are a reflection of their parents. When a mom and dad send their offspring out into the world, they can only hope that the reflection will be a positive one.

As believers, we are God's children. No one is perfect, and for this there is grace. However, we may be the only reflection of our heavenly Father that some will ever see. Our attitudes and actions on the job speak volumes to those around us. Although it may be tempting to do just enough to get by, we put forth our best effort when we remember we represent God to the world. A Christian's character on the job should be a positive reflection of the Lord.

This is true of our work at home as well. No one would disagree that daily chores are often monotonous, but we are called to face them with a cheerful spirit. God will give us the ability to do so when we ask Him.

Father, help me today to represent You well through my work. I want to reflect Your love in all I do. Amen.

Whom Do You Follow, Moses or Christ?

Therefore, holy brethren, partakers of a heavenly calling, consider Jesus, the Apostle and High Priest of our confession. He was faithful to Him who appointed Him, as Moses also was in all His house. For He has been counted worthy of more glory than Moses, by just so much as the builder of the house has more honor than the house. For every house is built by someone, but the builder of all things is God.

Hebrews 3:1–4

Do you ever wake up thinking about someone you may not have seen in years? Well, that's a "God call." God may be prompting your heart to respond to that person's need for encouragement.

One of Paul's great gifts was that of being an encourager. Yes, he spoke the truth unabashedly, yet he tempered it with praise and hope. "As you therefore have received Christ Jesus the Lord, so walk in Him, having been firmly rooted and now being built up in Him and established in your faith, just as you were instructed, and overflowing with gratitude" (Colossians 2:6–7).

The writer of the Book of Hebrews spoke with the same conviction and understanding. "Encourage one another day after day, as long as it is still called 'Today,' lest any one of you be hardened by the deceitfulness of sin. For we have become partakers of Christ, if we hold fast the beginning of our assurance firm until the end" (Hebrews 3:13–14).

Man's memory of his own disobedience is so quickly forgotten, Lord. The opportunity to follow Christ lays before me. Lord, help me respond.

Do Not Be Afraid

"Do not be afraid, for I have ransomed you. I have called you by name; you are mine. When you go through deep waters, I will be with you. When you go through rivers of difficulty, you will not drown. When you walk through the fire of oppression, you will not be burned up; the flames will not consume you."
Isaiah 43:1–2 NLT

Trials are inevitable, a part of life. God uses them to refine us, to burn up the dross, to mold us into the image of Jesus Christ. Even He was not immune to the difficulties of life. Jesus faced persecution, mocking, and death on the cross.

But in the midst of all trouble, Jesus walks beside us. He holds our noses above the water; He wraps us in flame-retardant clothing. We will not drown, nor will we be consumed in the fiery furnace. Why? Because He ransomed us. He paid sin's penalty, He delivered us from the slave market of sin, and He calls us by name.

So when you feel like you're drowning in a flood of trouble and difficulty, breathe deeply and relax. Bodysurf across those waves. Even if the fire of oppression singes you, remember that His promise says you will not be consumed. He will satisfy your desires in the "scorched places" (Isaiah 58:11).

Face life with no fear—you are God's.

Father, may I keep my focus on You today, not on the water that threatens to drown me or the fire that threatens to engulf me. I am Yours, and You will enable me to walk through the dangers that surround me.

Forgiven Much

She began to wet his feet with her tears. Then she wiped them with her hair, kissed them and poured perfume on them.
Luke 7:38 NIV

It was an extravagant, unacceptable event in Simon's eyes. To Jesus, it was a beautiful expression of love. How could the same actions be viewed so differently by host and guest?

Imagine it as a theatrical production. The stage is set. It's dinnertime in the home of Simon, a Pharisee well-versed in the law. Two main characters recline at the table—Simon and Jesus. Others are there as well.

Suddenly a woman with a questionable reputation bursts onto the scene. She was not invited and is poorly dressed. As she weeps, her tears fall upon Jesus' feet. Breaking custom, she lets down her hair. She wipes Jesus' feet, kisses them, and pours perfume on them. Gasps are heard. Such indiscretion! But Jesus smiles.

The horrified host mutters that if Jesus were truly a prophet, He would know this was a sinful woman.

Christ shares a story: "One man owed much, and another man little, but neither could pay their debts. The moneylender canceled both debts. Which will love the moneylender more?"

"Naturally," answered Simon, "the one who owed the greater debt."

Simon had not washed Christ's feet. In contrast, this woman of ill repute was beside herself with appreciation. The woman loved much because she was forgiven much.

Extravagant forgiveness and extravagant love were displayed that day. Christ told her to go in peace. Another life changed by the Master.

Lord, teach me to love You more.
I have been forgiven much. Amen.

Just Half a Cup

"I am coming to you now, but I say these things while I am still in the world, so that they may have the full measure of my joy within them."
John 17:13 niv

"Just half a cup, please." A friend is offered a cup of piping hot coffee, but she declines a full cup, accepting only a small amount. Perhaps she is trying to be polite, or maybe she feels as though she's had enough coffee already that day. But it is difficult and unnatural for her friend to stop pouring at half a cup, so she pours just a bit more than what was requested. She wants to give her friend the fullest possible measure of enjoyment that she can in that one cup of coffee.

That's how our Father feels when He longs to bestow His richest blessings and wisdom on us. He loves us, so He desires to fill our cup to overflowing with the things that He knows will bring us pleasure and growth. Do you tell Him to stop pouring when your cup is only half full? You may not even realize it, but perhaps your actions dictate that your cup remain half empty. Seek a full cup and enjoy the full measure of the joy of the Lord.

Dear Jesus, forgive me for not accepting the fullness of Your blessings and Your joy. Help me to see the ways that I prevent my cup from being filled to overflowing. Thank You for wanting me to have the fullness of Your joy. Amen.

Hide and Seek

"And do you seek great things for yourself? Seek them not, for behold, I am bringing disaster upon all flesh, declares the Lord."
Jeremiah 45:5 ESV

When we were little girls, we all dreamed big. Maybe we aspired to be a prima ballerina, to win an Oscar, or to own a mansion. Somewhere along the line our expectations fell into step with reality.

While the scope of our dreams may have narrowed, our desire for "great things" probably never changed. We'd like recognition for our talents, we want success at work, and we hope for more than just a minimum standard of living.

But God warns us: *Don't seek great things.* The more we seek them, the more elusive they become. As soon as we think we have them in our grasp, they disappear. If we commit to more activities than we can realistically handle, the best result is that we can't follow through. Worse, we might make them our god. Our God—the true God—wants to rearrange our priorities.

Jesus tells us what we should seek: the kingdom of God and His righteousness (Matthew 6:33). He won't hide from us. When we seek the right things, He'll give us every good and perfect gift (James 1:17). And that will be more than we can ask or dream.

*Lord, please teach me to seek not greatness,
but You. May You be the all in all of my life.*

For What Are You Zealous?

For am I now seeking the favor of men, or of God? Or am I striving to please men? If I were still trying to please men, I would not be a bond-servant of Christ.
GALATIANS 1:10

"Save the Whales," "Save the Rain Forests," read the placards of our times. But where are the billboards that proclaim, "Save the Human Soul"? Paul carried such a sign every day.

He was a "Jew's Jew" and proficient at keeping the law of Moses. Then Paul's life took an unscheduled detour. "But when He who had set me apart, even from my mother's womb, and called me through His grace, was pleased to reveal His Son in me, that I might preach Him among the Gentiles, I did not immediately consult with flesh and blood, nor did I go up to Jerusalem to those who were apostles before me; but I went away to Arabia, and returned once more to Damascus" (Galatians 1:15–17).

Paul didn't sit around asking men for their opinions. Christ's call was sufficient. Therefore, he devoted himself to study, prayer, and meditation alone with his Lord. For although he'd known the Scriptures, he had approached them from the wrong perspective. Paul would spend three years allowing his Lord to instruct him correctly in all that he'd missed the first time.

Lord, what are my own misconceptions concerning Your Word? Teach me the true meaning of the Scriptures.

Location, Location, Location

Those who live in the shelter of the Most High will find rest in the shadow of the Almighty. This I declare about the LORD: He alone is my refuge, my place of safety; he is my God, and I trust him.
PSALM 91:1–2 NLT

Where do you live? Where are you living right now, this instant?

If you are abiding in Christ, moment by moment, you are constantly safe under His protection. In that secret place, that hidden place in Him, you can maintain a holy serenity, a peace of mind that surpasses all understanding. If you are trusting in God, nothing can move you or harm you.

If money problems, physical illness, time pressures, job woes, the state of the world, or something else is getting you down, check your location. Where are you? Where is your mind? Where are your thoughts?

Let what the world has conditioned you to think go in one ear and out the other. Stand on the truth, the promises of God's Word. Say of the Lord, "God is my refuge! I am hidden in Christ! Nothing can harm me. In Him I trust!" Say it loud. Say it often. Say it over and over until it becomes your reality. And you will find yourself dwelling in that secret place every moment of the day.

God, You are my refuge. When I abide in You, nothing can harm me. Your Word is the truth on which I rely. Fill me with Your light and the peace of Your love. It's You and me, Lord, all the way! Amen.

An Hour Apart

And he cometh unto the disciples, and findeth them asleep, and saith unto Peter, What, could ye not watch with me one hour?
MATTHEW 26:40 KJV

An old hymn describes a "sweet hour of prayer," but let's be honest: Few of us have an hour to spend with the Lord every day. When those rare opportunities come, we don't even know how to handle them. But simply trying to fill an hour with spiritual things can be a real blessing.

Picture yourself sitting at a table, Bible in hand. You have an hour in front of you. What do you do?

First, choose a passage to study. Read through it at least five times, in different translations, if possible. Use a dictionary—both an English and a Bible dictionary—to check the meaning of any unusual words. Use a concordance to find other places where key words appear in the Bible. Check out the cross-references found in many Bibles.

Ask the five W's (*who*, *what*, *when*, *where*, and *why*) about the passage, and summarize what you've learned. List any lessons you can apply to your life.

Ask God to make you a doer of His Word, not only a hearer. Then, as a final step, share what God has taught you with someone else.

Lord and Savior, show me when and how to carve out an hour with You. Make me hungry for that intimate time.

Truth in Love

O LORD, I know the way of man is not in himself; it is not in man who walks to direct his own steps. O LORD, correct me, but with justice; not in Your anger, lest You bring me to nothing.
JEREMIAH 10:23–24 NKJV

A good friend will tell you the truth. "No, those pants do not flatter you." "He's not the right guy for you." "Yes, you need to update your hairstyle." Hopefully, she will go even further and gently help you see your missteps. Are you a gossip? A grumbler? Even when it is painful to hear, the truth is liberating.

Though confrontation is difficult, if we love someone, it is good and right to speak the truth in love. Jeremiah 17:9 tells us that our own hearts are wicked, and we can't understand our own feelings and actions. Our tendency is to rationalize our sinful behavior. Thankfully, God has given us the gift of the Holy Spirit to help us on our journey. If we ask, the Lord is faithful to His Word and He will reveal our motivations to us. We can use Jeremiah's words as our prayer, asking God to correct us, to show us what is true and how to live in light of it.

Thank You, Father, that You are the discerner of hearts, that You gently show me my sin, and that You have given me Your Holy Spirit to help me.

Get Those Hammers Ready

"Thus says the Lord of hosts, 'This people says, "The time has not come, even the time for the house of the Lord to be rebuilt." ' " Then the word of the Lord came by Haggai the prophet saying, "Is it time for you yourselves to dwell in your paneled houses while this house lies desolate?" Now therefore, thus says the Lord of hosts, "Consider your ways!"
Haggai 1:2–5

Since our winters here in California are fairly mild, a coat of paint can last about twenty years. The roof, however, is another story. When several severe rainstorms hit the coastline, we knew we'd ignored that roof long enough!

This same shabby state of affairs could be seen during the time of Haggai with God's temple. Although a small remnant had begun rebuilding, they had become overwhelmed. For about sixteen years the temple stood like a piece of unfinished furniture. Now God commissioned Haggai to bring His motivating Word to the people.

"So the Lord stirred up the spirit of Zerubbabel the son of Shealtiel, governor of Judah, and the spirit of Joshua the son of Jehozadak, the high priest, and the spirit of the remnant of the people; and they came and worked on the house of the Lord of hosts, their God" (Haggai 1:14).

The task loomed larger than life so the Lord spoke again:
" '. . . take courage. . .' declares the Lord, 'and work; for I am with you' " (Haggai 2:4).

Lord, whatever task is overwhelming me today You have the strength to see it through to fulfillment.

Light My Path

Your word is a lamp to my feet and a light for my path.
PSALM 119:105 NIV

Amy was walking a usually well-lit path around the lake. But tonight, the streetlamps had not come on—and the moon, though large and full, was covered by thick clouds. She had often walked around the lake, but this night, Amy stumbled over unnoticed tree limbs and half-buried rocks. Then the streetlamps flickered to life and a golden light illuminated the path. Amy could speed her pace, easily avoiding the dangerous obstructions.

God's Word is like a streetlamp. Often, we *think* we know where we're going and where the stumbling blocks are. We believe we can avoid pitfalls and maneuver the path successfully on our own. But the truth is that without God's Word, we are walking in darkness, stumbling and tripping.

When we sincerely begin to search God's Word, we find the path becomes clear. We see everything in a new light, a light that makes it obvious which way to turn and what choices to make. God's light allows us to live our lives in the most fulfilling way possible, a way planned out from the very beginning by God Himself.

Jesus, shine Your light upon my path. I have spent too long wandering through the darkness, looking for my way. As I search Your Word, I ask You to make it a lamp to my feet so that I can avoid the pitfalls of the world and walk safely along the path You have created specifically for me.

A Different Cup to Fill

O God, thou art my God; early will I seek thee.
PSALM 63:1 KJV

It is early morning and we stumble from our beds to take a shower, apply makeup, and blow-dry our hair. Meanwhile, coffee brews in the kitchen, and with a yawn we fill our cups. Busy women have limited time to relax, reflect, and pray. Yet a different and more significant type of cup longs to be filled—our spirit.

King David resided over the nation of Israel and all that that entailed. Yet he found time to seek the counsel, mercy, and direction of God daily. The more responsibilities he assumed, the more he prayed and meditated on God's precepts. Well before David was inundated with worldly concerns, nagging obligations, and his administrative duties, the Bible suggests that he sought the Lord in the early morning hours.

If the king of Israel recognized his need to spend time with God, how much more should we? When we seek our heavenly Father before daily activities demand our attention, the Holy Spirit regenerates our spirits, and our cups overflow.

Dear Lord, I take this time to pray and spend time with You before I attend to daily responsibilities. Fill my cup with the presence and power of Your Spirit. Give me the wisdom and direction I need today. Amen.

Power Up

The Spirit of God, who raised Jesus from the dead, lives in you.
Romans 8:11 NLT

God is the same yesterday, today, and forever. His strength does not diminish over time. That same mountain-moving power you read about in the lives of people from the Old and New Testaments still exists today. The same power that caused the walls of Jericho to fall, an ax to float, and a dead girl to live again is still available today. The force of God that formed the world, brought the dry land above the waters of the sea, and raised Jesus from the dead is available to work out the details of your life.

It's natural to want to do things on our own. We all want to be independent and strong. When faced with a challenge, the first thing we do is try to work it out in our own skill and ability—within our own power. But there's another way.

We don't have to go it alone. Our heavenly Father wants to help. All we have to do is ask. He has already made His power available to His children. Whatever we face—wherever we go—whatever dreams we have for our lives, take courage and know that anything is possible when we draw on the power of God.

Father, help me to remember that You are always with me, ready to help me do all things. Amen.

Comfort Food

For whatever things were written before were written for our learning, that we through the patience and comfort of the Scriptures might have hope.
ROMANS 15:4 NKJV

A big mound of ice cream topped with hot fudge; a full bowl of salty, buttery popcorn; grilled cheese sandwiches and warm chicken noodle soup fixed by Mom—comfort food. There is nothing like a generous helping of things that bring the sensation of comfort to a worn body at the end of a long day or to a bruised mind after a disappointment. Those comfort foods soothe the body and mind because, through the senses, they remind us of happier and more secure times.

Romans 15:4 tells us that the scriptures are comfort food for the soul. They were written and given so that, through our learning, we would be comforted with the truths of God. Worldly pleasures bring a temporary comfort, but the problem still remains when the pleasure or comfort fades. However, the words of God are soothing and provide permanent hope and peace. Through God's Word, you will be changed, and your troubles will dim in the bright light of Christ. So the next time you are sad, lonely, or disappointed, before you turn to pizza, turn to the Word of God as your source of comfort.

Thank You, Father, for the rich comfort Your Word provides. Help me to remember to find my comfort in scripture rather than through earthly things that will ultimately fail me. Amen.

The Fruit of the Spirit

But the fruit of the Spirit is love, joy, peace, patience, kindness, goodness, faithfulness, gentleness, self-control; against such things there is no law. Now those who belong to Christ Jesus have crucified the flesh with its passions and desires. If we live by the Spirit, let us also walk by the Spirit.
Galatians 5:22–25

When we become Christians we receive spiritual gifts as a result of our inward relationship with Jesus Christ. These gifts are known in the Bible as the fruit of the Spirit, but what does that really mean?

Inventoried in today's Scripture are qualities that, apart from God's power, would likely not be displayed in our character.

Take, for instance, joy. How many truly joyful people do you know? Most of us could probably count them on one hand. Joy is the inward peace and sufficiency that transcends life's circumstances.

So, what's the catch? Why is God showering us with these gifts? Because they prove that He can enter a human life and affect her or him with change, that others might also be won to Christ as they observe this miracle.

Lord, my greatest gift from You is salvation, Your grace enables me to begin life with a fresh start. And with this transformation of character, fruit becomes the yield, shared as I serve the body of believers with my unique spiritual gifts.

Creating Margin

"My Presence will go with you, and I will give you rest."
EXODUS 33:14 NIV

From the very first chapter of Genesis, God teaches us to take rest. He rested on the seventh day of creation and declared it good. Later, as the Israelites entered the Promised Land, God ordered the people to give the *soil* a rest every seven years.

When we short ourselves on rest, illness can result. That's our body's way of saying "Slow down! I can't keep up! If you won't listen to me, then I'm going to force you to."

God believes in rest! But most of us live lives that are packed to the brim with activities and obligations. We're overwhelmed. With such a fragile balance, unexpected occurrences, like a dead car battery, can wreck us emotionally, spiritually, and physically.

That's not the lifestyle God wants us to have. "He grants sleep to those he loves," wrote the psalmist (Psalm 127:2 NIV). God wants us to create a margin for the unexpected: a neighbor in need, a grandparent who requires extra attention, a friend who needs encouragement, our own kids as they grow and mature.

Life is busy. But in God's presence we find rest.

Help me, Father, to listen to Your instruction and heed Your words.

Power of the Word

The Spirit gives life; the flesh counts for nothing.
The words I have spoken to you are spirit and they are life.
JOHN 6:63 NIV

While waiting for a phone call regarding lab results from a recent blood test, Lisa meditated on Psalm 56:3 (NIV), "When I am afraid, I will trust in you." When Lisa was a little girl, her mother taught her to recite it in times of fear: a barking dog as she rode her bike, a dark room at bedtime, a first piano recital. Even now, it calmed her to remember how this verse had helped her conquer those childhood fears. She knew the Spirit gave life to those same words and stilled her anxiousness.

Jesus told His followers that His words were Spirit and life. How He works through His Word is a mystery, but He does. When we hear it, meditate on it, pray it, memorize it, and ask for faith to believe it, He comes to us in it and transforms our lives through it. Once the Word is in our mind or before our eyes and ears, the Holy Spirit can work it into our hearts and our consciences. Jesus told us to abide in His Word. That's our part, putting ourselves in a place to hear and receive the Word. The rest is the beautiful and mysterious work of the Spirit.

Thank You, Jesus, the Living Word,
who changes my heart and my mind
through the power of Your Word.

Nothing to Lose

Saul replied, "You are not able to go out against this Philistine and fight him; you are only a boy, and he has been a fighting man from his youth."
1 SAMUEL 17:33 NIV

Goliath, a pagan Philistine, defied Israel's army and challenged it to send a single man to fight him to decide who would rule the land. As the Israelites observed his giant body and fearsome war equipment, they quaked in their sandals. How could they win?

Victory lay in the hands of a visionary shepherd, David, who recognized that the battle was not his, but God's. The intrepid shepherd stepped forward to accept the challenge.

"Wiser" heads warned the youth of danger. King Saul counseled against fighting the Philistine warrior, then tried to deck the shepherd out in his own armor. But David had a better armor—the Lord God.

Sometimes we clearly hear the call of God to move ahead into spiritual battle. Others warn us against it, and their counsel seems wise. But God's call pulls at our hearts. Who are we listening to? Are these counselors godly people or discouraging, worldly wise Sauls, with at best a tenuous connection to God?

If God is fighting your battle for you, trust in Him, seek godly counsel, and follow His call implicitly. You have nothing to lose.

If You lead me, Lord, I cannot lose. Show me Your path and give me courage. Amen.

Taking a Real Sabbath

By the seventh day God had finished the work he had been doing; so on the seventh day he rested from all his work.
Genesis 2:2–3 niv

One of the Ten Commandments was to honor the Sabbath and keep it holy. God gives the example we can follow. In Genesis 2, He rested after His work was done.

What does honoring the Sabbath look like for women today? Some churches practice a literal Sabbath on Saturday and others take Sunday as their day of rest. Some Sabbath-keeping women rest from shopping and cooking, and many women who have to work on Sunday take another day as their personal Sabbath.

But too often we let our Sabbath day become as packed as the other six. We rush to get ready for church, then sing in the praise team, teach Sunday school, and (whew!) go to a meeting over lunch. The afternoon is for running errands, and our evening is spent in a discipleship group.

All those activities are fine in themselves. But when we overextend ourselves every single day, we run the risk of burning out—and forgetting why God created the Sabbath. He did it not so we could have another commandment to keep, but for our own good. Our bodies, minds, and emotions need rest. The Sabbath gives us a chance to take a breather. As we slow down our schedule and quiet our hearts, we can more easily hear from Him.

*God, forgive me for taking Your commands too lightly.
Help me to remember the Sabbath
and keep it holy, just as You did.*

Chosen Before the Foundation of the World

Blessed be the God and Father of our Lord Jesus Christ, who has blessed us with every spiritual blessing in the heavenly places in Christ, just as he chose us in Him before the foundation of the world, that we should be holy and blameless before Him.

Ephesians 1:3–4

The doctrine of predestination has baffled Christian theologians since the time the Bible was written. How can a woman have free will if God already knows what she'll choose? The fact that God knows the beginning from the end in no way diminishes our ability to choose.

To state this more simply, when God created the world He not only planned your place in it, but He also reserved a place in heaven for you. Now, you can either claim your ticket by accepting Christ's salvation on your behalf, or you can cancel the reservation by never responding to God's offer.

Remember Paul's encounter with that blinding light? He knew when Christ appeared to him that God had intervened to change the very course of his life: "Paul, an apostle of Christ Jesus by the will of God. . ." (2 Corinthians 1:1). God extended to Paul the truth about Jesus Christ and he responded in commitment.

Lord, help me and each woman reading this to enjoy the safety, protection, and sense of belonging that come from being chosen.

Lost and Found

"And the one who sent me is with me—he has not deserted me. For I always do what pleases him."
JOHN 8:29 NLT

We lose things on a daily basis. Each year we probably spend hours looking for things—keys, sunglasses, lipstick, or even the saltshaker that normally rests next to the stove. We know these items don't sprout wings and walk off but have been set somewhere and forgotten by you or someone you know.

You are God's most prized possession, and while He'll never forget where you are, sometimes we walk off from Him. We lose ourselves in the things we need to do, the places we need to go, and the people we need to see. Our calendars fill up with commitments we're obligated to keep. We often commit to too many things and exhaust ourselves trying to stay ahead of our schedules.

The further we displace ourselves from God—not necessarily on purpose—the more we become lost in our own space. While we're doing life on our own, we can forget that He is standing there waiting to do life every day with us. If you feel distant from Him today, look up. He's waiting for you to find your rightful place with Him.

God, I never want to become so busy that I lose sight of You. Show me what things I should commit to and what things are for someone else to do, so that I am available to You and ready to serve in the capacity You've prepared me for. Amen.

Pick Your Battles

To these four young men God gave knowledge and understanding of all kinds of literature and learning. And Daniel could understand visions and dreams of all kinds.
Daniel 1:17 niv

Daniel was one of the first Hebrew exiles taken from Jerusalem into friendly captivity (if there is such a thing) in Babylon. Separated from his family, forced into servitude, given a new identity and new gods, Daniel was probably only a teenager! He was now living in Babylon, the pagan center of the earth.

Did Daniel completely reject his new lifestyle? Did he argue with his master and refuse to learn? No! Amazingly, there were only a few areas where Daniel refused to compromise: he would not bow down and worship any other god or eat food that had been offered to idols.

We live in a type of Babylon, too. We're surrounded by anti-God behavior, customs, pop culture. It's easy to be offended by just about. . .everything. Everyday language is flavored with swear words, television shows mock our faith, schools introduce curricula that make us cringe.

Surprisingly, God didn't tackle every single issue in Babylon. He picked Daniel's battles for him, and Daniel was greatly used in the midst of a pagan culture. Not indignant or antagonistic, but compassionate and seeking the best for his captors.

Can we be Daniels in our communities today?

Lord, show me how to seek Your wisdom and discernment while picking my battles. Help me to love those who oppose You.

My Helper

So we say with confidence, "The Lord is my helper; I will not be afraid. What can man do to me?"
HEBREWS 13:6 NIV

Remember when you were a kid and you had a school project due? The whole thing seemed overwhelming until your father said, "Let me help you with that." He listened to your ideas, then helped you make the necessary purchases. Finally, the day arrived to put together your project. Instead of doing the work for you, your father simply made his presence known as you worked—encouraging you with, "That's great, honey!" and "Wow, I can hardly wait to see this when it's done!" His words boosted your confidence and spurred you on.

Your heavenly Father is a "That's great, honey" kind of encourager. Talk about building your confidence! When you're up against a tough situation, He's standing right there, speaking positive words over you, telling you you've got what it takes to be the best you can possibly be. And while He won't take the reins—He wants you to learn from the experience, after all—He will advise you as you go.

What are you facing today? Do you need a helper? God is the very best. Just knowing He's there will ease your mind and invigorate you for the tasks you face.

Father, I'm so glad You stand nearby, whispering words of encouragement. You're the best helper possible. Thank You for taking my fears and replacing them with godly confidence.

Can God Interrupt You?

In his heart a man plans his course,
but the LORD determines his steps.
PROVERBS 16:9 NIV

Before rushing out of the house each morning, we grab calendars. Our day is efficiently planned. We are eager to check off our to-do list. But wait! The phone suddenly rings. There is an unexpected knock at the door. The car tire is flat.

How do we react when our plans are interrupted? Do frustration, resentment, and anger quickly surface? We have places to go and people to meet. We do not have time for interruptions!

Have you ever considered that perhaps God has ordained our interruptions? A friend could be calling in need of encouragement. God knew you'd be just the right person to lift her spirits. Maybe the knock on the door is a lost child seeking help. Perhaps, just perhaps, God may be trying to get your attention.

There is nothing wrong with planning our day. However, we have such limited vision. God sees the big picture. Be open. Be flexible. Allow God to change your plans in order to accomplish His divine purposes. Instead of becoming frustrated, look for ways the Lord might be working. Be willing to join Him. When we do, interruptions become blessings.

Dear Lord, forgive me when I am so rigidly locked into my own agenda that I miss Yours. Give me Your eternal perspective so that I may be open to divine interruptions. Amen.

The Meaning of True Christian Fellowship

I thank my God in all my remembrance of you, always offering prayer with joy in my every prayer for you all, in view of your participation in the gospel from the first day until now. . . For it is only right for me to feel this way about you all, because I have you in my heart, since both in my imprisonment and in the defense and confirmation of the gospel, you all are partakers of grace with me.

PHILIPPIANS 1:3–5, 7

Paul was confined to prison when he wrote his letter to the Philippians. Yet rather than wallowing in self-pity, we see him reaching out to those he loves and reminiscing about their joyful times of fellowship together. The sheer memory of them causes warmth to invade his lonely prison. And though he longs to be with them, he is content in the place Christ has called him.

Paul's joy is not dependent upon circumstances. Rather, it overflows from the content of his heart, where the true source of joy resides, Jesus Christ. And because of this indwelling, Paul senses a oneness with other believers, despite the fact that they are far from him. It is the love of Christ that binds them together.

Paul's only aim in life was to be where God wanted him—so that he might spread the Gospel to all who would listen. And if this aspiration required suffering and isolation on his part, then Paul gladly paid the price.

Lord, might I pray as Paul, "I press on toward the goal for the prize of the upward call of God in Christ Jesus" (Philippians 3:14).

Trouble or Trust?

*"Don't let your hearts be troubled.
Trust in God, and trust also in me."*
JOHN 14:1 NLT

Trouble or trust? Which will you choose today? We women tend to be troubled in our hearts, worrying about our relationships, our appearance, our finances, our work, and perhaps especially about the future.

The disciples were worried about their future as well. Jesus had told them He would be going away from them. He was preparing them for His death, resurrection, and ascension into heaven. They were saddened when they heard Him say that they could not come with Him at that time, although they would follow later.

So Christ spoke these words to them in John 14:1, reminding them to trust in God and to trust in Him. He told them not to let their hearts be troubled. Sometimes we feel as if we can't control feeling troubled. But when we focus on the Lord and meditate upon His promises, we can gain control of our worries and replace them with trust.

You do not know what your future holds, but God does. He asks you to stop worrying. He asks you to trust in Him. He is faithful to provide for His own.

Father, please replace trouble with trust in this heart of mine that is sometimes lonely and unsure of the future. Thank You, Lord, that I can trust in You. Amen.

Marvelous Thunder

"God's voice thunders in marvelous ways;
he does great things beyond our understanding."
JOB 37:5 NIV

Have you ever reflected deeply on the power that God is? Not that He *has*, but that He is.

The ailing woman who simply touched Jesus' garment was healed. That's power. Lazarus walked out of the tomb alive. That's power. Jesus could walk on water and calm a storm with His words. That's power. Only a God who *is* power could do such things.

Job's friend Elihu made some false assumptions about his suffering companion, but he certainly understood God's power. Elihu described God as telling lightning where to strike (Job 36:32), and generating thunder with His own voice (Job 37:2–4). That's power—full-blown, mind-boggling, earthshaking power.

Now, consider this: The One who controls nature also holds every one of our tears in His hand. He is our Father, and He works on our behalf. He is more than enough to meet our needs; He does things far beyond what our human minds can understand.

This One who is power loves you. He looks at you and says, "I delight in you, My daughter." Wow! His ways are marvelous and beyond understanding.

Lord God, You are power. You hold all things in Your hand and You chose to love me. You see my actions, hear my thoughts, watch my heartbreak. . . and You still love me. Please help me trust in Your power, never my own.

Eye Care

For thus says the LORD of hosts. . .
"he who touches you touches the apple of His eye."
ZECHARIAH 2:8 NKJV

The apple of the eye refers to the pupil—the very center, or heart, of the eye. Consider the lengths we go to in order to protect our eyes. We wear protective glasses in some workplaces. We close our eyes or squint in windstorms or bright light. When dust blows, we turn our heads or put up our hands to keep the dirt from ending up in our eyes.

When we do get something in an eye, the ache and discomfort are instant. Tears form, and we seek to get the particle out as quickly as possible to stop the pain. If we are unable to remove the offending bit, we often become unable to do anything but focus on the discomfort.

To think that we are the apple of God's eye is incredible. Consider the care He must take for us. He will go to great lengths to protect us from harm. When something or someone does attack us, God feels our pain. He is instantly aware of our discomfort, for it is His own. When the storms of life come, we must remember how God feels each twinge of suffering. Despite the adversity, we can praise God for He is sheltering us.

Thank You, God, that You are so aware of what is happening to me. Thank You for Your protection. Amen.

Born Again to a Living Hope

In this you greatly rejoice, even though now for a little while, if necessary, you have been distressed by various trials, that the proof of your faith, being more precious than gold which is perishable, even though tested by fire, may be found to result in praise and glory and honor at the revelation of Jesus Christ.
1 Peter 1:6–7

"Religious fanatics!" "Jesus freaks!" "Bible thumpers!" These are just a few of the choice names hurled at those who dare to share their Christian faith. What degree of persecution are you willing to endure that the Gospel of truth might go forward to a needy world?

Remember Nicodemus? He came to Jesus by night, asking what he might do to be saved. Although he continued to watch from afar, this encounter with Christ had stirred something within the heart of Nicodemus. Christ's words had caused light to flood into his soul: " 'He who believes in Me, as the Scripture said, "From his innermost being shall flow rivers of living water" ' " (John 7:38). Then came the day when this Pharisee interceded for Christ.

When the multitude became divided as to Christ's true identity and many wanted to seize Jesus, Nicodemus, who could no longer remain silent, reminded them that their law couldn't judge a man without a proper hearing (John 7:51). At the foot of the cross Nicodemus publicly declared his belief.

Thank You, Jesus, for convicting my soul today.

God's Mountain Sanctuary

And seeing the multitudes, he went up into a mountain. . .and. . . his disciples came unto him: and he opened his mouth and taught them.
Matthew 5:1–2 KJV

Melissa felt crushed beneath work, home, and church responsibilities. So much so, she could no longer give or listen, let alone hear from God. So she decided to take a day trip to the mountains to try and unwind.

There the forest hummed with a symphony of sound as beams of sunlight filtered through the vast timberland. As she strolled a wooded path, she noticed how God's creation kept perfect cadence with its Creator. No one directed the wildflowers to bloom, no one commanded the trees to reach upward, and no one forced the creek to flow downstream. No one but God, and nature simply complied.

Jesus often retreated to a mountain to pray. There He called His disciples to depart from the multitudes so that He could teach them valuable truths—the lessons we learn from nature. Don't fret, obey God's gentle promptings, and simply flow in the path He clears.

Do you yearn for a place where problems evaporate like the morning dew? Do you need a place of solace? God is wherever you are—behind a bedroom door, nestled alongside you in your favorite chair, or even standing at a sink full of dirty dishes. Come apart and enter God's mountain sanctuary.

Heavenly Father, I long to hear Your voice and to flow in the path You clear before me. Help me to find sanctuary in Your abiding presence. Amen.

More Than Enough

Let us not become weary in doing good,
for at the proper time we will reap a harvest if we do not give up.
Galatians 6:9 niv

How often do we become impatient and give up? We stand in line at the coffee shop and find ourselves behind an indecisive person. Frustrated, we give up—but before we get to our car, that person—coffee cup in hand—walks past. If we'd only waited another minute, we, too, could be sipping a steaming caramel latte.

Or maybe we have a dream that we can't seem to make a reality—and rather than trying "just one more time," we give up. A piece of who we are drifts away like a leaf on the sea.

The Word of God encourages us to keep going, to press on, to fight off weariness and never give up. Jesus Christ has a harvest for each of us, and He eagerly anticipates blessing us with it—but we have to trust Him and refuse to give in to weariness.

We can only imagine what that harvest might be, because we know that God is the God of "immeasurably more than all we ask or imagine" (Ephesians 3:20 niv). We can be recipients of His "immeasurably more" if we press on in the strength He provides.

When you're tired, keep going—and remember that, in His perfect timing, you will reap an unimaginable harvest.

Father, You know that I'm tired and weary in this uphill struggle. Fill me with Your strength so I can carry on. I long to reap the harvest You have for me.

A Woman's Work

Well reported of for good works; if she have brought up children, if she have lodged strangers, if she have washed the saints' feet, if she have relieved the afflicted, if she have diligently followed every good work.
1 Timothy 5:10 KJV

With so many choices in today's world, what's a woman to do?

What's she to do with her time and her talents?

That's a tough question, especially in this me-centered, career-driven world. Women have so many opportunities that we can get ourselves quite confused as we look at all the options.

This confusion persists in our service to God. What does *He* want me to do? Wouldn't it be better to be working with orphans in Zambia than washing dishes in suburbia?

Who knows?

God does. His Word clearly explains a woman's work. This work includes keeping house, ministering to the poor, helping those in the church, and practicing hospitality. A widow who was worthy of church support had to have done all these things.

Such work is not very glamorous. It's not worthy of headlines or large paychecks. It is disdained by the world and even by some in the church.

But this is the humble work God honors, the work that will one day be praised.

Dear Lord, Your Word is so clear on what You expect of me. How can I miss it? And why do I so easily reject it? Teach me contentment in my calling as a woman, knowing that You will reward the humble labor of homemaking. Amen.

A Fragrant Offering

Be imitators of God, therefore, as dearly loved children and live a life of love, just as Christ loved us and gave himself up for us as a fragrant offering and sacrifice to God.
Ephesians 5:1–2 niv

Have you ever walked into a place that smelled beautiful? Scented candles, potpourri, or fresh cookies in the oven can be very inviting, drawing us in and making us want to stay for a while.

In a similar way, if we carry the scent of Christ in our daily walk, people will be drawn to us and want to "stay for a while." But how do we give off that amazing, inviting fragrance?

There's really only one way—by imitating God. By patterning our actions after His. By loving others fully. By seeing them through His eyes. By looking with great compassion on those who are hurting, as Jesus did when He went about healing the sick and pouring out His life for those in need.

As we live a life of love in front of those we care for, we exude the sweetest fragrance of all—Christ. That's one aroma that can't be bottled!

Dear Lord, I long to live a life that points people to You. As I care for those in need, may the sweet-smelling aroma of You and Your love be an invitation for people to draw near.

Halloween, Day of Evil or Innocent Fun?

Therefore, let us fear lest, while a promise remains of entering His rest, any one of you should seem to have come short of it. For indeed we have had good news preached to us, just as they also; but the word they heard did not profit them, because it was not united by faith in those who heard.
HEBREWS 4:1–2

Halloween is here again. Time for Christians to espouse their polarized viewpoints concerning this mysterious and/or magical time of year. Halloween isn't just about dressing up and collecting candy. Today it's become an issue that each Christian must address.

Realizing that a child's objective is not to indulge in the occult but instead to have fun, Christian writers are exercising their creativity. To go along with the "harvest festival" idea, already fostered by many churches, is a drama book by Louis Merryman entitled *Halloween Alternatives*, containing ideas for reaching young minds with the Gospel. A book by Liz Curtis Higgs, *The Pumpkin Patch Parable*, relates how God plants the seed of belief in our hearts.

Today's Scripture is about "entering into God's rest," something which those who do not choose Him will never experience.

Dear God, I know You have kept Your part of the bargain, in obtaining salvation for me through Christ's death on the cross. Whether I respond to this salvation or not is up to me.

Godly Beauty

Like a gold ring in a pig's snout is a beautiful woman who shows no discretion.
Proverbs 11:22 NIV

Today's society has redefined beauty, and it certainly does not include discretion. There is nothing discreet about the advertisements for sexy lingerie we see in magazines and even on television during prime time.

Some of the most attractive female stars fail to use discretion in their choices regarding their apparel, child-rearing, materialism, drugs, and relationships with men. Yet these women are teenage girls' role models. What happened to "pretty is as pretty does"? What happened to modesty?

We are called to honor the Lord by demonstrating discretion. In doing so, we also guard our hearts. The Bible calls the heart the "wellspring of life." It is difficult to live a pure life for Jesus while lacking modesty in choices of clothing, language, and lifestyle.

A gold ring is a thing of beauty, but in a pig's snout, it quickly loses its appeal! A beautiful woman without discretion may attract a crowd, but not the right one. She may appeal to a man, but not a godly one. She will receive attention, but sadly it will come in the form of shock, rather than respect.

As a single Christian woman, no matter your shape or size, your height or hair color, you are *beautiful*. Beauty is in the heart first. It shines forth through attitudes and actions that honor God. This is true beauty.

Lord, when I am tempted to use beauty to attract the world to my body, remind me that a godly woman uses modesty to point the world to You. Amen.

Quiet Hope

It's a good thing to quietly hope, quietly hope for help from God.
Lamentations 3:26 msg

Hope is essential to life. Without it, life has no meaning, no purpose.

How much truer that is in our spiritual lives. The hope of eternal life in heaven grows more powerful the longer we live in our earthly bodies. Hope keeps us going in the midst of trouble and heartache. It allows us to live in expectation of life with no pain, no sorrow, no trouble of any kind to mar our eternal existence.

Jeremiah is often called the "weeping prophet." Yet even in his lament over Judah's sin and turning away from God, he wrote these words: "It's a good thing to quietly hope. . .for help from God." Dwelling on the confusion and chaos of his day only added to Jeremiah's distress. The prophet knew that keeping his focus on the Lord was essential to seeing the hope of his people's salvation that God had promised.

God calls us to "cease striving" (Psalm 46:10), so that we can know Him and understand the hope of His calling (Ephesians 1:18). He wants us to quietly hope and wait on God's promises for strength (Isaiah 40:31), for endurance (1 Corinthians 10:13), for peace (Romans 15:13), for salvation (1 Thessalonians 5:8), for eternal life in heaven (Titus 1:2)—for others as well as for ourselves.

Lord, help me to be quiet before You today no matter what is going on around me. I look to the hope I have in Christ Jesus for all I need to do Your will today.

Being of One Mind

Do nothing from selfishness or empty conceit, but with humility of mind let each of you regard one another as more important than himself; do not merely look out for your own personal interests, but also for the interests of others.
Philippians 2:3–4

While vacationing in the Midwest this past fall, my husband and I toured several Amish communities. How well these people live out the teaching of today's Scripture on unity. Forsaking the modern world that surrounds them, with a deep sense of community, the Amish labor together for the good of all.

As Christians we are called to encourage one another in the faith. Paul, who spent so much of his own life in prison, had a deep understanding of the need for the reassurance and hope which the Lord richly supplied. This reliance on God's abundant source of blessings overflowed from his heart, spilling out to his fellow Christians.

What if we used the greeting time in church, during the worship service, to find out the specific needs within the body of Christ? Many of our brothers and sisters are wounded, both physically and spiritually. Yet they come to Sunday services with a deceptive smile on their faces, their return trip home as lonely as the rest of their week will probably be. Do you care?

Who is my source of strength?
Lord, help me encourage others.

Masterpiece

*You made all the delicate, inner parts of my body
and knit me together in my mother's womb.*
Psalm 139:13 NLT

At the moment of your conception, roughly three million decisions were made about you. Everything from your eye color and the number of your wisdom teeth, to the shape of your nose and the swirl of your fingerprints was determined in the blink of an eye.

Now consider that there are approximately six billion human beings alive on this planet today, and each of *them* was as individually crafted as you. If that thought isn't staggering enough, think about this: It's estimated that as many as 100 billion people have walked the earth at one time or another—and each of *them* was uniquely made. Wow. How can we even begin to fathom the God who is responsible for all that?

He is a big God. Unfathomable. Incomparable. Frankly, words just don't do Him justice. And He made *you*. You were knit together by a one-of-a-kind, amazing God who is absolutely, undeniably, head-over-heels crazy-in-love with you. Try to wrap your brain around that.

Heavenly Father and Creator, thank You for the amazing gift of life, for my uniqueness and individuality. Help me to use my life as a gift of praise to You. Amen.

Finding Real Rest

And I said, Oh that I had wings like a dove!
for then would I fly away, and be at rest.
Psalm 55:6 kjv

There are days. . .

. . .when the family gets sick and the dog disappears,
. . .when the phone doesn't stop ringing,
. . .when your favorite sweater ends up in the dryer,
. . .when your boss takes his frustration out on you,
. . .when you think things can't get any worse, but they do.

There are days.

On such days, it's tempting to wish for an easy way out. If only you could get away from phones and responsibilities and people who want more of you than you have to give.

If only you could fly away! Then you could be at rest.

Really?

It takes more than a quiet place or a time away to bring true rest. Often, even if we go away from the noise and demands of family, we find ourselves thinking of the very ones we wanted to leave. Instead of being at peace, we're full of guilt and regret.

Instead of flying away, we must jump into God's everlasting arms and dive into His Word. Rest is found in knowing Christ and understanding that through His sacrifice, we are at peace.

As we allow God's peace to fill us, we will find real rest.

Father God, there are many days when I don't have time to sit. And too often my house is Crisis Central. In all these times, remind me that peace comes from knowing You and resting in the work You have done. Amen.

Finding Confidence in Christ

Let us then approach the throne of grace with confidence, so that we may receive mercy and find grace to help us in our time of need.
Hebrews 4:16 NIV

Celebrities have it. So do CEOs, professional athletes, and musicians. No, not money—confidence. So how can we modern women cultivate confidence in a world that rewards thinness, talent, and tabloid-readiness over character and virtue?

First, we can take our eyes off the world and focus them on God. The world says that you have to be beautiful and successful to be worthy—but God says we are worthy because He created us and He loves us. The world makes a big deal out of scandals and bad news. God has given us the good news of Jesus Christ through the scandal of the cross.

Second, we can resolve to put our confidence in Christ, because He is trustworthy. His Word says all the promises of God are "yes" in Christ Jesus. He will never leave or forsake us, and since He lives in our hearts, He will give us the peace and contentment we need to follow Him. We can take our requests to God, knowing that He hears us and approves them because of Jesus Christ. What freedom there is in that!

So when you wonder why in the world God placed you here, remember: We can approach His throne with confidence, finding all we'll ever need to live—and thrive.

Lord, help me to remember that Your arms are open wide, and I need only to walk into them.

How About Some Fun?

*A twinkle in the eye means joy in the heart,
and good news makes you feel fit as a fiddle.*
Proverbs 15:30 msg

"Have you had any fun this week?"

This query, in and of itself, might sound odd, but two friends agreed to ask each other this question periodically because both had the tendency to plow through an entire week of school, work, church, and community commitments forgetting—or neglecting—to plan an activity or two for the sole purpose of recharging their own burnt-out batteries. Both women realized they would have to make an effort to carve out time for activities that brought them joy. For one, it was kayaking and hiking; for the other, it was settling into her favorite reading chair with a mystery novel.

God does not want His kids to be worn out and stressed out. He did not design us to be like little Energizer Bunnies that keep on going and going and going. We need time to *recreate*—to revive and refresh our bodies and minds. A little relaxation, recreation—and yes—*fun* are essential components of a balanced life. Even Jesus and His disciples found it necessary to get away from the crowds and pressures of ministry to rest.

There's a lot of fun to be had out there—playing tennis or golf, jogging, swimming, painting, knitting, playing a musical instrument, visiting an art gallery, playing a board game, or going to a movie, a play, or a football game. Have you had any fun this week?

*Lord, You are the One who gives balance to my life.
Help me to find time today for a little relaxation,
recreation, and even fun. Amen.*

Babes in Christ

Therefore, putting aside all malice and all guile and hypocrisy and envy and all slander, like newborn babes, long for the pure milk of the word, that by it you may grow in respect to salvation, if you have tasted the kindness of the Lord.
1 PETER 2:1–3

When you have a new baby, you're starting with a clean slate. And although babies have inherited Adam's bent toward sinning, they haven't as yet exercised this "family affliction."

If we grow physically but ignore our spiritual needs, the potential for becoming a well-rounded human being is severely diminished, if not permanently stunted. This is the issue that Peter addresses in this passage.

As mothers, grandmothers, stepmothers, and aunts, we have a God-ordained call to teach children the Word of God that they might someday enter the kingdom of God. Jesus said: " 'Whoever causes one of these little ones who believe in Me to stumble, it is better for him that a heavy millstone be hung around his neck, and that he be drowned in the depth of the sea' " (Matthew 18:6).

That's pretty strong language. But look at the stakes! A child's whole life can be altered by someone who turns them away purposely from the truth of Jesus Christ.

Lord, lead me to spiritual growth, as I read " 'every word that proceeds out of the mouth of God' " (Matthew 4:4).

Inside Out

"Don't you understand either?" he asked.
"Can't you see that the food you put into your body cannot defile you?
. . . It is what comes from inside that defiles you."
MARK 7:18, 20 NLT

People have generally focused on keeping the outside clean. The Jews of Jesus' day made sure they washed the same hand first each time. In keeping with the law, they refused to eat certain foods, declaring them "unclean."

We act in much the same way today. Some foods turn our stomach and become "unclean" to us. Americans consider daily baths the norm.

If only we exercised the same care in keeping our *minds* clean. Jesus listed some of the unclean things that flow from our minds: lust, pride, envy, and slander, among others. Unfortunately, once we have allowed images or thoughts into our minds, we can't "scrub" them away the way soap washes away dirt.

Safeguarding our thought-life starts with what we allow into our minds. As much as possible, we should "see no evil" and "hear no evil." Music, television, movies, books, even our friendships must be filtered.

We can't erase bad thoughts from our minds, but we can crowd them out—by filling our minds with noble, lovely, and true thoughts. "How can a [single mom] stay pure? By obeying your word" (Psalm 119:9 NLT).

The blood of Christ cleanses us and the Bible helps to keep us clean.

Lord, search my thoughts, and show me my impurities.
Fill me with Your Word.

Pace Your Race

Let us strip off every weight that slows us down, especially the sin that so easily trips us up. And let us run with endurance the race God has set before us.
HEBREWS 12:1 NLT

Nervously, the young woman approached the starting line. It was her first footrace since she began jogging a few months before. At the sound of the gun, she bolted forward in stride with the advanced runners. And then it hit: exhaustion. Shuffling and gasping for breath, she realized she had not paced herself.

The apostle Paul likened our spiritual journey to an endurance run. The race begins with faith in Christ. As we allow God to lift the weight of sin, we become swifter and more efficient with each step.

Often, though, we fight to stay ahead of those who appear more "spiritually mature" than we are. Meanwhile, God desires to train us at a pace developed exclusively for us.

Those who train at their own level of ability and maintain realistic expectations are the true winners. The key to finishing the course takes a balance of patience, perseverance, and an unfaltering dependence on our heavenly trainer. God promises an eternal prize for those who persevere, at their own pace, to the end.

So run the race at your own pace!

Heavenly Father, help me to run this spiritual race balanced with patience, perseverance, and faith. I rely on You to strengthen me on the road of life toward my heavenly reward. Amen.

Desires

The eyes of all look to you, and you give them their food at the proper time. You open your hand and satisfy the desires of every living thing.
PSALM 145:15–16 NIV

Anita pulled into her driveway to be greeted by her two dogs, standing side by side and staring into the driver's side window. The young black mutt's tail frantically wagging and the old yellow Lab's slower wag showed their excitement for their mistress. When Anita stepped out of the car, the two pets knew that within minutes food would be in their bowls.

The dogs' eager and trusting faces made Anita consider her own trust in God. He made every creature. He designed their appetites and their tastes. He provides in the earth all that is needed for their fulfillment. Will He not satisfy them?

We can give to God every desire of our heart, every longing, and every appetite. He can satisfy them. Prayer is the link. Start by telling Him what you long for and what you desire. As you commune with Him, you will find your desires are either fulfilled or they begin to change to the blessings He wants to give you.

Lord, help me to be open and honest before You with all my yearnings. Enable me to trust You to fulfill or change the desires of my heart.

Stand Firm and Receive the Crown

Therefore, my beloved brethren whom I long to see, my joy and crown, so stand firm in the Lord, my beloved. I urge Euodia and I urge Syntyche to live in harmony in the Lord.
PHILIPPIANS 4:1–2

Church committee meetings can either be a blessing or a bear, depending, of course, upon whether the members are working together for a common goal. Evidently, two of the church women at Philippi, Euodia and Syntyche, were less than harmonious. Therefore, Paul admonished them.

It is significant that Paul took the time to address this issue. Left unchecked, such arguing would wreak havoc in the church. Perhaps you have encountered someone who, although she professes belief in Christ, has treated you without charity or love. Fast, pray for guidance, and then go to her and pray again. Failure to do so gives Satan an opportunity to get a foothold within the church, as the argument escalates and people choose sides.

Speaking like a proud father, Paul refers to these believers at Philippi as his "joy and crown." He brought the Gospel message to them. And then he stood back to watch them grow in their faith. He doesn't want it all to turn to ashes.

Lord, help me to remember that You surrendered all Your rights that I might know true freedom. Please show me how to persevere, make amends, and live in harmony.

Stand in the Gap

"I looked for a man among them who would build up the wall and stand before me in the gap on behalf of the land so I would not have to destroy it, but I found none."
EZEKIEL 22:30 NIV

Each prayer request you offer up to God is important to you, and when you ask others to pray, you're counting on them to help carry you through the tough times.

Do you give the same consideration to those who ask you for prayer? It's easy in the busyness of life to overlook a request someone else has made. Maybe you don't know the person very well or you don't really have an understanding of what he or she is going through. Perhaps the request came in an e-mail that you quickly glanced at and then deleted. Yet even with e-mailed prayer requests, others trust you to stand in the gap for them during difficult times in their lives.

Don't delay. Take time right when you receive a request to talk to the Lord on the requester's behalf. Be the bridge that carries that person through the valley of darkness back to the mountaintop of joy.

Heavenly Father, help me to have a heart of compassion for those I know and even for those I don't know who need Your comfort and love. Help me never to be too busy to pray for them. Amen.

The Lesson of the Luggage

"Bring the whole tithe into the storehouse, so that there may be food in My house, and test Me now in this," says the Lord of hosts, "if I will not open for you the windows of heaven and pour out for you a blessing until it overflows."
Malachi 3:10 NASB

Even though finances would be tight, Sharon finally decided to give her tithe to the church, beginning the first of the month. A few days preceding the first, she visited the mall and noticed a set of luggage at 25 percent off. The luggage was perfect for her business trips. The price was exactly the amount that she would be tithing. *Perhaps I can wait one more month.*

She picked up the luggage and carried it to the cashier. As Sharon waited in line, she envisioned herself at the airport looking savvy. Finally, no more embarrassment with tattered luggage. However, as the line shortened, she remembered her promise. With a pang of guilt, she stepped out of line and returned the luggage to the shelf.

On Sunday Sharon placed her tithe in the offering plate. It felt good to be obedient to the Lord. Nevertheless, she still dreaded using her old luggage on business trips.

Driving home Sharon spotted a garage sale. Out of curiosity, she pulled over. She couldn't believe her eyes. There was a set of luggage almost identical to what she had seen at the mall.

"How much are you asking for that luggage?" she queried.

"For you, five dollars," came the reply.

Lord, help me to faithfully tithe and never to doubt Your abundant provision. Amen.

Ladies in Waiting

I will wait for the Lord. . . . I will put my trust in him.
Isaiah 8:17 niv

Modern humans aren't good at waiting. In our fast-paced society, if you can't keep up, you'd better get out of the way. We have fast food, speed dialing, and jam-packed schedules that are impossible to keep. Instant gratification is the name of the game—and that attitude can creep into our lives as Christians.

The Lord Jesus Christ doesn't care about instant gratification. Our right-now attitudes don't move Him. Maybe He finds the saying, "Give me patience, Lord, *right now*," humorous—but He rarely answers that particular prayer.

Do we want joy without accepting heartache? Peace without living through the stress? Patience without facing demands? God sees things differently. He's giving us the opportunity to learn through these delays, irritations, and struggles. What a wise God He is!

Like Isaiah, we need to learn the art of waiting on God. He will come through every time—but in *His* time, not ours. The wait may be hours or days, or it could be years. But God is always faithful to provide for us. It is when we learn to wait on Him that we will find joy, peace, and patience through the struggle.

Father, You know what I need, so I will wait.
Help me be patient, knowing that You
control my situation and that all good
things come in Your time.

God's Precious Promises

His divine power has granted to us everything pertaining to life and godliness, through the true knowledge of Him who called us by His own glory and excellence. For by these He has granted to us His precious and magnificent promises, in order that by them you might become partakers of the divine nature, having escaped the corruption that is in the world by lust.

2 PETER 1:3–5

From the moment a baby is conceived it has everything it needs to grow into a complete human being, everything except time. For time acts as a refiner. Our spiritual growth is the same. From the moment we accept Christ, He infuses His Spirit within us, giving us right standing with the Father and making us a child of God. "He made Him who knew no sin to be sin on our behalf, that we might become the righteousness of God in Him" (2 Corinthians 5:21). As we walk in step with Him, learning His ways, we will eventually reflect these changes in our character.

Peter reminds us that Jesus Christ is the Savior. "Therefore, brethren, be all the more diligent to make certain about His calling and choosing you; for as long as you practice these things, you will never stumble; for in this way the entrance into the eternal kingdom of our Lord and Savior Jesus Christ will be abundantly supplied to you" (2 Peter 1:10–11).

*God, You promised me a Savior
and You sent Jesus. Hallelujah!*

A Godly Guest List

"But when you give a banquet, invite the poor, the crippled, the lame, the blind, and you will be blessed. Although they cannot repay you, you will be repaid at the resurrection of the righteous."
LUKE 14:13–14 NIV

You may not host banquets, but what about barbeques? Dinner parties? Pizza and movie nights? Now we're talking.

It is tempting to carefully select a few people to invite to a dinner party. You know the routine—a close girlfriend, a guy she thinks is attractive, a guy you are interested in, and then a couple of "fillers" just so that the plot is not obvious.

The Bible admonishes us to get more creative with our guest lists. You may read the words *crippled* and *lame* and think they sound like old-fashioned Bible words. In actuality, there are those all around us with physical limitations. Their eyes, ears, or legs that don't work properly do not make them any different on the inside.

Expanding our guest lists requires us to consider others, not just ourselves. Reaching out to someone who looks or seems a bit different from you will feel good. Likely you will notice that you have more in common than you'd imagined.

There is certainly reward in heaven for believers who demonstrate this type of kindness. The reward on earth is sweet as well. It may provide you with an unexpected new friend.

Father, remind me to reach out to others and to be a friend to all types of people. Amen.

When I Think of the Heavens

When I consider your heavens, the work of your fingers, the moon and the stars, which you have set in place, what is man, that you are mindful of him, the son of man that you care for him?
PSALM 8:3–4 NIV

Do you ever spend time thinking about the vastness of God? His greatness? His majesty? When you ponder His creation—the heavens, the moon, and the stars—do you feel tiny in comparison? Do you wonder how, in the midst of such greatness, He even remembers your name, let alone the details of your life or the problems you go through?

Daughter of God, you are important to your heavenly Father, more important than the sun, the moon, and the stars. You are created in the image of God, and He cares for you. In fact, He cares so much that He sent His Son, Jesus, to offer His life as a sacrifice for your sins.

The next time you look up at the heavens, the next time you *ooh* and *aah* over a majestic mountain or emerald waves crashing against the shoreline, remember that those things, in all of their splendor, don't even come close to you—God's greatest creation.

Oh Father, when I look at everything You have created, I'm so overwhelmed with who You are. Who am I that You would think twice about me? And yet You do. You love me, and for that I'm eternally grateful!

Sharpening Friendships

Iron sharpeneth iron; so a man sharpeneth the countenance of his friend.
Proverbs 27:17 KJV

One of the first casualties of a busy life is friendship.

Often we don't even realize it is missing, because the more activities we have, the more people surround us. Yet because we are in a hurry, we don't form real friendships with most of these people.

We all have a need for close friendships. We need others in our lives who will challenge us to make us sharper, bolder, gentler, and more Christlike.

For married women, husbands provide much of this needed intimacy. But no man can meet every need for female interpersonal communication; women need women.

Some may think that a sharpening friendship is characterized by leisurely conversation and prayer over a cup of tea. And sometimes this does happen. But the greater honing comes when abrasives are applied. Days spent helping a needy friend or nights spent beside the bed of a dying one develop patience, strength, and courage.

Friendships like these take time. It's beneficial for our health and countenance—and those of our friends—to make that time.

Dear Jesus, I know You are a friend who sticks closer than a sister, yet sometimes I need the comfort of friends I can see and touch. Help me to say no to extra activities so I have time to invest in friends. Amen.

Hold to God's Truth, Not to Visions

You have died and your life is hidden with Christ in God. When Christ, who is our life, is revealed, then you also will be revealed with Him in glory. Therefore consider the members of your earthly body as dead to immorality, impurity, passion, evil desire, and greed, which amounts to idolatry. For it is on account of these things that the wrath of God will come, and in them you also once walked, when you were living in them.
Colossians 3:3–7

Some Christian testimonies really stir your heart. Some are from individuals who have turned from lives of debauchery and waste to become true seekers of God.

Our churches are comprised of redeemed sinners. "For all have sinned and fall short of the glory of God, being justified as a gift by His grace through the redemption which is in Christ Jesus; whom God displayed publicly as a propitiation in His blood through faith" (Romans 3:23–25).

Paul's message is that Christ in us should cause a change in our lives. For we have been delivered from the "wrath of God." This metamorphosis should make a visible difference in how we are living our lives. For Christ has set up residence within us.

There cannot be any detours or distractions from the truth. "Let no one keep defrauding you of your prize by delighting in self-abasement and the worship of the angels" (Colossians 2:18).

Let me be cautious of bypassing the Word of God and the Spirit of God to substitute visions of angels for the Gospel.

Perfect Prayers

Pray, therefore, like this: Our Father. . .
Out of the depths have I cried to You, O Lord.
Matthew 6:9 amp; Psalm 130:1 amp

How many messages have you heard on prayer? Have you ever come away thinking, *Did you hear how eloquently they prayed? How spiritual they sounded? No wonder God answers their prayers!*

Sometimes we take the straightforward and uncomplicated idea of prayer—the simple give-and-take of talking with God—and turn it into something hard. How many times have we made it a mere religious exercise, performed best by the "holy elite," rather than what it really is—conversation with God our Father.

Just pour out your heart to God. Share how your day went. Tell Him your dreams. Ask Him to search you and reveal areas of compromise. Thank Him for your lunch. Plead for your family and friends' wellbeing. Complain about your car. . . . Just talk with Him. Don't worry how impressive (or unimpressive!) you sound.

Talk with God while doing dishes, driving the car, folding laundry, eating lunch, or kneeling by your bed. Whenever, wherever, whatever—tell Him. He cares!

Don't allow this day to slip away without talking to your Father. No perfection required.

Father God, what a privilege it is to unburden my heart to You. Teach me the beauty and simplicity of simply sharing my day with You.

The Dream-Maker

"No eye has seen, no ear has heard, no mind has conceived what God has prepared for those who love him."
1 CORINTHIANS 2:9 NIV

Dreams, goals, and expectations are part of our daily lives. We have an idea of what we want and how we're going to achieve it. Disappointment can raise its ugly head when what we wanted—what we expected—doesn't happen like we thought it should or doesn't happen as fast as we planned.

Disappointment can lead to doubt. Perhaps questions tempt you to doubt the direction you felt God urging you to pursue. Don't quit! Don't give up! Press on with your dream. Failure isn't failure until you quit. When it looks like it's over, stand strong. With God's assistance, there is another way, a higher plan, or a better time to achieve your dream.

God knows the dreams He has placed inside of you. He created you and knows what you can do—even better than you know yourself. Maintain your focus—not on the dream but on the Dream Maker—and together you will achieve your dream.

God, thank You for putting dreams in my heart. I refuse to quit. I'm looking to You to show me how to reach my dreams. Amen.

Ethnic Barriers

There is no distinction between Greek and Jew, circumcised and uncircumcised, barbarian, Scythian, slave and freeman, but Christ is all, and in all. And so, as those who have been chosen of God, holy and beloved, put on a heart of compassion, kindness, humility, gentleness and patience; bearing with one another; just as the Lord forgave you, so also should you.
Colossians 3:11–13

To say we love Christ and yet maintain deeply rooted prejudices against others is inconsistent with everything He taught. For Christ came to reconcile all peoples to Himself, not separate us into factions.

Above all, God wants us to be harmonious in worship of Him and also in working with Him. "Now may the God who gives perseverance and encouragement grant you to be of the same mind with one another according to Christ Jesus; that with one accord you may with one voice glorify the God and Father of our Lord Jesus Christ. Wherefore, accept one another, just as Christ also accepted us to the glory of God" (Romans 15:5–7).

Lord, let the true peace of Christmas, which is Christ, be found in my heart as I am obedient to Your command to love one another, just as You have loved me (John 13:34).

A Heavenly Party

"I tell you that in the same way there will be more rejoicing in heaven over one sinner who repents than over ninety-nine righteous persons who do not need to repent."
Luke 15:7 NIV

God is a major party animal. Want proof? He throws the biggest bash in all of creation every time a baby Christian is born into His family. Can't you just imagine it? Angels and saints join together at the foot of the throne in sheer praise and celebration over one more soul saved for all eternity!

The Father threw your very own party on the moment you accepted His Son as your Savior. Did you experience a taste of that party from the response of your spiritual mentors here on earth? As Christians, we should celebrate with our new brothers and sisters in Christ every chance we get.

If you haven't yet taken that step in your faith, don't wait! Heaven's party planners are eager to get your celebration started.

Father, I am so grateful that You rejoice in new Christians. Strengthen my desire to reach the lost while I am here on earth. Then, when I reach heaven, the heavenly parties will be all the sweeter! Amen.

Thin Entering Wedge

Joyful are those who obey his laws and search for him with all their hearts. They do not compromise with evil, and they walk only in his paths.
Psalm 119:2–3 NLT

It started out small. Every few months or so, Kara would go to the library and check out a couple romance novels. Occasionally a chapter would contain a steamy love scene, and she would just skip over those pages. One afternoon she read one in its entirety and was surprised at how much she enjoyed it. She began stopping by the library more often, and soon she was reading several novels a week. She'd long since stopped skimming through the steamy scenes. The steamier the better. She would often stay up all night on the weekends to finish her latest reads.

One Sunday morning Kara woke up late again and was shocked when she realized that it had been two or three months since she'd been to church, and even longer since she'd picked up a Bible. It happened so gradually. . .she couldn't believe this was where she was.

Most people don't set out to become addicted to romance novels, rack up thousands in credit card debt, or get caught in a cycle of unfulfilling relationships. These things generally happen gradually—often with one compromise at a time. This is why we must continually be on guard against making small compromises. Many small compromises can lead to devastation. Be on guard and live wisely.

Father, help me to stay connected to You regularly. Help me to stay on the wise path and to guard myself against compromise. Amen.

Tuesday
November 26

Choosing Wisely

Our mouths were filled with laughter.
Psalm 126:2 niv

Amanda stared glumly at the rock-hard turkey parked on the kitchen counter. She'd miscalculated defrosting time; it was now Thanksgiving morning, and the entrée of honor was still obstinately ossified.

The twenty-two-pound bird was too large for the micro-wave, so she tried the blow dryer. Warm air only deflected into her face from the turkey's impenetrable skin. Dunking the bird in a warm bathtub merely cooled the water down, leaving dinner's main course as nonpliable as a cement block.

In a rush of frantic desperation, Amanda grabbed the tool-box from the garage and whacked the turkey with a hammer. It only jarred her budding headache into full bloom.

Dinner was at noon. Guests would soon be arriving. What to do?

We women often plan perfect family events, only to find out how imperfectly things can turn out. The soufflé falls, the cat leaps onto the counter and licks the cheese ball, little Johnny drops Aunt Martha's crystal gravy dish (full of gravy, of course). Our reactions to these surprise glitches can make or break the event for everyone present. Mom's foul mood sucks the joy from the room.

The Bible says that Sarah laughed at the most unexpected, traumatic time of her life—when God announced that she would have a baby at the age of ninety (Genesis 18:12). At this unforeseen turn of events, she could either laugh, cry, or run away screaming.

She chose to laugh.

Lord, give us an extra dollop of grace and peace to laugh about unexpected dilemmas that pop up. And to remember that our reaction is a choice. Amen.

The Father Has Bestowed a Great Love

See how great a love the Father has bestowed upon us, that we should be called children of God; and such we are. For this reason the world does not know us, because it did not know Him. Beloved, now we are children of God, and it has not appeared as yet what we shall be. We know that, when He appears, we shall be like Him, because we shall see Him just as He is. And every one who has this hope fixed on Him purifies himself, just as He is pure.

1 JOHN 3:1–3

Have you ever looked into the mirror and thought, *I wish I had a new body?* Well, Christ has one reserved for you in heaven. This body is imperishable, undefiled, and will not fade away (1 Peter 1:3–4).

While we don't know when Jesus is coming again, we do know that our new bodies will coincide with this event. "When Christ, who is our life, is revealed, then you also will be revealed with Him in glory" (Colossians 3:4).

Yet the gift of our new bodies is only one aspect of the Father's incredible love for His children. His love prompts His children to purify themselves just as He is pure (1 John 3:3). They also abide in Him and practice righteousness (1 John 3:6–7), for they have been born of God (1 John 3:9; John 3:7).

Lord, as I prepare to celebrate Your birth,
the greatest gift I can lay beside the manger
is an act of my will that makes me Your child.
Yes, I have been born again.

Available 24/7

I call on you, O God, for you will answer me;
give ear to me and hear my prayer.
PSALM 17:6 NIV

No one is available to take your call at this time, so leave a message and we will return your call—or not—if we feel like it. . .and only between the hours of 4:00 and 4:30 p.m. Thank you for calling. Have a super day!

We've all felt the frustration of that black hole called voice mail. It is rare to reach a real, honest-to-goodness, breathing human being the first time we dial a telephone number.

Fortunately, our God is always available. He can be reached at any hour of the day or night and every day of the year—including weekends and holidays! When we pray, we don't have to worry about disconnections, hang-ups, or poor reception. We will never be put on hold or our prayers diverted to another department. The Bible assures us that God is eager to hear our petitions and that He welcomes our prayers of thanksgiving. The psalmist David wrote of God's response to those who put their trust in Him: "He will call upon me, and I will answer him" (Psalm 91:15 NIV). David had great confidence that God would hear his prayers. And we can, too!

Dear Lord, thank You for always being there for me. Whether I am on a mountaintop and just want to praise Your name or I am in need of Your comfort and encouragement, I can count on You. Amen.

Amnon and Tamar

And Tamar lived in her brother Absalom's house, a desolate woman.
2 SAMUEL 13:20 NIV

Second Samuel 13 tells the tragic story of Amnon and Tamar. Amnon, one of King David's sons, raped his half sister, Tamar. Verse 18 says that Tamar dressed appropriately as a virgin daughter of the king. But after she was raped, Tamar exchanged her beautiful robe for the ashes of mourning.

Absalom, Tamar's other brother, was kind to her and took her into his home. Although she lived with him, scripture says that Absalom never said a word about her pain. The last time we read of Tamar is in 2 Samuel 13:20, "And Tamar lived in her brother Absalom's house, a desolate woman." Unfortunately, because of the culture of the time, Tamar would no longer be considered marriageable. The stigma of rape would remain with her, and this one event would shape the rest of Tamar's life.

Many women today also have been victimized. After experiencing pain and victimization, they, like Tamar, live desolate lives, allowing the experience to define them and determine their future. This does not have to be. Unlike Tamar, women today have choices.

No matter how dark your circumstances, God can redeem them. He can weave your pain into the tapestry of your life and provide hope, help, and healing. You can begin by speaking of the pain, then refusing to carry it. Open your heart to God today and receive the gift of healing.

Father, thank You for offering me hope and healing. Help me to let go of the pain of my past so that it does not define me. Redeem it for Your glory. Amen.

Treasure Vault

"For where your treasure is, there your heart will be also."
Luke 12:34 niv

Where is your greatest treasure? Do you own something so valuable it sits in a safe-deposit box in your bank? Maybe you take it out once in a while then return it for safekeeping.

If that's really your life's greatest treasure, you're in trouble, for according to this verse, your heart is locked up in a narrow, dark safe-deposit box, where it's awfully difficult to love others and enjoy the world God has given you.

Maybe you don't own that kind of valuable, but you're inordinately proud of the vehicle you drive. Would you really want your heart to sit out in all weather, where it could eventually rust away? Even the best care will never make a car last forever. Hide it in a garage, but it still has a limited life.

But when your best treasure is your relationship with Christ and His eternal reward, you don't have to worry about where your heart is. It's safe with Jesus, free to love others, and valuable to both you and the people with whom you share Christ.

Are you gathering earthly treasures or eternal ones? Those on earth won't last. Sending treasures before you to heaven is the wisest thing you can do. Worldly goods fade, but not those in Jesus' treasure vaults.

Lord, help me send treasures ahead of me into eternity instead of grabbing all the earthly items I can get. Amen.

Christmas Joy

And we have seen and bear witness and proclaim to you the eternal life, which was with the Father and was manifested to us—what we have seen and heard we proclaim to you also, that you also may have fellowship with us; and indeed our fellowship is with the Father, and with His Son Jesus Christ.

1 JOHN 1:2–3

The countdown to Christmas has begun. Are your cards in the mail yet? What message have you extended to friends and family? Illustrations of cats in floppy red Santa caps or snowy winter scenes cannot effect a change in the lives of those who do not know the Christ of Christmas. For only the Word of God has the power to reach into searching hearts and bring hope.

Where will you find joy this Christmas? It's not in brightly colored packages under the tree. And unless your loved ones know the Lord, jubilation probably won't be present at your family gatherings either. For we cannot partake of this commodity apart from Christ.

Consider today what printed message you will send to loved ones this Christmas. . .a message of hope about Christ the Savior, or a scene in which He is nowhere to be found?

Dear Lord, thank You for the knowledge that Jesus is still the "reason for the season."

The Reason for Job's Suffering

Job. . .was blameless, upright, fearing God, and turning away from evil. And seven sons and three daughters were born to him. His possessions also were 7,000 sheep, 3,000 camels, 500 yoke of oxen, 500 female donkeys, and very many servants.
JOB 1:1–3

This, of course, was life as Job used to know it, before his character was tested. "And the LORD said to Satan, 'Have you considered My servant Job? For there is no one like him on the earth, a blameless and upright man, fearing God and turning away from evil.' Then Satan answered the LORD, 'Does Job fear God for nothing? Hast Thou not made a hedge about him and his house. . .and all his possessions have increased in the land. But put forth Thy hand now and touch all that he has; he will surely curse Thee to Thy face' " (Job 1:8–11).

Satan intimated to God that Job only loved Him because of all the blessings Job had received. "Then the LORD said to Satan, 'Behold, all that he has is in your power, only do not put forth your hand on him' " (Job 1:12).

Job's life became an unwelcome ride on a trolley called tragedy. In one day he lost all his children and his house, servants, and livestock. And through all of this Job refused to blame God or sin.

Lord, as a Christian, lead me so that I do not expect You to be my "celestial Santa Claus." Lead me so I continue to follow, no matter the circumstances.

Password, Please

And if we are [His] children, then we are [His] heirs also: heirs of God and fellow heirs with Christ [sharing His inheritance with Him].
Romans 8:17 amp

Passwords are required everywhere, it seems: ATM machines, computer settings, bill paying. Passwords identify the user. They are intended to keep others out of our business. We're urged to change them frequently to protect our identity.

Christians have but one password: *Jesus.* Once we acquire this password through salvation, we become heirs of God with Him. We're children of the king. Precious saints. The Father gives us His own name to set us apart from the world.

Unlike computer or ATM passwords, this special name can never be compromised. We are safe and secure in the Father's arms, able to access every gift promised. Read the scriptures to see all that is available to you as a believer: eternal life, provision, promise after promise, blessing upon blessing.

Do you have your password, ready to swing open the gates of heaven? It's *Jesus.* Jesus, *period*. No other name is needed, no other combination.

You can take that to the bank.

Dear heavenly Father, today I choose to follow You. I give You my life, my all. Teach me Your ways and guard my heart.

Ordinary Transformed

Now when the Sabbath was past, Mary Magdalene, Mary the mother of James, and Salome bought spices, that they might come and anoint Him.
MARK 16:1 NKJV

Mary Magdalene, Mary the mother of James, and Salome bought burial spices and headed to Jesus' tomb to perform an ordinary task after the death of a loved one. In their darkest hour, as they grieved, they went about doing the job at hand. What a surprise they had in store when they got to the tomb and found that Jesus had risen from the dead!

A sleepless woman got up from bed, her mind troubled with a problem. Wandering around her house, she saw a stack of wrinkled clothes on the ironing board, a tiresome task she had left unfinished. As she prayed and asked for God's help, she remembered a phrase she'd heard on the radio earlier that day: "Do the next thing." In the middle of the night, with a heart heavy with care, she began the repetitive chore. Pressing shirt after shirt, her head cleared and she found a solution to her problem. Soon her ironing was finished and she went to bed.

That night the sleepless woman learned what Christian monks have known for centuries: There is spiritual value in the monotonous tasks essential to our lives. Often, it's in these times that we are surprised by the Lord, just as the women at His tomb were. As we engage our bodies in work, our minds are free to feel His presence and sense His leading.

Lord, help me to look and listen for You during the ordinary moments of my daily work.

He Is Coming with the Clouds

Behold, He is coming with the clouds, and every eye will see Him, even those who pierced Him; and all the tribes of the earth will mourn over Him. Even so. Amen.
REVELATION 1:7

Cecil B. DeMille was known for his extravagant movie productions. Who can forget his version of Moses parting the Red Sea? However, the appearance of Christ in the clouds will surpass every event that has ever taken place on earth. This future event will be a worldwide phenomenon in which every eye will see Him. And the hearts of those who refused to examine the evidence and refused to know Him will ache with the agonizing pain of conviction that it's simply too late. The purpose for His appearance this time will be to judge the world of its greatest sin, the rejection of His great gift of salvation.

Those who are "unprepared" for this global happening will be in shock! "For the Lord Himself will descend from heaven with a shout, with the voice of the archangel, and with the trumpet of God; and the dead in Christ shall rise first. Then we who are alive and remain shall be caught up together with them in the clouds to meet the Lord in the air, and thus we shall always be with the Lord" (1 Thessalonians 4:16–17). It doesn't get any better than this!

Father, when humans have failed me I tend to blame You for their choices. Please break down the barriers in my heart that I might worship Your Son this Christmas.

Late-Night Counseling

*I will praise the Lord, who counsels me;
even at night my heart instructs me.*
Psalm 16:7 NIV

For us women, the nighttime hours are often difficult. When the chaos of the day settles down and our head hits the pillow, we're free to think. . .about everything. Problems. Relationship issues. Job concerns. Decisions. The "what ifs." The "I should haves." Sometimes our thoughts wander for hours. We toss and turn, and sleep won't come.

If you're like this, if you find nighttime difficult, then it's time for a change of thinking. Instead of looking at the night as problematic, look at it as your one-on-one time with the Lord. He longs to meet you in the wee hours of the night. He wants to chase away any unnecessary worries and give you everything you need to sleep like a baby.

How encouraging to know that God longs to counsel us—to advise. And He's fully aware that nighttime is hard. So, instead of fretting when you climb into bed, spend that time with Him. Use the nighttime as your special time with God. Meet with Him and expect to receive His counsel.

Lord, nighttimes are hard sometimes. I want to trust You. I want to put my head on the pillow and fall fast asleep. But the cares of the day overwhelm me. Father, I trust Your counsel. Speak to me in the night. Instruct my heart.

Grace versus the Law

I am amazed that you are so quickly deserting Him who called you by the grace of Christ, for a different gospel; which is really not another; only there are some who are disturbing you, and want to distort the gospel of Christ.
GALATIANS 1:6–7

Christmas will be here before we know it. Perhaps there will be a big red package under the tree for you, perhaps a brand-new bathrobe? Doesn't your family know how comforting and warm your old robe is? Are they trying to rip away this "nucleus of your solace"? No, they just want to replace one that is threadbare, faded, and otherwise tacky with a better-looking model.

Jewish believers were transitioning from the Law, filled with regulations, and beginning to follow the Gospel of grace. However, they easily fell into the trap of "desiring their old robes back." A group called the Judaizers began wooing them back to the old covenant rites, including circumcision.

Therefore, Paul, God's apostle to the Gentiles, left on his missionary journeys to bring the Gospel of grace to those who were being seduced by this group.

Paul, teacher of the Law, now speaks to them of his own conversion. "The gospel which was preached by me is not according to man. For I neither received it from man, nor was I taught it, but I received it through a revelation of Jesus Christ" (Galatians 1:11–12).

Paul played a central role in the "persecution of the church of God beyond measure." But seeing Christ, face-to-face, reduced him to heartfelt repentance. Lord, strengthen my own commitment to You.

Creation's Praise

For you created my inmost being;
you knit me together in my mother's womb.
PSALM 139:13 NIV

God didn't spend seven days creating things and then put His creation abilities on the shelf. He is continually creating wonderful things for His people. He created each of us with a special design in mind. Nothing about us is hidden from Him—the good parts or the bad.

Before you had a thought or moved a muscle, God was working out a plan for your existence. Maybe He gave you brown hair and a sweet smile or good genes for a long life, or He gave you dark hair and clever fingers that are artistic. Perhaps He gave you a musical voice that worships Him daily in song. Whatever His gifts, He designed them just for you, to bring ministry to His hurting world.

When we look at the seven days of Creation, let's thank God that He didn't set things working and then walk away. Adam and Eve were important to Him, but so are we. He has personally created everything in this wonderful world—including us.

Do we need any more reason to praise the Lord who brought into existence every fiber of our beings?

Thank You, Lord, for detailing every piece of my body, mind, and spirit. I'm glad nothing that happens to me or in me is a surprise to You. Help me use all Your gifts to Your glory. Amen.

Take Five

The LORD God formed man of the dust of the ground, and breathed into his nostrils the breath of life.
GENESIS 2:7 NKJV

How would you describe your physical and mental state today? Are you rested and refreshed, or do you feel weary, worn down by the unrelenting demands and pressures of doing life? We tend to think that the longer and harder we work, the more productive we will be. But when we become fatigued spiritually and emotionally, we eventually reach a point of exhaustion.

You *are* in control and you *can* stop the world from spinning. Even if you know that it is impossible to take a day off, it helps tremendously to make time for a personal "time-out."

Pause from whatever you are doing for just a few moments and breathe deeply. Shut your office door, close your eyes, or pause for a second or two in the bathroom. Ask God for a sense of calm and clarity of mind to deal properly with your next assignment. Take time to unwind from a stressful day by a few minutes of "me time" in the car as you drive home. If your commute is short, pull over for a few minutes and let the weight of the day fall off.

Sometimes the most active thing we can do is rest, even if for only a short time.

Father, help me not to push myself so hard. Help me to remember to take five and breathe. Amen.

Smiles Bring Joy

A cheerful look brings joy to the heart,
and good news gives health to the bones.
Proverbs 15:30 niv

The teenage girl nervously walked backstage. It was her turn next. She had practiced for hours. This song was perfect, her teacher had said. But the butterflies in her stomach were telling a different story. Fear began to grip her throat. She couldn't breathe. It was then that she saw her mother sitting in the front row. There she was, eyes sparkling, smiling that goofy smile, and proudly saying, "My daughter is next! She is so talented!" The young girl took a deep breath and closed her eyes. The fear melted and confidence took over. *I can do this,* she thought as she boldly walked onstage.

Smiles can say so many things in a quiet, gentle form. They can give comfort and support and bring joy and strength to someone who is weary. Courage and confidence are given by the love that smiles portray. They can simply remind a person that someone really does care. And more often than not, a smile is immediately returned to the giver.

Joy is contagious; spread it around. Smile at someone today. Go ahead and chuckle at that joke. Laugh with someone. Not only will you be blessing another, but also you will be blessed yourself.

Dear Lord, fill me with Your joy today that I may bless others with my smile and laughter and portray Your love to those around me. Amen.

God's Message to the Churches

*"But I have this against you,
that you have left your first love."*
Revelation 2:4

One of my favorite questions to ask couples over dinner is "How did you meet?" Each story invariably presents a set of impossible circumstances that had to be orchestrated in order to bring this man and woman together. As these details are relayed, a glow begins to come back into the eyes of those remembering. There is nothing to compare with that "first bloom of love."

This is the kind of love that God desires from us. That on-fire, totally consuming, single focus of our attention. His call to the church at Ephesus then was that they remember their first love—and rekindle their purpose to seek Him first.

His message, however, to the church at Smyrna was very different. " 'I know your tribulation and your poverty (but you are rich). Do not fear what you are about to suffer. . . . Be faithful until death, and I will give you the crown of life' " (Revelation 2:9–10).

Throughout history, God's church has suffered persecution. But here is a message of hope to all for whom cruelty is a constant companion: "Remain faithful. God's reward is at hand."

O Lord, may Your Light be the fire in my soul!

Jesus as Our Arbitrator

If only there were someone to arbitrate between us. . .
so that his terror would frighten me no more.
Job 9:33–34 NIV

Penny took her daily walk, trying to clear her thoughts. Her sister Susie had been diagnosed with stage 3 breast cancer. . .not a death sentence, but a serious and frightening diagnosis, nonetheless. Not only that, but Penny's job was in jeopardy, her parents had needs of their own, and Penny's car was in the shop—again. "I don't know how much more I can take," Penny said out loud. "God, help—if You're even listening!"

When our world caves in, it's tempting to blame God and push Him away. Though such a reaction is all-too-human, God longs for us to seek Him during times of struggle. We may never know this side of heaven why He allows certain things to happen, but we can be sure that He loves us and will never leave us.

As Job noted, God knew of our need for someone to bridge the gap between us and our perfect heavenly Father. So He sent Jesus to be our arbitrator and the perfect sacrifice for our sins. Because of His death, we don't have to fear God's wrath.

Today, instead of looking at your circumstances, lift your head and look to Jesus. He wants to spare you the terror you are experiencing. When you surrender your situation to Him, He will comfort you with His presence.

Lord, thank You for sending Jesus to be the bridge between us. Help me to turn to Him—and not run away—in times of fear and doubt.

Behave Yourself!

I will behave myself wisely in a perfect way. O when wilt thou come unto me? I will walk within my house with a perfect heart.
PSALM 101:2 KJV

Home is where the heart is.

Home is a refuge, a place of rest.

Home is the smell of fresh-baked bread, the sound of laughter, the squeeze of a hug.

Because home is a place of comfort and relaxation, it is also the place where we are most likely to misbehave. We would never think of yelling at family members in public, for example, but if one of them pushes our buttons *just once* at home, we will instantly level her or him with a verbal machine gun.

David himself knew the danger of walking unwisely at home. He was home—not in battle—when he saw Bathsheba on the rooftop. His psalm cited above reminds us that we must behave wisely all the time, but especially at home.

Because more is caught than taught, our family must see mature behavior from us. We must model integrity—we must keep our promises and act the way we want those around us to act. Hypocrisy—"Do as I say, not as I do"—has no place in the home of a mature Christian woman who has been made complete in Christ.

May God grow us up into mature women, and may we walk accordingly, especially at home.

Father God, how often I fail at home. Make me sensitive to the Spirit so that I will recognize when I am straying from the path of maturity. I'm the adult here; help me to act as one. Amen.

Anxiety Check!

Do not be anxious about anything, but in everything, by prayer and petition, with thanksgiving, present your requests to God.
Philippians 4:6 niv

Twenty-first-century women are always checking things. A bank balance. E-mail. Voice messages. The grocery list. And, of course, that never-ending to-do list. We routinely get our oil, tires, and brake fluid checked. And we wouldn't think of leaving home for the day without checking our appearance in the mirror. We even double-check our purses, making sure we have the essentials—lipstick, mascara, and the cell phone.

Yes, checking is a part of living, isn't it? We do it without even realizing it. Checking to make sure we've locked the door, turned off the stove, and unplugged the curling iron just comes naturally. So why do we forget some of the bigger checks in life? Take anxiety, for instance.

When was the last time you did an anxiety check? Days? Weeks? Months? Chances are, you're due for another. After all, we're instructed not to be anxious about anything. Instead, we're to present our requests to God with thanksgiving in our hearts. We're to turn to Him in prayer so that He can take our burdens. Once they've lifted, it's bye-bye anxiety!

Father, I get anxious sometimes. And I don't always remember to turn to You with my anxiety. In fact, I forget to check for anxiety at all. Today I hand my anxieties to You. Thank You that I can present my requests to You.

The Rainbow Surrounding Christ

Behold, a throne was standing in heaven, and One sitting on the throne. And He who was sitting was like a jasper stone and a sardius in appearance; and there was a rainbow around the throne, like an emerald in appearance.
REVELATION 4:2–3

God promised Noah that He would never again destroy the world by a flood. As a reminder, God set a rainbow in the clouds (Genesis 9:13–16). Now we see that there is also a rainbow in heaven, but it's not the half-bow we're used to seeing. This rainbow is a complete circle because in heaven all things are whole and finished. Yet the most amazing thing about this prism of color is that it surrounds Christ.

We know this because there He is "sitting on the throne," which is the posture of judgment, and He is being worshiped. " 'Holy, holy, holy, is the Lord God, the Almighty, who was and who is and who is to come' " (Revelation 4:8). In this passage Christ is referred to as the Creator. "And He is the image of the invisible God, the first-born of all creation. For in Him all things were created, both in the heavens and on earth, visible and invisible, whether thrones or dominions or rulers or authorities—all things have been created through Him and for Him. And He is before all things, and in Him all things hold together" (Colossians 1:15–17). Jesus Christ, God Almighty, who resides in heaven and sits on the throne of judgment, is surrounded by the rainbow.

Lord, thank You that the Babe of Christmas will one day judge the whole world.

Have You Been with Jesus?

Now when they saw the boldness of Peter and John, and perceived that they were uneducated and untrained men, they marveled. And they realized that they had been with Jesus.
ACTS 4:13 NKJV

A young woman grew up in the Deep South but attended college in another part of the country. With time, she began to lose her Southern drawl. When she returned to her hometown for extended visits, however, she found herself picking up the regional dialect again. Her friends would tease her, saying, "We can tell you've been down South again!" Words like *y'all* and phrases such as *fixin' to* made it apparent that she had spent time with her family. This didn't bother her, though. The woman was proud of her Southern roots.

In Acts we read that Peter and John healed a crippled man and, when questioned by the authorities, boldly responded that the healing had been done in Jesus' name. They went on to preach the gospel. Extraordinary courage was seen in these ordinary men. The rulers were astounded. They took note that Peter and John *had been with Jesus*.

When we meditate on scripture and seek the Lord in prayer regularly, we naturally become a little more like Him. Just as slow Southern speech points clearly to a particular region on the map, may our lives undeniably reflect that we have been with the Son of God.

Jesus, make me more like You today. Amen.

Healthy Habits

Since we have these promises, dear friends, let us purify ourselves from everything that contaminates body and spirit, perfecting holiness out of reverence for God.
2 Corinthians 7:1 niv

Tanya woke up Monday morning with a terrible headache. She washed down a couple aspirin with a cup of coffee, showered, and tried her best to go to work with a smile plastered on her face. By noon the pain lessened, and she grabbed a sandwich from the vending machine. By 2 p.m. she was ready to call it a day. Diet soda kept her going through the afternoon. Dinner was a frozen entrée, eaten over the sink. After some mindless television she fell into bed, but her sleep was restless. As she stared at the numbers on her digital clock glowing in the dark, she knew the next day would be no better than this one.

What Tanya doesn't realize, and what many fail to understand, is that the way we feel today is directly related to the habits we practiced yesterday. A weekend of staying up until all hours of the night and eating junk food will likely produce a Monday morning of misery. On the other hand, the investment of exercising, getting enough sleep, and eating properly reaps countless benefits in helping us be more productive, clearheaded, and energetic. God created our earthly bodies to be temples, and we only get one.

Father, thank You for my temple. Help me to care for it to the best of my ability and honor You with healthy habits. Amen.

Difficult People

Do not turn your freedom into an opportunity for the flesh,
but through love serve one another.
GALATIANS 5:13 NASB

In the classic movie *An Affair to Remember*, Deborah Kerr asks Cary Grant, "What makes life so difficult?" to which he responds, "People?"

Yes, people tend to make our lives difficult. But they also make life worth living. The trick is not to let the biting words or nefarious deeds of others become glaring giants that make us flee or weigh us down with hate and resentment.

The only way David stood up to the giant Goliath was by turning his problem over to the Lord and relying on His strength and power. Then, acting in faith, David prevailed with the weapons at hand—a slingshot and one smooth stone.

Sometimes, like David, we need to turn our skirmishes with others over to the Lord. Then, by using our weapons—God's Word and a steadfast faith—we need to love and forgive others as God loves and forgives us.

Always keep in mind that, although we may not like to admit it, we have all said and done some pretty awful things ourselves, making the lives of others difficult. Yet God has forgiven us *and* continues to love us.

So do the right thing. Pull your feet out of the mire of unforgiveness, sidestep verbal retaliation, and stand tall in the freedom of love and forgiveness.

The words and deeds of others have left me wounded and bleeding. Forgiveness and love seem to be the last thing on my mind. Change my heart, Lord. Help me to love and forgive others as You love and forgive me. Amen.

A Strong Heart

Whom have I in heaven but you? And earth has nothing I desire besides you. My flesh and my heart may fail, but God is the strength of my heart and my portion forever.
PSALM 73:25–26 NIV

Do you ever feel like you have a weak heart? Feel like you're not strong? You crater at every little thing? Do you face life's challenges with your emotions in turmoil instead of facing them head-on with courage and strength? If so, you're not alone. Twenty-first-century women are told they can "be it all" and "do it all," but it's not true. God never meant for us to be strong every moment of our lives. If we were, we wouldn't need Him.

Here's the good news: You don't have to be strong. In your weakness, God's strength shines through. And His strength surpasses anything you could produce, even on your best day. It's the same strength that spoke the heavens and the earth into existence. The same strength that parted the Red Sea. And it's the same strength that made the journey up the hill to the cross.

So how do you tap in to that strength? There's really only one way. Come into His presence. Spend some quiet time with Him. Acknowledge your weakness, then allow His strong arms to encompass you. There's really nothing else in heaven or on earth to compare. God is all you will ever need.

Father, I feel so weak at times. It's hard just to put one foot in front of the other. But I know You are my strength. Invigorate me with that strength today, Lord.

Renewing Our Minds

Present your bodies a living and holy sacrifice, acceptable to God, which is your spiritual service of worship. And do not be conformed to this world, but be transformed by the renewing of your mind, that you may prove what the will of God is, that which is good and acceptable and perfect.
ROMANS 12:1–2

Mary had lived an exemplary life and was betrothed to Joseph. Then an angel came with an announcement that would cast a shadow of doubt on her impeccable character. God had asked Mary to bear His Son.

Leaving the results of this decision in the hands of her powerful God, Mary accepted her role as the mother of the Messiah. And during the difficult days which followed, she allowed the Word of God to renew her mind. But was that enough to give her sufficient power to obey the Lord?

The apostle Paul answers this question for us. "For though we walk in the flesh, we do not war according to the flesh, for the weapons of our warfare are not of the flesh, but divinely powerful for the destruction of fortresses. We are destroying speculations and every lofty thing raised up against the knowledge of God, and we are taking every thought captive to the obedience of Christ" (2 Corinthians 10:3–5).

The weapons that God provides for us are spiritual. We must become proficient with such an arsenal before such can be effective. So, if the Lord says His Word is a weapon to be used against the enemy, we've got to read it, know it, and follow it.

Lord, I am grateful for Mary's example.

The Practice of Praise

Bless the Lord, O my soul; and all that is within me. . . .
Bless the Lord, O my soul, and forget not all his benefits:
who forgiveth all thine iniquities; who healeth all thy diseases;
who redeemeth thy life from destruction.
Psalm 103:1–4 KJV

Trials come to all of us, and when they do, it's easy to forget all that God has done for us in the past. Often our adverse circumstances sabotage our efforts to praise God in every situation.

The psalmist practiced the power of praise as he acknowledged God's faithfulness to forgive, heal, and restore. He blessed the Lord with his whole heart because he trusted in God's divine plan.

Positive acclamations of our faith produce remarkable results. First, praise establishes and builds our faith. It decrees, "No matter what is happening, no matter how I feel, I choose to praise God!" Second, praise changes our perspective. As we relinquish control, praise redirects our focus toward God rather than on our problems. And third, praise blesses the heart of God. It brings God joy for His children to acknowledge His presence and power through praise.

The Bible admonishes us to praise God in every circumstance, saying, "In every thing give thanks: for this is the will of God in Christ Jesus concerning you" (1 Thessalonians 5:18 KJV). To bless the Lord in all things is to receive God's blessings. Begin the practice of praise today!

Heavenly Father, You are worthy of all my praise.
I thank and praise You for my current circumstances,
knowing that You are at work on my behalf. Amen.

Honor Your Parents

Honour thy father and thy mother: that thy days may be long upon the land which the Lord thy God giveth thee.
Exodus 20:12 kjv

Honoring your parents is a lifelong duty. It looks different at four, fourteen, and forty, but it is a commandment important enough that almighty God chose to include it in a list of just ten.

This commandment may be difficult for an adult woman to know how to obey. You know you should honor your mother and father, and yet it is not always simple. What exactly does honor entail? You are an adult, and yet they are still your parents. What if your parents are unbelievers?

These are not easy questions to answer, but the commandment is fairly cut and dry. Honor them, respect them, treat them well, listen to them, and never speak ill of them to others. You may not follow all of your parents' advice. Now that you are an adult, you are not required to do so. It is still admirable to seek it at times. They know you well, and they have lived longer than you have. They may have helpful input.

If your parents are not believers, honor them in every way possible so long as it does not cause you to stumble in your walk with the Lord. We are always called to put the Lord first.

God, help me to honor my parents as You have instructed me to do. Amen.

Sharing Our Blessings

Divide your investments among many places,
for you do not know what risks might lie ahead.
ECCLESIASTES 11:2 NLT

Daphne stacked the boxes of canned goods against the pantry wall, singing praise songs while she worked. God had transformed the bare-boned Christmas that she expected into an overwhelming abundance. First her church and then her workplace brought box after box of food and gifts. The last, crowning gift came from her husband's workplace, a leftover Christmas tree. Green branches and Christmas cards replaced the strands of light she had hung on the front window.

Many of us have experienced times when God's people have stepped in with a much-needed gift of transportation or food or a car repair.

Maybe that's why God tells us to give as much of ourselves and our belongings to as many people as possible. We need the grace of giving *and* receiving.

Later Daphne had more to offer. An abused woman stayed in her home. She invited friends over for holiday meals and bought gifts for needy children. She started small during that memorable Christmas. There was so much more than she could use. One out of every ten cans went to a local food bank.

As we have freely received from God's goodness, may we freely give.

Father, You provide for our needs. Use us to provide
for others. Give us wisdom as to how
and to whom to give. Amen.

TUESDAY
DECEMBER 24
CHRISTMAS EVE

The Temple Is Rebuilt

Now. . .the LORD stirred up the spirit of Cyrus king of Persia, so that he sent a proclamation throughout all his kingdom, and also put it in writing, saying, "Thus says Cyrus king of Persia, 'The LORD, the God of heaven, has given me all the kingdoms of the earth, and He has appointed me to build Him a house in Jerusalem, which is in Judah. Whoever there is among you of all His people, may his God be with him! Let him go up to Jerusalem which is in Judah, and rebuild the house of the Lord, the God of Israel; He is the God who is in Jerusalem.' "

EZRA 1:1–3

Is there a Christmas that really stands out in your memory, one for which the anticipation nearly drove you crazy?

Now transfer that degree of excitement to how Israel felt when this proclamation finally went out. The Israelites were on the fringe of being brought back to the land God had given them, and now, their center of worship was about to be restored! Thus, the prophecy recorded in Jeremiah was fulfilled: " 'For thus says the LORD, "When seventy years have been completed for Babylon, I will visit you and fulfill My good word to you, to bring you back to this place" ' " (Jeremiah 29:10–11).

Approximately 175 years before King Cyrus was even born, God had spoken through the prophet Isaiah concerning him. "Thus says the Lord. . .'It is I who says of Cyrus, "He is My shepherd! And he will perform all My desire." ' And he declares of Jerusalem, 'She will be built,' And of the temple, 'Your foundation will be laid' " (Isaiah 44:24, 28).

Lord, my world is filled with uncertainty.
But I can be absolutely sure that what
You have said will come to pass.

Happy Birthday, Jesus!

And Joseph also went up from Galilee, from the city of Nazareth, to Judea, to the city of David, which is called Bethlehem, because he was of the house and family of David, in order to register, along with Mary, who was engaged to him, and was with child. And it came about that while they were there, the days were completed for her to give birth. And she gave birth to her first-born son; and she wrapped Him in cloths, and laid Him in a manger, because there was no room for them in the inn.

LUKE 2:4–7

Joy fills our hearts as we celebrate Christmas. But are we mindful of the sacrifices surrounding this tiny Savior's birth? First, Christ, the Son of God, willingly left heaven's throne, took on a human body, and grew to manhood so He could die on the cross.

Next, consider Mary, a young girl filled with dreams of Joseph, the man to whom she'd just been betrothed. An angel announced to Mary that she had been chosen as the mother of the Messiah (Luke 1:35). Putting her own desires aside, she accepted God's plan.

God also sent an angel to prepare Joseph's heart. "Behold, an angel of the Lord appeared to him in a dream, saying, 'Joseph, son of David, do not be afraid to take Mary as your wife; for that which has been conceived in her is of the Holy Spirit. And she will bear a Son; and you shall call His name Jesus, for it is he who will save His people from their sins' " (Matthew 1:20–21).

Father, Your Word is all I need today: " 'Behold, a virgin will be with child and bear a son, and she will call His name Immanuel' "(Isaiah 7:14).

Blessing, Not Blasting

*Bless the LORD, O my soul: and all that is within me,
bless his holy name.*
PSALM 103:1 KJV

Many people in our country claim they do not believe in God; others shrug and say they don't know if He exists. But whenever a copier jams at work, or a dish is dropped in a restaurant, or a flight is delayed, atheists and agnostics include God in the midst of their misery. They yell His name as if *He* messed up on the job—even though they believe He doesn't officially exist.

We, as Christians, are called to invest all our emotional energy in blessing God, rather than blasting Him. When others demean their day as "god-awful," we can choose to experience a "God-wonderful" day. When others swear at traffic, we can sing praises along with a CD or radio. With His help—because no one can praise God without tapping in to the power of His Spirit—we can develop spiritual radar that detects daily God-moments worthy of applause: rainbows and roses, clean water to drink, and belly laughs with our friends.

Every day God stacks His gifts around us as if it were Christmas. Like children, we can't give Him much. But we can offer all we are to bless His holy name. And that's the present He loves most.

*Lord, each day I encounter thousands of
opportunities to bless You, the Lord of the universe.
Help me seize the day and praise You
whenever I can!*

King Forever

You, O God, are my king from ages past,
bringing salvation to the earth.
PSALM 74:12 NLT

Sometimes it seems like every part of our lives is affected by change. From the economy and headline news to friendships and family relationships, nothing ever seems to stay the same. Even our leaders are in a constant state of flux. Every election cycle we see politicians come and go. Generation after generation, monarchs succeed their elders to the throne. Ministers move from one church to the next, and bosses get promotions or transfers.

These changes can leave us feeling unsteady in the present and uncertain about the future. With more questions than answers, we wonder how these new leaders will handle their roles.

It's different in God's kingdom. He's the King now, just as He was in the days of Abraham. His reign will continue until the day His Son returns to earth, and then on into eternity. We can rely—absolutely depend on—His unchanging nature. Take comfort in the stability of the King—He's our leader now and forever!

Almighty King, You are my rock. When my world
is in turmoil and changes swirl around me,
You are my anchor and my center of balance.
Thank You for never changing. Amen.

Order in Our Prayers

First of all, then, I urge that entreaties and prayers, petitions and thanksgivings, be made on behalf of all men, for kings and all who are in authority, in order that we may lead a tranquil and quiet life in all godliness and dignity. This is good and acceptable in the sight of God our Savior, who desires all men to be saved and to come to the knowledge of the truth.
1 Timothy 2:1–4

The demands of this world, and the pace at which our technology is racing, can sometimes overwhelm us, causing feelings of panic, powerlessness, and even paranoia. Is there a solution that brings life back into perspective? Yes. And God calls it prayer.

Our human sense of ineptness—we simply aren't equal to the task of being in charge of the universe—causes us to react to pressure. So, we've got to release the hand controls back to God. And when we practice this on an individual level, the prayers we offer within our congregations become more effective.

Prayer isn't some mystical entity to be attained by a few saintly little ladies in the church. Instead, it is an act of worship on the part of the created toward the Creator. Prayer is simply "talking to God" about everything that affects our lives.

Spirit of God, fall afresh on me that I might lift my voice in petition to You.

Keeping Christmas

"For there is born to you this day in the city of David a Savior, who is Christ the Lord."
LUKE 2:11 NKJV

Christmastime comes. It comes every year right after Thanksgiving. It comes with noise and crowds and gift wrap. It comes with fudge and mistletoe and shopping—lots of shopping—whether we are ready for it or not. December brings a new type of "busy" into our days. It is a busy that is pine-scented and sparkly and, if we are lucky, snow-blanketed.

Christmas goes. It goes as quickly as it came, with crumpled tissue paper and leftover ham. It goes with the last surprise, the final carol, and the taking down of lights. It goes out to the curb, pine-scented still—but over.

This Christmas season, among the wonderful hustle and bustle of one more party and one more gift to purchase, take time to rest in the true meaning of the celebration. God's only Son was born in Bethlehem and laid in a manger, sent from heaven to save us from our sin and give us everlasting life.

This year let Christmas stay. As December melts into January and a new year begins, *keep Christmas.* Let the Christ of Christmas make every day a little happier, a little brighter, a little bigger. Make *life* the special occasion, not just December 25.

Keep Christmas this year—all year.

Father, thank You for the gift of Your only Son, sent that I might have life instead of death. Help me to keep the spirit of Christmas in my heart and celebrate Jesus all year long. Amen.

Going Above and Beyond

Now to him who is able to do immeasurably more than all we ask or imagine, according to his power that is at work within us, to him be glory in the church and in Christ Jesus throughout all generations, for ever and ever!
Ephesians 3:20–21 NIV

Are you one of those people who goes above and beyond—at work, in your relationships, and at play? Maybe you like to do all you've promised to do, and then some. If this is true of you, then you're more like your heavenly Father than you know. His Word promises that He always goes above and beyond all that we could ask or imagine.

Think about that for a moment. What have you asked for? What have you imagined? It's amazing to think that God, in His infinite power and wisdom, can do immeasurably more than all that! How? According to the power that is at work within us. It's not our power, thankfully. We don't have enough power to scrape the surface of what we'd like to see done in our lives. But His power in us gets the job done. . .and more.

Praise the Lord! Praise Him in the church and throughout all generations! He's an immeasurable God.

Heavenly Father, I feel pretty powerless at times. It's amazing to realize You have more power in Your little finger than all of mankind has put together. Today I praise You for being a God who goes above and beyond all I could ask or imagine.

A New Day

God, treat us kindly. You're our only hope. First thing in the morning, be there for us! When things go bad, help us out!
Isaiah 33:2 msg

There are days that start off wrong and finish worse. Days in which we feel out of sorts, like a tire out of balance, clumsy and inefficient. We say things we shouldn't say, using a voice that is too harsh, too loud. We experience days full of failure, tinged by sin. Wouldn't it be great to redo our bad days?

We have that opportunity. It's called *tomorrow*. Lamentations 3:22–23 tells us that by God's mercies, He gives us a fresh canvas every twenty-four hours. Anger, grudges, irritations, and pain don't have to be part of it. No matter how stormy the day before, each new day starts fresh. And He is there for us first thing in the morning and every step of the way in our day, even if things begin to go wrong—again.

Every day is a new day, a new beginning, a new chance to enjoy our lives—because each day is a new day with God. We can focus on the things that matter most: worshipping Him, listening to Him, and being in His presence. No matter what happened the day before, we have a fresh start to enjoy a deeper relationship with Him. A fresh canvas, every twenty-four hours.

Before I get out of bed in the morning, let me say these words and mean them: "This is the day the Lord has made; let us rejoice and be glad in it" (Psalm 118:24 niv).

Contributors

Banks, Tracy: March 19

Biggers, Emily: January 31; February 4; April 1, 7; May5, 8; June 16, 18, 22; July 3, 8; August 20; September 27, 30; October 23; November 1, 17; December 16, 22, 29

Bloss, Joanna: January 19, February 16; March 29; May 1; June 20; July 13, 21; August 19, 23; September 21; November 4, 25, 29; December 17

Coty, Debora M.: March 24; November 26

Douglas, Katherine: January 3; April 13

Dyer, Dena: February 8; April 28; June 14; October 16; November 6; December 12

Elacqua, Tina: January 23; August 13; September 16

Farrier, Nancy J.: March 27; August 26; September 26; October 25

Fisher, Suzanne Woods: January 2, 27; February 20; March 11; April 30; May 7, 26; June 6, 11; July 25; September 1, 22; October 13, 19; December 31

Fitzpatrick, Carol Lynn: January 1, 5, 8, 13, 17, 20, 25, 29; February 2, 6, 10, 12, 17, 21, 25, 28; March 4, 7, 9, 14, 17, 20, 23, 26, 31; April 3, 6, 8, 11, 15, 20, 23, 25, 29; May 2, 6, 10, 12, 15, 20, 28; June 1, 5, 10, 15, 19, 24, 29; July 4, 9, 14, 19, 23, 29; August 1, 7, 12, 17, 22, 25, 30; September 3, 7, 11, 15, 19, 23, 28; October 3, 7, 12, 17, 22, 26, 31; November 3, 8, 12, 16, 20, 23, 27; December 1, 2, 5, 7, 11, 15, 20, 24, 25, 28

Franklin, Darlene: February 3, 11; March 15; April 4, 22, 16; May 11; July 10; August 29; October 2, 5; November 9; December 23

Germany, Rebecca: February 27; May 24; June 26

Gregor, Shanna D.: July 22; October 10, 18; November 13, 22; December 9
Gyde, Judy: March 25

Hanna, Janice: January 14, 21, 24; February 18, 19; April 5; June 8, 12; July 5, 15; August 9; September 4; October 20, 30; November 18; December 6, 14, 19, 30

Hetzel, June: May 23; June 30; November 14

Key, Eileen: January 18, 22; February 5, 13; March 6, 22; April 26; May 21; July 27; August 4, 15; September 13; December 3

Krause, Tina: March 10; July 6, 20; August

16; September 10; October 9, 27; November 10; December 21
Keller, Austine: January 11; May 3; June 3; November 7, 28

Kucera Jones, Shelly: March 1; April 9; May 22; July 1; December 10
Lehman, P. J.: March 28; August 10; September 17

Maltese, Donna K.: February 15; April 17; June 6; August 3; September 6; October 4; December 18

McDonald, Faith Tibbetts: June 4

McGlone, Becky: May 14; June 17; July 7, 12; August 2, 11, 14; September 20; November 21

McQuade, Pamela: March 16; May 25; June 27; July 11, 31; October 15; November 30; December 8

Middlebrooke, Helen Widger: February 26; April 12; June 13; August 5, 27; September 9; October 29; November 5, 19; December 13

Nydegger, Mandy: February 24; September 24

O'Dell, Nicole: January 12; February 9; March 18; April 27; May 16, 29; June 2, 21; August 28; September 2, 25; October 1, 11

Phillips, Rachael: February 7, 14; March 5; April 2, 10; June 23; July 30; August 24; December 26

Ratliff, Sarah Mae: March 8; July 28
Rayburn, Julie: January 10; February 1, 23; March 2, 12; May17, 19; July 2; August 8; September 18; October 21

Redenbo, Judy: January 4; July 24; September 5

Reid-Matchett, Kimm: January 16, 28; March 21; April 21; June 25; July 18; October 8, 24, 28; November 15

Richards, Ramona: April 24; May 4; July 17

Schmelzer, Kate E.: March 13; May 13; September 12

Slawson, Leah: January 6, 15; April 14; May 9, 30; June 28; July 16; August 6, 21, 31; September 8; October 6, 14; November 11; December 4
Thomas, Christan: February 22; May 31

Tipton, Annie: January 9, 26; April 18; July 26; September 14; November 24; December 27

Vawter, Marjorie: January 7, 30; March 3; April 19; May 18; August 18; September 29; November 2

Willey, Martha: March 30

Wise, Jean: May 27; June 9

TRACY "BOBO" BANKS is a freelance writer, award-winning poet, licensed minister, business owner, and Web site administrator. Her greatest blessings: God's unconditional love, family, friends, and autistic niece, Hailie. www.tracybobobanks.com

EMILY BIGGERS is a gifted education specialist in a north Texas public school district. She enjoys travel, freelance writing, and serving in a local apartment ministry through her church.

JOANNA BLOSS lives with her four children in the Chicago area. She is coauthor of *Grit for the Oyster: 250 Pearls of Wisdom for Aspiring Writers* and author of *God's Gifts for the Graduate*. Joanna is also a personal trainer and a graduate student in clinical psychology.

DEBORA M. COTY is an events speaker, columnist, author of *The Distant Shore* and *Hugs, Humor, and Hope for Harried Moms*, contributor to *Heavenly Humor for the Woman's Soul*, and coauthor of *Grit for the Oyster: 250 Pearls of Wisdom for Aspiring Writers*.

Author and speaker KATHERINE DOUGLAS started writing creatively in the third grade. Her publications include six books and dozens of articles. You may visit her Web site at www.katherinedouglas.com.

DENA DYER is a writer who resides in the Texas Hill Country. She has contributed to more than a dozen anthologies and has authored or coauthored three humor books. www.denadyer.com

TINA ELACQUA teaches, writes, and publishes journal articles, books, conference papers/presentations, and technical reports/presentations. She has held roles of research scientist, professor, and consultant in industrial/organizational psychology.

NANCY J. FARRIER is the author of twelve books and numerous articles and short stories. She is married and has five children. She lives with her family in Southern California.

SUZANNE WOODS FISHER's debut novel, *Copper Star*, released in 2007. The sequel, *Copper Fire*, will release in May 2008. Fisher is a contributing editor to *Christian Parenting Today* magazine.

CAROL LYNN FITZPATRICK is a bestselling author of nine books that have totaled nearly three quarters of a million books sold. Her book *Daily Wisdom for Women* appeared on the CBA (Christian Booksellers Assoc.) Ten Best Sellers List for many years.

DARLENE FRANKLIN resides in the Colorado foothills with her mother and her Sia-Ti (Siamese/ Tiger) cat, Talia. An author and speaker, she has two grown children and two grandchildren. Darlene has published novels, magazine articles, and children's curriculum.

REBECCA GERMANY works full-time as a fiction editor and has written and compiled several novellas and gift books. She lives in Ohio, where she enjoys tending a kitchen garden.

SHANNA D. GREGOR is a writer and editor who helps ministries and publishers develop books that express God's voice for today through the doors of opportunity He sets before her.

JUDY GYDE and her husband, Bruce, have been married for four decades and have three children and seven grandchildren (so far). They serve as leaders in their church and enjoy their RV and motorcycle. Judy's writing has been published in more than forty publications.

JANICE HANNA (who has also written under the name Janice Thompson) is the author of more than thirty novels and nonfiction books. She enjoys writing books that touch lives. Janice lives in Texas.

JUNE HETZEL, Ph.D., is professor of education at Biola University. She enjoys the roles of wife, friend, author, editor, and professor. She and her husband, Geoff, reside in Southern California.

AUSTINE KELLER resides in Tampa, Florida, writing and publishing as ministry to others as well as for her own enjoyment. She also enjoys a newly emptied nest and fishing with her husband.

EILEEN KEY resides in Texas near her three grown children and two wonderful grandchildren. She taught school for thirty years and now pursues her interests of writing and editing.

SHELLY KUCERA JONES is a training specialist with a farm insurance company. A freelance writer, she has contributed to Barbour's *Daily Wisdom for Single Mothers* project. Shelly and her husband live in Texas.

TINA KRAUSE is an award-winning newspaper columnist and author of the book *Laughter Therapy*. She is a wife, mom, and grandmother of four. Tina and her husband, Jim, live in Valparaiso, Indiana.

P. J. LEHMAN has written for three devotional books from her home in Valrico, Florida. She teaches writing, enjoys the arts, and her all-time favorite—a hammock and a good book. Her most fulfilling role is being a wife and the mother of three children.

DONNA K. MALTESE is a writer, editor, and the author of *Power Prayers to Start Your Day*. She is married, has two children, and resides in Silverdale, Pennsylvania.

FAITH TIBBETTS McDONALD lives in Pennsylvania with her husband and three children. She teaches writing at the Pennsylvania State University and is coauthor of the book *Grit for the Oyster: 250 Pearls of Wisdom for Aspiring Writers.*

BECKY McGLONE is a passionate follower of Christ, a home-schooling mom, and freelance writer. Her previous work includes the self-published *Devotions for Difficult Days,* as well as writing published in the Billy Graham Evangelistic Association's *Decision* magazine. Becky lives in central Ohio.

PAMELA McQUADE is a freelance writer and editor with several books to her credit, including *Prayers and Promises for the Graduate* and *Daily Wisdom for the Workplace.* She and her husband live in the New York metropolitan area.

HELEN WIDGER MIDDLEBROOKE is the mother of nine home-educated children, including a daughter with Down syndrome. She lives on Guam, where she is a freelance writer and an advocate for the disabled.

MANDY NYDEGGER lives with her husband, David, in Waco, Texas. She loves Christmas, snow, and the Indianapolis Colts.

NICOLE O'DELL is an accomplished writer of books, devotions, and Bible studies. She has been an in-depth studier, Bible study leader, and teacher for more than twelve years. Nicole lives in central Illinois with her husband, Wil, and their children.

RACHAEL PHILLIPS is an award-winning fiction and humor writer who has authored four biographies published by Barbour Publishing. Rachael and her husband live in Indiana. Visit her website at www.rachaelwrites.com.

SARAH MAE RATLIFF enjoys worshipping God, writing, working with children, and spending time with her family. Sarah and her husband, Ryan, are high school sweethearts who are expecting a son in April.

JULIE RAYBURN is a public speaker and an area director for Community Bible Study. She lives in Atlanta with her husband, Scott. They have two grown children and one granddaughter.

JUDY REDENBO is a wife and mother of four from the Toledo, Ohio, area. She wants to share with others the grace God has given her through many experiences in caregiving. Judy spends her free time writing and encouraging older people.

KIMM REID-MATCHETT put herself through university while raising three active boys. After receiving a psychology degree, she remarried and now finds her newly combined family of nine to be exhilarating. Kimm continues to work on writing projects while volunteering at a women's shelter. She resides in Alberta, Canada.

RAMONA RICHARDS is an award-winning author and editor who has worked on more than 350 publications. Ramona's articles have appeared in *Today's Christian Woman* and *Chicken Soup for the Caregiver's Soul,* and her books include *A Moment with God for Single Parents.* She lives in Nashville with her daughter Rachel.

KATE E. SCHMELZER graduated from Taylor University in 2008 with a double major in professional writing and counseling and a minor in Christian education. She hopes to be an author, counselor, and missionary.

LEAH SLAWSON has been married to her husband, Guice, for more than twenty years and they have two teenagers, a son and daughter. She lives in Montgomery, Alabama.

CHRISTAN THOMAS is a writer and editor

whose work has appeared in magazines and newspapers across Texas and Tennessee. Originally from the Indianapolis area, Christan now lives in Tennessee with her husband, Brock, and dogs Tucker and Suzy Q. She recently began doctoral studies at East Tennessee State University.

ANNIE TIPTON is an editor and writer living in small-town Ohio. A former newspaper reporter, she loves her family, friends, sushi, and beach vacations.

MARJORIE VAWTER is a full-time freelance writer, editor, and proofreader. She lives with her husband in Colorado and enjoys hiking and snowshoeing near their cabin in the mountains. The Vawters have two adult children.

MARTHA WILLEY is married with three sons. By age twelve, Martha knew she wanted to be a writer. She lives in northwest Ohio.

JEAN WISE is a freelance journalist/writer and a speaker at retreats and gatherings. Her background as an RN led to work in public health and gerontology. She lives in Edon, Ohio, with her husband. Find out more at her web site: www.jeanwise.org.

Scripture Index

Old Testament

Genesis
1:27—January 1
1:27, 31—May 31
2:2–3—May 26; October 16
2:7—December 9
9:13, 16—April 6
12:1–2—February 20
21:17—February 7
31:34—June 7
45:4–5—January 13

Exodus
12:21–23—March 26
14:13—August 3
16:4—September 20
18:17–18—January 27
18:19—August 23
20:8—June 30
20:12—December 22
20:17—May 5
33:14—October 13

Deuteronomy
6:6, 9—March 29
16:17—May 25
29:2–6—June 14

Joshua
2:11—May 4
6:17—June 11

Judges
12:7–10—April 28

1 Samuel
1:20—May 12
17:33—October 15
31:1–2—July 9

2 Samuel
9:7—July 30
11:2–5—July 23
13:20—November 29
22:5, 7—February 8
22:20—March 16

2 Kings
5:3—June 23

Ezra
1:1–3—December 24

Nehemiah
13:14—March 5

Esther
2:2–4—August 25

Job
9:33–34—December 12
12:7–10—September 23
37:5—October 24
37:14–16—September 1

Psalms
1:3—September 21
5:3—January 3, March 7
5:11–12—January 22
8:3–4—November 18
10:4—February 9
16:7—December 6
17:3—July 5
17:6—November 28
18:29—August 19
19:1–2—September 22
22:1—January 29
22:26—January 4
23:2–3—March 15
23:3—August 15
25:8–9—September 16
28:7—August 5
29:11—September 13
33:9—July 26
34:2–3—August 6
34:18—April 17
37:4—March 18
37:7—August 18
38:15—June 20
42:5–6—February 16; March 13
46:1—January 18
46:10—November 2
55:6—November 5
56:1–4—February 28
56:8—May 27
57:1—April 28
61:1–4—January 17
63:1—October 9
66:5—March 30
68:19—April 22
69:1–3—January 2
73:25–26—December 19

74:12—December 27
78:4—March 24
84:11—January 31
91:1–2—October 4
91:5—February 18
91:11—March 19
92:1–4—March 20
102:1—December 13
103:1—December 26
103:1–4—December 21
105:40—March 14
111:2—August 31
118:24—December 31
119:2–3—November 25
119:9—November 9
119:26–29—April 3
119:50—June 9
119:105—October 8
126:2—November 26
127:2—October 13
130:1—November 21
139:13—November 4; December 8
139:13–16—April 8
145: 15–16—November 11
150:1–2, 6—April 11

Proverbs
1:3–6—January 8
2:6–8—April 23
8:1–2—August 24
8:1–4, 11—January 20
8:13—September 12
9:13–18—January 25
11:22—November 1
14:33—March 9
15:13—July 20
15:30—November 7; December 10
16:9—May 24; October 21
17:22—March 22; June 22
19:23—July 8
20:3—June 12
24:16—June 17
27:9—January 9
27:17—November 19
31:15, 18—July 25
31:30—June 2

Ecclesiastes
2:1–3—May 6
3:1, 4—May 20
8:5—March 10
9:11—April 5
11:2—December 23
12:1, 13–14—May 28

Song of Solomon
1:15—August 26

Isaiah
1:1–3—June 5
8:17—November 15
12:3—June 28
25:1—May 23
26:3–4—May 13
30:15—January 7
33:2—December 31
40:5—July 4
40:8—April 21
40:29—July 21
41:13—May 30
42:16—February 15
43:1–2—September 29
49:16—May 9
50:4—May 11
53:7—August 21
55:9—March 6
58:11—August 10; September 29
66:2—July 16
Jeremiah
1:5—April 19
10:23–24—October 6
23:23–24—April 13
29:5—August 29
29:11—January 12
31:25—May 18
45:5—October 2

Lamentations
3:22–23—April 27
3:26—November 2
3:40—January 15

Ezekiel
1:1–3—July 14
3:4—July 19
22:30—November 13
34:14–15—July 12

Daniel
1:17—October 19
2:23—April 24
3:17—April 30
3:17–18—May 22
11:21–24—August 1

Hosea
8:7—June 6

Joel
2:13—February 5

Amos
4:13—March 21

Jonah
1:3—June 27

Micah
6:6, 8—September 15

Zephaniah
3:17— January 6; March 3

Haggai
1:2–5—October 7

Zechariah
2:8—October 25

Malachi
1:2—April 16
3:10—November 14

NEW TESTAMENT

Matthew
4:19—February 10; September 18
5:1–2—October 27
5:14—January 26
6:7—March 17
6:9—November 21
6:10—May 19
6:24—March 8
6:34—April 18
7:12—August 13
11:28–30—January 23; May 18
15:28—September 6
16:25—April 12
17:20—July 10
19:27–28—January 5
20:31–32—April 4
22:2–3—June 10
25:35, 40—May 13
26:40—October 5

Mark
5:25–28—February 2
5:34—September 8
6:31–32—July 6
7:18, 20—November 9
10:21–22—March 28
12:35–38, 40—February 12
14:51–55—February 21
16:1—December 4

Luke
2:4–7—December 25
2:11—December 29
2:36–38—May 2
4:3–4—February 6
5:20—January 24
6:41—September 14
7:37–38—July 31
7:38—September 30
9:1–3—February 17
10:36–37—April 26
10:38–40—February 25
10:41–42—August 2, 28
11:1–3—February 22
12:34—November 30
14:13–14—November 17
15:6—September 4
15:7—November 24
15:8–10—March 4
18:31–33—March 31
23:45—June 26

John
1:41—March 23
4:5–7—April 20
4:28–29—May 8
5:2–4—April 25
6:44—May 7
6:57–58—May 10
6:63—October 14
7:2–5—May 15
8:29—October 18
9:3—May 29
10:2–3—June 1
10:27—January 28
11:1, 3—June 15
11:35—May 27
14:1—January 18; October 23
14:2—June 19
14:16—July 27
15:13—July 15
16:33—June 18
17:3–5—June 24
17:4—June 13
17:13—October 1
18:19–21—June 29

Acts
4:13—December 16
7:59–60; 8:1—July 29
9:36—April 12
9:39—April 12
16:15—April 7
20:35—May 16
28:5—July 1

Romans
4:2–3—August 7
5:1–2, 6—August 12
8:1—April 9
8:1–4—August 17
8:11—October 10

8:15—January 21
8:17—December 3
8:26–27—January 30
8:28—March 2; May 29
10:1—August 22
12:1–2—December 20
12:9—July 2
13:1, 6—April 15
15:4—October 11

1 Corinthians
1:25—March 11
1:26–27—July7
2:9—November 22
2:10, 12—August 30
2:14—March 12
3:12–13—February 11
3:16–17—September 3
6:19—July 28
8:3—April 14
10:1–6, 8—September 7
12:3—September 11
12:4–5—June 8
13:1—September 19
15:55—August 8

2 Corinthians
1:3–4—September 25
4:18—February 23
5:7—September 5
5:17—January 16
7:1—January 11; December 17
10:12—July 17
12:9—January 19

Galatians
1:6–7—December 7
1:10—February 19; October 3
3:11—September 10
3:26—June 16
5:13—December 18
5:22–25—June 21; October 12
6:9—August 16; October 28

Ephesians
1:3–4—October 17
3:20—October 28
3:20–21—December 30
5:1–2—October 30
5:15–17—September 2
5:16-17—August 9
6:18—August 11

Philippians
1:3–5, 7—October 22
2:3–4—April 1; November 3
4:1–2—November 12
4:6–7—August 20; December 14
4:11—March 25

Colossians
3:3–7—November 20
3:11–13—November 23
3:23—September 27
4:6—January 10

1 Thessalonians
2:14—February 1

2 Thessalonians
3:5—June 3

1 Timothy
2:1–4—December 28
5:10—August 27; October 29

2 Timothy
1:11–12—February 13

Philemon
1:7—March 27

Hebrews
3:1–4—September 28
3:4—June 4
4:1–2—October 31
4:16—November 6
5:13—May 1
6:15—March 1
10:23–24—June 25
10:25—May 17
11:13—April 10
12:1—July 13; November 10
12:12–13—April 2
13:6—October 20

James
1:2–4—July 18
1:12—May 21
1:17—February 4
1:19–20—July 3
1:22—February 24
1:27—February 26
2:14—July 22
5:16—August 4

1 Peter
1:6–7—October 26

2:1–3—November 8
3:3-4—February 27
5:7—August 14

2 Peter
1:3–5—November 16
1 John
1:2–3—December 1
1:9—April 9
3:1–3—November 27
3:20—April 9
4:10—February 14

2 John
1:9—July 11

3 John
1:2—January 14

Jude
1:24—September 26

Revelation
1:7—December 5
1:8—September 9
2:4—December 11
2:17—February 3
4:2–3—December 15
19:5—May 3
21:6—September 24